PRENTICE HALL

Language Teaching Methodology Series

Teacher Education
General Editor: Christopher N. Candlin

# Language Teaching Methodology

A textbook for teachers

**Other titles in this series include**

ELLIS, Rod
*Classroom second language development*

ELLIS, Rod
*Classroom language acquisition in context*

KENNEDY, Chris
*Language planning and English language teaching*

KRASHEN, Stephen
*Second language acquisition and second language learning*

KRASHEN, Stephen
*Principles and practice in second language acquisition*

KRASHEN, Stephen
*Language acquisition and language education*

KRASHEN, Stephen and TERRELL, Tracy
*The natural approach*

MARTON, Waldemar
*Methods in English language teaching: frameworks and options*

McKAY, Sandra
*Teaching grammar*

NEWMARK, Peter
*Approaches to translation*

NUNAN, David
*Understanding language classrooms*

PECK, Antony
*Language teachers at work*

ROBINSON, Gail
*Crosscultural understanding*

STEVICK, Earl
*Success with foreign languages*

SWALES, John
*Episodes in ESP*

TOMALIN, Barry and STEMPLESKI, Susan
*Video in action*

WENDEN, Anita
*Learner strategies for learner autonomy*

WENDEN, Anita and RUBIN, Joan
*Learner strategies in language learning*

YALDEN, Janice
*The communicative syllabus*

# Language Teaching Methodology

## A textbook for teachers

**DAVID NUNAN**

National Centre for English Language Teaching and Research,
Macquarie University, Sydney

ENGLISH LANGUAGE TEACHING

**Prentice Hall**

New York  London  Toronto  Sydney  Tokyo  Singapore

First published 1991 by
Prentice Hall International (UK) Ltd
Campus 400, Maylands Avenue,
Hemel Hempstead,
Hertfordshire HP2 7EZ
A division of
Simon & Schuster International Group

Typeset in 10 on 12pt Times Roman
by Keyboard Services, Luton.

Printed in Great Britain by
Redwood Books, Trowbridge, Wiltshire

Library of Congress Cataloging-in-Publication Data

Nunan, David.
    Language teaching methodology: a textbook for teachers / David
    Nunan.
        p.   cm. – (Prentice Hall International English language
    teaching)
      Includes bibliographical references.
      ISBN 0-13-521469-6
      1. Language and languages–Study and teaching.   I. Title.
    II. Series: English language teaching.
    P51.N85   1991
    418'.007–dc20                         90–48530
                                             CIP

British Library Cataloguing in Publication Data

Nunan, David
    Language teaching methodology: a textbook for teachers.
    1. Foreign languages. Teaching. Methodology
    I. Title
    428.0071

    ISBN 0-13-521469-6

5   95 94

For my family, as ever.

# Contents

# General Editor's Preface

A glance at the available literature for teachers-in-training in a range of educational subject matters reveals a strong tendency towards revealed truth. Unfortunately for these trainees, however, the pathway towards this goal is not couched in terms of personal exploration but is expressed more as sets of precepts for teachers' actions, tied to injunctions and homilies about desirable (and very frequently undesirable) classroom behaviours. Prescriptions for practice abound and are presented unquestioningly, placing the teacher/reader in a characteristically mimetic role, expected to mark and follow what has been laid down, often by writers unfamiliar to these readers and from culturally and educationally alien worlds. Very often these prescriptions are bundled together to constitute a *method*, a pathway to presumed effectiveness in the classroom. Language teaching, among all disciplines, has suffered particularly from these recipes for ills.

Although such an approach has been hugely successful in terms of publication, it has been much less so in terms of teacher conversion to innovative classroom action. Despite what they may appear to support in theory, or say they are in favour of in training seminars, teachers seem in actuality strangely resistant to changes to their established practices. It sometimes seems as if they operate in two worlds, a world of apparent acceptance in one plane and one of actual rejection in the other. There is undoubtedly some correlation between being presented with someone else's answers to what they perceive to be your problems and your likely unwillingness to adopt such nostrums and to convert them to your personal intellectual and practical philosophy.

If this disparity is as prevalent as it appears to be, then there are serious questions to be raised about the nature and process of language teacher education, and about the delivery modes and vehicles for pre- and in-service teacher development. Ways need to be found where the experiences of successful teaching, the results of relevant research into language and learning and the exigencies and demands of the classroom can be woven into a set of principles for practical experimentation and challenge by classroom teachers and their learners.

It is this objective that David Nunan sets himself in this latest contribution to the Language Teaching Methodology Series. First and foremost the reader is introduced, through carefully chosen and apt extracts, to the world of language teaching classrooms, which, if not directly identifiable, are at least familiar in outline to the practising teacher, whatever her or his context. From these extracts, problems and issues arise to illustrate and exemplify what research and experience tell us about the teaching of the various components of the language teaching curriculum: the teaching of skills, the teaching of grammar and phonology, the exploration of the roles and potential of the learner, the strategies and management of the teacher, and the innovative ways in which relevant materials can be developed for classroom use.

In short, *Language Teaching Methodology: A Textbook for Teachers* provides a valuable counterpoint to the author's already very successful action research book for language teachers, *Understanding Language Classrooms*, also in the Language Teaching Methodology Series. It shares a similar philosophy of exploration and doing; a commitment to the teacher trying out new ways of teaching content and enhancing learner skills and strategies through constructing appropriate curricula for her or his classroom. Suggestions and insights for reflective teaching abound and are always linked to practical tasks and relevant action, while the references cited serve to underpin the techniques and researches David Nunan carefully exemplifies.

PROFESSOR CHRISTOPHER N. CANDLIN
NCELTR
Macquarie University, Sydney

# *Preface*

Frank Lloyd Wright, the great American architect, once walked into his studio and announced that he had just completed his latest project. Mystified, his students looked around the studio for the plans, which were no where in evidence, when Wright said, 'All I need to do now is get it down on paper.' *Language Teaching Methodology* is a book I have been writing for many years – the major problem was getting it down on paper.

When I became involved in second language teacher education in the 1970s, I was struck by the discrepancy between the prescriptive statements by methodologists about what ought to go on in language classrooms, and what actually went on in the classrooms where I taught and where I observed others teach. During the 1970s and early 1980s there was a preoccupation with methods, and the focus of attention was on finding the right method. While I must confess to flirtations with Suggestopedia, Total Physical Response, the Silent Way, and even the rather obscure, and now largely defunct, All's Well, I was uneasy with the notion of classroom practices which were based on prescriptions which were imported from outside the classroom itself. It seemed to me that in developing pedagogical tasks for the classroom we needed to meld insights into the nature of language learning and use from source disciplines such as linguistics and psychology, with insights from the classroom itself.

In this book, I have tried to achieve such a synthesis. The two questions which motivated the book were: what does current theory and research have to tell us about the nature of language learning and use, and what is it that teachers and learners actually do in language classrooms? In seeking answers to the second question, I spent many hours observing, recording and transcribing classroom interactions. While not all of the material I collected has found its way into the book, the final product was informed by insights from over thirty classrooms. I should point out that my purpose was not to provide instances of exemplary practice, that is, to show what should be done, but to demonstrate what actually is done in language classrooms. To adopt a normative approach would have been to fall into the very trap I was trying to avoid. This is not to say that there is no such thing as successful practice. However, success can only be evaluated against criteria such as curriculum goals, teacher aims, learner intentions and learning outcomes. Ultimately, it is up to individual teachers and learners to develop and apply their own criteria for determining what is or is not successful practice.

This brings me to my final goal in writing this book. It is not enough to set out what others have discovered and written about the nature of language learning and use. Nor is it sufficient to point out what others have done. The final step is for teachers to identify what works for them and their learners, in their own particular context, through the collaborative exploration of their own classrooms. In this book I have attempted to provide the concrete steps through which such exploration might be carried out.

I should like to thank Kathi Baily for the detailed and discerning comments and criticisms she made on an earlier draft of this book. Thanks are also due to Chris Candlin, David Haines and Isobel Fletcher de Tellez for their advice, criticism and support.

DAVID NUNAN
Macquarie University
March 1991

# Classroom Extracts

# Chapter One

# *An Empirical Approach to Language Teaching Methodology*

## 1.1 Introduction

An important task confronting applied linguists and teachers concerned with second and foreign language learning is to overcome the pendulum effect in language teaching. This effect is most evident in the area of methodology where fads and fashions, like theories of grammar, come and go with monotonous regularity. The way to overcome the pendulum effect is to derive appropriate classroom practices from empirical evidence on the nature of language learning and use and from insights into what makes learners tick. The major purpose of this book is to introduce teachers and student teachers to an empirically-based approach to language teaching methodology. Such an approach integrates theory and research into the nature of language learning and use, with insights derived from the observation and analysis of what actually goes on in classrooms (as opposed to what some say should go on), and uses this knowledge to inform the issues raised and points made.

In this chapter I attempt to define methodology and relate it to the broader field of curriculum development. I also give some indication of the themes to be pursued in the book and provide an overview of its contents. The chapter answers the following questions:

1. What is methodology, and how does it relate to other important concepts such as curriculum and syllabus design?
2. What does recent research have to say about the nature of language processing and production?
3. Why is it important to relate theory and research to what actually goes on in the classroom?
4. Why is 'task' an important element in language learning and teaching?
5. How can teachers and student teachers explore the ideas in this book to their own classrooms?

## 1.2 Defining methodology

Traditionally, a distinction has been drawn between syllabus design and methodology: the former concerning itself with the selection and grading of linguistic and experiential content, the latter with the selection and sequencing of learning tasks and activities. In other words, syllabus design is concerned with what, why and when; methodology is concerned with how. However, with the development of communicative approaches to language teaching, the traditional distinction between syllabus design and methodology has become difficult to sustain. As Breen points out, while syllabus design, as traditionally conceived, is concerned with the learner's destination, communicatively oriented syllabuses should:

> prioritize the route itself; a focusing upon the means towards the learning of a new language. Here the designer would give priority to the changing processes of learning and the potential of the classroom – to the psychological and social resources applied to a new language by learners in the classroom context . . . a greater concern with capacity for communication rather than repertoire of communication, with the activity of learning a language viewed as important as the language itself, and with a focus upon the means rather than predetermined objectives, all indicate priority of process over content. (Breen 1984: 52–3)

(For a detailed account of the effect of communicative language teaching on syllabus design and methodology, see Nunan 1988a, 1989a.)

It is also worth looking at the original formulation of the relationship between the different variables in the curriculum equation proposed by Breen and Candlin in their seminal 1980 paper 'The essentials of a communicative curriculum in language teaching'.

In the *Longman Dictionary of Applied Linguistics*, methodology is defined as follows:

> (1) . . . the study of the practices and procedures used in teaching, and the principles and beliefs that underlie them.
> Methodology includes:
> (a) study of the nature of LANGUAGE SKILLS (e.g. reading, writing, speaking, listening) and procedures for teaching them
> (b) study of the preparation of LESSON PLANS, materials, and textbooks for teaching language skills
> (c) the evaluation and comparison of language teaching METHODS (e.g. the AUDIOLINGUAL METHOD)
> (2) such practices, procedures, principles, and beliefs themselves. One can, for example criticize or praise the methodology of a particular language course.
>
> (Richards *et al.* 1985: 177)

In this book I consider methodology from the perspective of the classroom. The major focus is on classroom tasks and activities and the management of learning. In Chapters 2, 3, 4 and 5 we study the nature of language skills and the procedures for teaching them. I have presented the skills in separate chapters both for convenience and for the purposes of exposition; I am not suggesting that they should be treated separately in the classroom. In fact, we see that even in lessons which are explicitly devoted to the development of one or other of the macro-skills, the other skills usually also feature prominently. (For a detailed treatment of the sequencing and integration of skills see Nunan 1989a.)

There has been a tendency historically to equate methodology with method. As Richards (1987:11) points out, the goal of many language teachers is to find the right method: 'the history of our profession in the last hundred years has done much to support the impression that improvements in language teaching will come about as a result of improvements in the quality of methods, and that ultimately an effective language teaching method will be developed.' He goes on to say that for many years it was believed that linguistic or psycholinguistic theory would uncover the secrets of second language acquisition, and that then the problem of how to teach a second language would be solved once and for all.

In this book I have comparatively little to say about methods, and one chapter only will be devoted to a comparative analysis and critique of the more prominent methods. Without wishing to pre-empt what I have to say later, I should indicate my general orientation. Despite their diversity, all methods have one thing in common. They all assume that there is a single set of principles which will determine whether or not learning will take place. Thus they all propose a single set of precepts for teacher and learner classroom behaviour, and assert that if these principles are faithfully followed, they will result in learning for all. Unfortunately, little evidence has been forthcoming to support one approach rather than another, or to suggest that it is the method rather than some other variable which caused learning to occur. There is also little evidence that methods are realised at the level of classroom action in the ways intended by their creators. For example, Swaffar *et al.* (1982) found that although the teachers who took part in their study were specifically trained in a particular method, their actual classroom practice was characterised by a range of activities and tasks which transcended the method in question. Their study underlines the importance of collecting evidence directly from the classroom rather than assuming that what teachers are taught to do, or what they say they do, accurately reflects what goes on in their classrooms (see also the study by Long and Sato (1983), which underlines the importance of collecting classroom data).

## 1.3 Research into language processing and production

An important aspect of methodology is the development of teaching routines, materials and tasks for use in the classroom. In this book we look at the growing body of literature on language learning and use by both first and second language learners which can be drawn on by methodologists in the process of formulating principles for the design of classroom materials and learning tasks. In this section I review a selection of the literature which addresses most readily the concerns of second language education. The research is presented more fully in the chapters on language skills and strategies, and their applications to the classroom processes and teaching materials are spelled out.

In terms of language processing, it is now generally accepted that learners need access to both top-down as well as bottom-up processing strategies. Bottom-up processing strategies focus learners on the individual components of spoken and written messages, that is, the phonemes, graphemes, individual words and grammatical elements which need to be comprehended in order to understand these messages. Top-down processing strategies, on the other hand, focus learners on macro-features of text such as the writer's or speaker's purpose, the topic of the message, the overall structure of the text and so on.

In comprehending spoken messages, it has been suggested that learners need the following bottom-up and top-down strategies:

> Bottom-up listening involves the listener in scanning the input to identify familiar lexical items; segmenting the stream of speech into constituents, for example, in order to recognise that 'abookofmine' consists of four words; using phonological cues to identify the information focus in an utterance; using grammatical cues to organise the input into constituents, for example, in order to recognise that in 'the book which I lent you' [the book] and [which I lent you] are major constituents, rather than [the book which I] and [lent you].

> Top-down listening strategies, on the other hand, involve the listener in assigning an interaction to part of a particular event, such as story telling, joking, praying, complaining; assigning persons, places and things to categories; inferring cause and effect relationships; anticipating outcomes; inferring the topic of a discourse; inferring the sequence between events; inferring missing details. (Adapted from Richards 1990: 51)

Until fairly recently, the focus in the language classroom was firmly on the development of bottom-up processing strategies. However, in recent years, the need for a balance between both types of strategy has been recognised. A major task confronting the curriculum developer, materials writer and classroom teacher is to sequence and integrate these strategies in ways which facilitate learning. In this book we explore ways in which this might be achieved.

Issues and factors similar to those we have seen in relation to listening comprehension also appear in the research into reading comprehension. For quite a few years there has been a lively debate on the relative claims of bottom-up and top-down approaches to reading comprehension. The central notion behind the bottom-up approach is that reading is basically a matter of decoding a series of written symbols into their aural equivalent. According to this approach, the reader processes every letter as it is encountered. These letters or graphemes are matched with the phonemes of the language, which it is assumed the reader already knows. These phonemes, the minimal units of meaning in the sound system of the language, are blended together to form words. The derivation of meaning is thus the end process in which the language is translated from one form of symbolic representation to another. More recent interactive models of reading give much greater prominence to top-down reading strategies, which obviate some of the shortcomings of a purely bottom-up approach by enabling readers to use their background knowledge of the content of a text as well as knowledge of text structure to reconstruct the writer's original communicative intentions in writing the text.

The importance of interactive approaches to second language reading has been demonstrated in a growing body of empirical research. Nunan (1985), for example, found that the lack of appropriate background knowledge was a more significant factor in the ability of second language learners to comprehend school texts than linguistic complexity as measured by various readability formulae. Carrell *et al.* (1988) also contains a wealth of data on the significance of interactive models of reading for second language reading programs.

It is worth noting that for most of its history, language teaching has focused on written language (see, for example, Kelly 1969; Stern 1983; Howatt 1984). With a few exceptions, it is only comparatively recently that the focus has turned to spoken language. Interest in spoken language was kindled, among other things, by the development of tape recorders which made it possible for researchers to record, transcribe and study in detail oral interactions between people. This research highlighted some of the contrasts between spoken and written language. Thus, while written texts are characterised by well formed sentences which are integrated into highly structured paragraphs, spoken language consists of short, fragmentary utterances in a range of pronunciations. There is often a great deal of repetition and overlap between one speaker and another, and speakers frequently use non-specific references. (They are more likely to say 'it' and 'this' than 'the left-handed monkey wrench' or 'the highly perfumed French poodle on the sofa'.) This is not to say that spoken language is unstructured, but that it is structured differently from written language (Halliday 1985a).

Brown and Yule (1983b) suggest that in contrast with the teaching of written language, teachers concerned with teaching the spoken language must address the following types of question:

1. What is the appropriate form of spoken language to teach?
2. From the point of view of pronunciation, what is an appropriate model?
3. How important is pronunciation?
4. Is it any more important than teaching appropriate handwriting in the foreign language?
5. If so, why?
6. From the point of view of the structures taught, is it all right to teach the spoken language as if it were exactly like the written language, but with a few 'spoken' expressions thrown in?
7. Is it appropriate to teach the same structures to all foreign language students, no matter what their age or their intentions in learning the spoken language?
8. Are those structures which are described in standard grammars the structures which our students should be expected to produce when they speak English?
9. How is it possible to give students any sort of meaningful practice in producing spoken English?

Brown and Yule distinguish between two basic language functions, the transactional function and the interactional function. The transactional function is primarily concerned with the transfer of information, and the getting of goods and services, while the primary purpose of interactional language is to maintain social relationships (Brown and Yule 1983b; Richards 1990). In Chapter 3 we look in greater detail at the methodological implications of this distinction.

Another basic distinction is between monologues and dialogues. The ability to give an uninterrupted oral presentation requires different skills from those involved in having a conversation with one or more other speakers: skills which many native speakers never master adequately (Brown and Yule 1983b). Researchers undertaking conversational and interactional analysis have also shown that interactions do not unfold neatly like textbook dialogues, and that meanings do not come ready made. Participants have to work together to achieve mutual understanding, and conversational skills include the ability to negotiate meaning with one's interlocutors. These are skills which learners must acquire or transfer from their first language, just as they must acquire lexical and morphosyntactic knowledge.

There is also a growing body of research into the development of writing skills. Bell and Burnaby (1984) point out that writing is an extremely complex cognitive activity which requires the writer to demonstrate control of several variables at once. At the sentence level, these include control of content, format, sentence structure, vocabulary, pronunciation, spelling and letter formation. Beyond the sentence, the writer must be able to structure and integrate information into cohesive and coherent paragraphs and texts. These discourse level skills are probably the most difficult of all to master, not only for foreign language learners but for native speakers as well. Some of the most interesting work on the development of writing skills is being carried out by researchers investigating the development of writing in first language users and using Halliday's systemic–functional model as their theoretical framework (see, for example, Martin 1985), and it is time for such a model to be applied to second language research.

To summarise this section, I set out some of the skills which research shows are needed by learners if they are to become successful users of the language. These have been extracted from Nunan (1989a).

In relation to listening, learners need skills in segmenting the stream of speech into meaningful words and phrases; the ability to recognise words, phrases and word classes; ways of relating the incoming message to one's own background knowledge, and identifying the rhetorical and functional intent of an utterance or parts of an aural text; skills in interpreting rhythm, stress and intonation to identify information focus and emotional/attitudinal tone; the ability to extract the gist/essential information from longer aural texts without necessarily understanding every word.

Successful reading involves using word attack skills such as identifying sound/symbol correspondences; using grammatical knowledge to recover meaning, for example interpreting non-finite clauses; using different techniques for different purposes, for example skimming and scanning for key words or information; relating text content to one's own background knowledge of the subject; identifying the rhetorical or functional intention of individual sentences or text segments, for example recognising when the writer is offering a definition or a summary, even when these are not explicitly signalled by phrases such as 'X may be defined as . . .'.

In relation to speaking and oral interaction, learners need the ability to articulate phonological features of the language comprehensibly; mastery of stress, rhythm, intonation patterns; an acceptable degree of fluency; transactional and interpersonal skills; skills in taking short and long speaking turns; skills in the management of interaction; skills in negotiating meaning; conversational listening skills (successful conversations require good listeners as well as good speakers); skills in knowing about and negotiating purposes for conversations; using appropriate conversational formulae and fillers.

Lastly, successful writing involves mastering the mechanics of letter formation and obeying conventions of spelling and punctuation; using the grammatical system to convey one's intended meaning; organising content at the level of the paragraph and the complete text to reflect given/new information and topic/comment structures; polishing and revising one's initial efforts; selecting an appropriate style for one's audience.

An area of increasing significance to language teaching methodology is that of learning strategies, and there has been a marked increase in recent years in research into the learning strategy preferences of second and foreign language learners. Published coursebooks and teaching materials are also begining to utilise tasks designed to increase learners' sensitivity to their own preferred learning strategies as well as to develop more efficient learning strategies. Relevant theory and research and practical applications of this research are explored in Chapter 9.

## 1.4 The context and environment of learning

The context and environment of learning, as well as the management of language classrooms, are relatively under-represented in the literature on language teaching methodology, and one of the aims of this book is to redress the balance by providing a detailed and comprehensive overview of teacher and learner action in the classroom. In keeping with the rest of the book, the discussion is informed by theory and research, and supported by detailed extracts from a wide variety of language classrooms.

In all types of classrooms, teacher talk is important, and has been extensively researched and documented. In language classrooms it is particularly important because the medium is the message. The modifications which teachers make to their language, the questions they ask, the feedback they provide and the types of instructions and explanations they provide can all have an important bearing, not only on the effective management of the classroom, but also on the acquisition by learners of the target language. In this book we explore the language which teachers use in the management of learning and evaluate the effectiveness of different types of teacher talk.

In the preceding section I provided a brief summary of what is currently known about the nature of language in use. In order to develop an effective, empirically based methodology, this knowledge needs to inform and guide classroom practice. In Nunan 1989a, I argue that the concept of the communicative task can provide a way of integrating the research on language learning and use, as well as give practical effect to the research at the level of pedagogical action. The communicative task is described as:

> a piece of classroom work which involves learners in comprehending, manipulating, producing or interacting in the target language while their attention is principally focused on meaning rather than form. The task should also have a sense of completeness, being able to stand alone as a communicative act in its own right. (Nunan 1989a: 10)

Tasks can be typified in many different ways. In analytic terms, tasks will contain some form of input data which might be verbal (for example, a dialogue or reading passage) or non-verbal (for example, a picture sequence) and an activity or procedure which is in some way derived from the input and which sets out what learners are to do in relation to the input. The task will also have (implicitly or explicitly) a goal and roles for teachers and learners.

In this book we look at the research which has provided a theoretical rationale for different types of classroom task. We also look at ways of organising learners, the efficacy of different types of group work, individualised instruction and mixed ability groups. In this analysis, our focus will be on managerial aspects of organising learners for learning as well as the types of organisation and tasks which maximise the potential for second language acquisition.

## 1.5  Classrooms in action

One of the naive assumptions underpinning a great deal of speculative writing on language teaching is that curriculum plans will be faithfully realised at the level of classroom action. There is the further assumption that what teachers present to learners is (more or less) what they learn. This assumption, that planning equals teaching equals learning, has been shown to be simplistic (Nunan 1988b). In this book we see that classrooms are extremely complex places where the moment-by-moment decisions which teachers have to make transform and translate plans into action. In order to capture the realities of the classroom in action, we need to spend time in classrooms observing, documenting and analysing what goes on there. While this might seem like a relatively uncontroversial statement, few books on language teaching methodology actually ground their proposals in the day-to-day realities of the classroom. I have attempted to go some way towards providing a fuller context for the theory and research, as well as the themes, issues and concerns of this book by incorporating into the text classroom transcripts and ethnographic accounts of classrooms in action. The empirical database for this book is derived from observations and transcripts from many classrooms containing a wide variety of learner and teacher types. The great majority of these are reported here for the first time, and were specifically collected for this book. In producing these accounts, I have transcribed all of the teacher and learner language verbatim, and have tried to provide enough information on the context and setting in which the teaching and learning took place to ensure the coherence of the transcriptions.

The flavour of these classroom snapshots is captured in the following extract. It has been taken from a lesson with a group of advanced EFL learners who are undertaking an intensive summer course on English for Business. Like most extracts, it illuminates a number of pedagogical and methodological concerns, and it could be utilised to inform discussion in more than one chapter. For example, if the extract were to occur in a section on group work and learner language, it could illustrate the way in which advanced learners can be stimulated to negotiate content by providing contradictory information. In the context of a discussion on task grading, it could be utilised to show the way in which text, task and learner factors interact to determine difficulty. In a chapter on listening and group interaction, it could provide evaluative data on the potential of jigsaw listening tasks to stimulate interaction. Lastly, in the context of a discussion on grammar, one could look at the use (and misuse) of modality choices by the speakers, and consider the ways in which the interaction could be used in a follow-up grammar lesson focusing on modality.

### Pre-reading task

This extract is from a lesson based on a jigsaw listening task. The students have spent forty minutes working in two groups of ten. The students in each group were given a taped conversation and the following worksheet. While the worksheet for the two groups was identical, the tapes contained different, and, in some instances, conflicting information.

Before reading the extract, make a note of the language you would expect this sort of task to elicit (think in particular of the language of negotiation and expressing agreement/disagreement).

---

SITUATION You work for a printing firm which produces weekly magazines. Your firm is going through a period of contraction, and the manager is in the process of deciding on a number of redundancies. At present there are three foremen in the Works Department: Alan Larkin, Geoffrey Richards and Philip Green. At least one, and possibly two of these men are going to be made redundant.

TASK The Managing Director has asked you to put forward a joint recommendation saying which of the three men should be sacked and which should definitely be kept on.

PROCEDURE
1. Listen to the tape and fill in the information table.
2. Rank the information from most to least important in terms of its value in deciding whether the individual should be retained.

3. Decide who should be sacked and who should be retained.
4. Discuss your conclusion with a member of the other class group. You have to reach a joint agreement which is satisfactory to both of you.
5. Having reached agreement, complete and sign the memorandum.

INFORMATION TABLE

| Alan Larkin | Geoffrey Richards | Philip Green |
| --- | --- | --- |
|  |  |  |

MEMORANDUM

To:      The Managing Director

From:    The Works Manager/Personnel Manager

Having given lengthy consideration to your request, we have come to the following decision:

_____ Should be made redundant.

_____ May be made redundant if the financial situation deteriorates.

_____ Should be retained.

Signed:

Dated:

### *Classroom extract 1.1: A jigsaw listening task*

Having completed steps 1–3, the students regroup into pairs. As the members of the pairs are drawn from different groups, they have access to rather different information. The following discussion is between one of the students and a native-speaking student teacher who joined in the task to make up the numbers.

[Michael and George are sitting in a corner of the classroom facing each other across a desk. They have been trying to resolve a difference of opinion engendered by the different versions of the tape they have heard.]

M:  Are you talking about Alan or Geoffrey? Just the first name.

G:  Well, I understood I was talking about Geoffrey, yeah. Is that correct?

M:  Not at all.

[At several points in the interaction, M, the second language learner exhibits weaknesses in modality choices which makes his disagreements seem abrupt, even confrontationist.]

G:  Not at all. So I have confused the man, have I? I've made a mistake here. Who . . . who are you . . . can you. . . . What notes do you have on Richards? See if we can get this sorted out first.

M:  We're talking about Geoffrey, right? And he's certainly the man that had a very good report. He knows the job, and I don't see why we should at all discuss this because it is so obvious to me that he should be on the payroll.

G:  Well, it could very well be that I'm confusing the names of the people involved, so let's make sure we're talking about the same people, shall we?

[They study their notes for a few minutes, and, after some discussion, finally agree on who to eliminate. They then begin discussing Alan Larkin.]

G:  But he is a foreman, rather than a supervisor, I understand, and this is basically a union job, is it not? I mean, I . . . my information is that all these people are occupying more or less the same rank.

M:  Yes, but I mean, er, I agree, they are all, erm, foremen. Supervisor, by the way, is the same to me. Isn't it to you?

G:  Um. no, it's not quite the same thing to me. A foreman is, uh, somewhat lower on the, er, range, right?

M:  All right, so he himself is not a supervisor and he is in the same rank as Geoffrey, yeah?

[Here, the participants spend several minutes negotiating to resolve a misunderstanding of the role and functions of 'foreman' and 'supervisor'. The misunderstanding is finally resolved when George insists that he knows best.]

G: Yeah.

M: But they, they all three have some kind of a
leading operator or a foreman's job, right?
We can't have a foreman doing a union job.

G: Well, actually, I must say on this issue that
foremen are, in fact, um, key figures – usually
in the union . . . the trade union set up.

[G, as the native speaker, finally claims privileged knowledge, in the process providing a good model of how to use modality to soften disagreement.]
[The teacher claps his hands]

T: Okay, can we, can we just reformulate now
into one group?

[There is shuffling and noise as chairs and desks are rearranged.]

T: Okay, then, what did you agree on?

M: Not much.

[Laughter.]

T: Who did you think should get the . . . should
be made redundant?

M: Philip Green.

T: And who should be kept on?

M: We didn't finish that.


### Post-reading task

1. To what extent were your predictions about the type of language generated by the task borne out?
2. If you were designing a follow-up lesson to this, with highly proficient second language learners, what would you focus on?


Most classroom extracts demonstrate the complexity of the classroom, and the multiple events which occur within them. Extract 1.1 is no exception, and could provide analytical data for many different aspects of language learning and teaching, including listening comprehension, modality choices by advanced learners (for example, using 'may' or 'might' to soften the force of disagreeing with one's interlocutor), negotiation of meaning and pedagogical task, group and pair work and so on. In presenting each extract, I limit my comments to those issues and events pertinent to the chapter in which the extract occurs. Further analysis by the reader will reveal many other interesting things going on, and most of the extracts will repay more study and analysis.

## 1.6  Exploring language classrooms

It is all very well to find out what has been said about a particular subject, and how this knowledge has been applied in the development of teaching materials and classroom tasks. However, from the perspective of practical methodology, such information is of limited value to readers unless they have the opportunity to explore the ideas in relation to their own classroom context or to their own development as practitioners. In order to provide this essential third step in the process of professional engagement – from ideas, to application, to exploration – each of the chapters concludes with a series of tasks which are designed to encourage readers to apply and assess the ideas, materials and methods presented in the body of the chapter. The notion of teachers researching their own classrooms has been current for a number of years. As far back as 1975, Stenhouse argued that it was not enough for teachers work to be researched, that they need to research it themselves. More recently, Larsen-Freeman and Long (1991) have commented on the growing interest in teacher-initiated action research, and the value of such research in helping teachers gain understanding of and enhance their teaching. They see cause for optimism in this trend, and express the hope that eventually all language teacher preparation programmes will contain a 'train the teacher as classroom researcher' component.

Action research as an integral part of teachers' professional practice has been argued for most recently and forcefully by Kemmis and McTaggart (1988: 10) who provide a four-stage cycle for carrying out such research. They suggest that to do action research, a group and its members must first develop an action plan to improve what is already happening. The next step is to implement the plan. Step three is to observe the effects of the intervention in the context in which it occurs. The final step is to reflect on these effects and use this as a basis for a further cycle of planning, action, observation and reflection.

Of course, it is not necessary for every exploratory investigation to take the shape of a fully formulated action research project along the lines suggested by Kemmis and McTaggart. However, such projects, in the appropriate circumstances and with adequate support, can be immensely valuable as a way of contesting ideas and fuelling professional growth, and are one of the most effective ways of counteracting the pendulum effect referred to at the beginning of the chapter.

The following example of an action research project illustrates the various steps in the process, and shows how the process might operate in the context of language education.

**Step 1: Problem identification.** In a staffroom, a teacher is talking to me about the problems she is having with one of her classes. The major problem seems to be that the students do not seem interested or motivated.

**Step 2: Preliminary investigation.** The teacher and I decide that we will collaborate to investigate the classroom and obtain a record of what is going on. I spend several hours in the classroom over the next few days, recording and observing the teacher and the students. The teacher and I review the material I have gathered and discuss it.

**Step 3: Hypothesis.** On the basis of our review, we decide that the content does not seem to stimulate students, nor do they seem to make connections between the content of the lessons and their own needs and interests.

**Step 4: Plan intervention.** A conscious effort is made by the teacher to make links between the content and the learners. She does this principally by modifying the types of question she asks, in particular increasing the number of open, referential questions. (Referential questions are those to which the teacher does not know the answer. For an extended discussion of their role in second language classrooms see Long and Sato 1983.)

**Step 5: Outcome.** Recordings made a week later show that more complex interactions are taking place in the classroom. There is more involvement and interest on the part of the students, there is more 'natural' discourse (e.g. students nominate topics, they disagree with teacher, and there is more student–student interaction), and the language learners use is more complex syntactically.

**Step 6: Reporting.** The teacher conducts a staff development session in which she describes the project and its outcomes.

As already indicated, I am not suggesting here that all observations and investigations need to assume the proportions of a full-scale action research project. However, this case study does illustrate a number of important points. In the first place, such research has the potential to address practical problems affecting teachers' everyday lives. Secondly, that it can provide a link between theory, research and practice. In the example you have just read, the teacher reflected on the nature of teacher–student interaction, and read several research reports on teacher questions and their effect on learner output. In short, the study illustrates the potential of classroom observation and research to act as a professional development tool. (For a detailed description and analysis of the use of action research in language classrooms see Nunan 1989b.)

In the chapters which follow, we see that published research can be a useful point of departure for teachers interested in researching their own classrooms. Teachers can either replicate published research to evaluate its usefulness for their own context, or they can take the research one step further, modifying and adapting it to explore questions of importance in their classrooms.

## 1.7 How to use this book

This book has been designed to provide maximum flexibility for teachers, teacher educators and student teachers. The chapters can be worked through sequentially, or individual chapters can be studied discretely. In fact, the materials on which this book is based have been used on a number of courses in a modular format. That said, I would recommend that the first five chapters be dealt with sequentially because a model of language and learning is built up over the course of the chapters, and it will be easier to understand this model if the chapters are read in sequence.

Each chapter follows a similar pattern. The initial sections are devoted to an over-view of the theory and research which has been conducted. This provides a basis for exploring how the ideas and research outcomes have been applied in teaching, task design and materials development. The chapter concludes with a series of action research tasks which invite you to explore the ideas in the context of your own classroom.

The book can be either used individually or collaboratively. In the latter case, it is a good idea to read the initial sections individually. This can be followed by group work, in which the classroom extracts and sample teaching tasks and materials are evaluated against the theory and research. Because of the centrality of the classroom extracts to the philosophy of the book as a whole, I have provided pre- and post-reading tasks to help focus your reading of the tasks. Lastly, if you are currently teaching, you can take one or two of the exploration/application tasks to try with your own students. A final group discussion session can then enable you to provide and receive feedback on the outcomes of the application tasks.

## 1.8  Conclusion

I have argued that language teaching methodology needs to be placed on a more secure empirical footing. Materials, learning tasks and pedagogical exercises need to be based not on ideology or dogma, as is too often the case now, but on evidence and insights into what constitutes effective language teaching. I have tried to show that a considerable body of knowledge exists and can be readily exploited by materials designers and methodologists.

In the long run, research will be effective only to the extent that it is embraced by teachers. Therefore, there needs to be a much closer relationship between teaching and research and between teachers and researchers, and teachers themselves need to be involved in the research process. Such involvement is consonant with the vision of Barnes, who said:

> To frame the questions and answer them, we must grope towards our invisible knowledge and bring it into sight. Only in this way can we see the classroom with an outsider's eye but an insider's knowledge, by seeing it as if it were the behaviour of people from an alien culture. Then, by an act of imagination we can both understand better what happens and conceive of alternative possibilities. (Barnes 1975: 13)

In the rest of this book we shall be taking up and extending some of the themes and issues which have been briefly touched upon here. Chapters 2–9 look at the nature of language learning and use, and include chapters on listening, speaking and oral interaction, the development of literacy, vocabulary and pronunciation, the role of grammar within language teaching methodology, and learning strategies and styles. In Chapter 10 the focus of attention is the context in which language learning and teaching take place: and here we shall address issues related to classroom management and organisation. Chapter 11 looks at resources for teaching, particularly the development of teaching materials. Chapter 12 provides a critical analysis of a number of prominent methods, along with an evaluation of the place of methods within language teaching methodology. The final chapter summarises the major issues which have emerged in the book, and points the way to future developments.

This book differs in several significant ways from other texts on language teaching methodology. I have already indicated some of these, including the empirical approach based on research and real classroom data, and the active involvement of the reader. In concluding, I should like to highlight other important distinguishing features of this book. This book is not intended as a book of recipes for tired teachers. Nor is it a prescription for practice. Rather, readers are invited, through the critical reading, evaluation and informed application of the research and ideas set out here, to discover and develop their own philosophy of teaching, and to create their own methodological practices.

# Chapter Two

## *Communicative Approaches to Listening Comprehension*

### 2.1 Introduction

In this chapter we address issues relating to listening comprehension. In the first section, we shall examine different views on the nature of listening comprehension and look at recent research into listening. This is followed by a section in which we shall see how views on the nature of listening and the results of research into listening have been applied to listening programmes, materials and pedagogical tasks. This will provide a basis for you to explore listening processes in your own context. The chapter addresses the following questions:

1. What is meant by bottom-up and top-down approaches to listening?
2. How can we characterise different types of listening task?
3. What is it that distinguishes texts from non-texts?
4. What makes listening difficult for language learners?
5. How can insights from theory and research be incorporated into listening materials and pedagogical tasks?

### 2.2 Bottom-up and top-down views of listening

What happens when we comprehend aural messages? What is it that good listeners do to derive meaning from the texts they hear? According to one view, they segment the stream of speech into its constituent sounds, link these together to form words, chain the words together to form clauses and sentences and so on. This view is known as the bottom-up approach to listening, and its inadequacy can be easily demonstrated. Consider the following text from Bransford and Johnson (1972):

**Text 1**
The procedure is actually quite simple. First you arrange things into different groups. Of course, one pile may be sufficient, depending on how much there is to do. If you have to go somewhere else due to lack of facilities that is the next step, otherwise you are pretty well set.

It is important not to overdo things. That is, it is better to do too few things at once than too many. In the short run this may not seem important, but complications can easily arise. A mistake can be expensive as well. At first the whole procedure will seem complicated. Soon, however, it will become just another facet of life. It is difficult to see any end to the necessity for this task in the immediate future, but then one can never tell. After the procedure is completed, one arranges the materials into different groups again. Then they can be put into their appropriate places. Eventually they can be used once more, and the whole cycle will then have to be repeated. However, that is a part of life.

While most native speakers of English would have little trouble in comprehending the sounds, words and clauses in this messages, it is unlikely that they would be able to demonstrate comprehension by listening to the text and writing a precis or providing a verbal account. However, if they are provided with a context for making sense of the text then the task becomes relatively simple. For example, if the listener is told that text 1 is about 'washing clothes', then the individual constituents are much more readily interpretable, and the task of recalling the information in it is much easier.

In effect the title 'Washing Clothes' enables the listener to bring knowledge from outside the text to the task of interpreting and comprehending the text itself, and this illustrates an important point: that meaning does not reside exclusively within the words on the tape recorder or on the page. It also exists in the head of the listener or reader. Successful listeners and readers are those who can utilise both 'inside the head' knowledge and 'outside the head' knowledge to interpret what they hear and see. The use of inside the head knowledge, that is, knowledge which is not directly encoded in words, is known as the top-down view of listening.

In their book on listening, Anderson and Lynch (1988) contrast the bottom-up view of 'listener as tape recorder' with the top-down view of 'listener as model builder'. The view of listener as tape recorder suggests that the listener takes in and stores aural messages in much the same way as a tape recorder. However, research shows that this is not the way that listening works. If you ask someone to listen to a message and write down as much of the message as they can recall, you will generally find that they have remembered some bits of the message, they have forgotten other bits, and they have added in bits which were not in fact in the message at all. In addition, those bits which are successfully recalled will not be in the exact words of the original message. It seems that when we comprehend messages, we store the meanings but not the linguistic forms. The alternative to the listener as tape recorder view, that of listener as active model builder, accords a much more active role to listeners as they construct an interpretation of a message by utilising both bottom-up and top-down knowledge.

## 2.3 Identifying different types of listening

One of the underlying themes of this book is that language exists to fulfil communicative and functional purposes, and that these purposes will be reflected in language structures themselves. In other words, the context in which language is used and the purposes to which it is put will play a large part in shaping language. Given this view, a logical place to start in our investigation of listening is to consider the different purposes for listening and attempting to come up with a taxonomy of listening tasks. As a preliminary exercise, you might like to examine the following texts and consider the ways in which they might be grouped together.

## Text 2

Weatherwise for the city, continuing mild to warm conditions. Cloudy at times. There's the slight chance of a late shower or thunderstorm. Local overnight fogs inland. The predicted temperature ranges: 17–26 near the coast; 15–29 inland. Currently it is 25 degrees in town. That's 3 degrees above the average. Further outlook, sunny and warm on Friday, a cool change with showers on Saturday, and rain on Sunday.

## Text 3

| | |
|---|---|
| Helga: | Er, excuse me. |
| Receptionist: | Yes? |
| Helga: | Can you tell me how to get from the Youth Hostel to the Zoo? |
| Receptionist: | Are you going by public transport or what? |
| Helga: | Yes, I want to go by public transport. |
| Receptionist: | Your best bet is just to walk out to Paramatta Road. |
| Helga: | Yes. |
| Receptionist: | Turn left. |
| Helga: | Mmm . . . |
| Receptionist: | Get the bus to Circular Quay. |
| Helga: | Yes. |
| Receptionist: | Then get a ferry straight over to the Zoo. |
| Helga: | Great! Good! What number bus would that be? |
| Receptionist: | Oh, they've got it on the front – 'Circular Quay'. There're about half a dozen buses that go through on Paramatta Road, so you've got no problems. |
| Helga: | Right! Great! Thanks a lot. Oh, and, er, how much is it? |
| Receptionist: | Let's see – it's three sections. That's $1.20. |
| Helga: | Okay. |
| Receptionist: | Bye. |

## Text 4

Oh, anything – I'm terrible, you know – *EastEnders* – I'm terrible for the soapies. I'll watch real rubbish – *Sale of the Century* – anything like that . . . I should be saying the News, and all the current affairs programmes, documentaries and that kind of thing, but I've got to be in the mood for them, 'cause they take more effort. I use the TV to relax, you know, after work. I just want to put my feet up and watch a load of rubbish. I feel ashamed but it's true . . . But at least I don't watch the video clips until 4 am!

## Text 5

A forty-year-old fisherman has died after being swept off the rocks at Malabar this afternoon. He and a friend were both swept into the sea. The friend struggled to safety, but the victim died after being airlifted from the water to the Prince Henry Hospital.

**Text 6**

Sue:      Hang on [yell] . . .
          [Door opens] Sorry. Ah, you must be Yumiko. . . . We . . . .
Yumiko:   Hello, yes. And you are Sue.
Sue:      Yes, yes. And this is Dave, my husband.
Dave:     How do you do?
Sue:      And the kids are in watching TV. Come in, come in . . . Let me help you with your
          cases – Is that all?
Yumiko:   Thank you.
Sue:      Here, Dave, take these to Yumiko's room. Your room's downstairs – first on the
          right. I'll show you later. Come on into the kitchen and we'll have a drink.
          [footsteps] Kids, this is Yumiko from Japan.
Kids:     Hi!
Sue:      Come on, turn off the telly. Come on and have a drink, Yumiko. Are you tired? The
          flight was late wasn't it?

**Text 7**

Alice:    Hi there . . . . hi!
Bruce:    Oh, Alice, hi – slaving over a hot barbecue. The wood's wet – not burning [coughs].
          All this rain. Come in – yeah – I nearly thought we'd have to . . . you know, call the
          party off.
Alice:    Yes, I almost rang yesterday. But the weather looks okay. I almost got stranded on the
          Gladesville Bridge – I could hardly see anything.
Bruce:    Alice – you know Alex and Jan, don't you?
Alice:    Well, no – I know you both by sight . . .
Alex:     . . . yes . . .
Alice:    You live next door to Jerry and Sharon, don't you?
Jan:      Yes – hi – it's awful – we've all been here for years but . . .
Alex:     . . . and this is David, our three year old.

(Texts 2–7 adapted from Nunan and Lockwood 1989)

The first thing to notice is that some texts are monologues, being produced by only
one speaker, while others are created by the joint endeavour of two or more
speakers. Obviously, comprehending monologues involves different listening skills
from those required to take part in interactional tasks involving speaking as well as
listening. This suggests that we can classify listening tasks into those which involve
only listening and those which demand some form of oral interaction.

In considering the three monologues (that is, texts 2, 4 and 5), most people would
agree that that texts 2 and 5 seem to have more characteristics in common than
text 4. They are more carefully structured and planned than text 3 which consists
of fragmentary utterances and which seems to have been created on the spot in
response to an initial question. Texts 2 and 5, in contrast, look as though they were
written out beforehand. Notice also the clipped, elided language of text 2 which is
designed to convey the maximum amount of information in the shortest possible
time.

Texts 3, 6 and 7 can also be subdivided. In this case, texts 6 and 7 seem to have more in common than text 3. Texts 6 and 7 seem to be basically social in their purpose, while the purpose of text 3 is to obtain and provide information. This reflects the broad distinction between 'interactional' talk and 'transactional' talk (Brown and Yule 1983b; Richards 1990). Of course, both interactional and transactional functions can coexist in any given interaction, and interactions themselves are more-or-less interactional and more-or-less transactional (in fact, many utterances have both an interactional *and* a transactional function). In a sense, all three texts are interactional, and it might be better to use the term 'interpersonal' for the socially oriented talk.

Texts 6 and 7 can be further subdivided. Text 6 is created by people who are strangers to each other, whereas the interactions in text 7 are between people who know each other. This is reflected in the level of formality in the language used and the shared knowledge of the interactants in text 7. This can be schematised as in Figure 2.1.

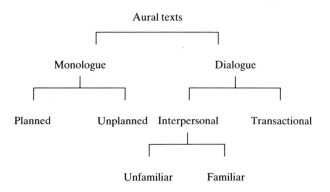

FIGURE 2.1 *A classification of aural texts.*

## 2.4 Textual connectivity

Since the 1960s, there has been a broadening of focus from linguistic analysis at the level of the sentence, to analysis at the level of discourse: that is, to an analysis of sentences in combination. A major problem confronting discourse analysts is that of defining discourse and determining what it is that distinguishes coherent discourse from random sentences. (Coherence refers to the sense in which the individual sentences or utterances of a text 'hang together'.) In some instances, it seems fairly obvious that a piece of language forms a coherent text. Consider, for example, texts 8 and 9.

**Text 8**

A fortnight ago, I walked into a gloomy isolation shelter constructed of black plastic stretched over eucalyptus poles. Sprawled on the dirt floor was a young lad we had nicknamed Snakebite. He was brought in by one of the nurses early in the morning, after being bitten on the foot by a snake which had slithered into his shelter. Snakebite survived that incident, but he looked close to death through shock and hunger.

**Text 9**

The offspring born, some say, of a marriage of convenience, died in infancy last Sunday. Walk into any office and you are likely to be offered a cup of Chinese tea or a cup of coffee. It is becoming acceptable for women to visit – either in groups or alone – discos and lounges for an enjoyable night out.

Most people immediately, and correctly, identify that the sentences which make up text 8 seem to cohere, whereas those in text 9 do not. What is it that gives text 8 its coherence? A cursory inspection indicates that there are certain expressions within the text which help to bind the sentences together. Some of these expressions, and the way they provide vertical integration are illustrated below.

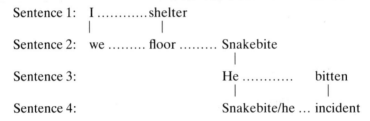

In text 9, however, there are no such devices. From this, it would seem that texts are given their coherence, that is, their sense of unity, by certain relationships between the different sentences or utterances in the text which are marked by particular words and expressions. This view is proposed by Halliday and Hasan (1976), who define texts, as opposed to random sentences, in terms of the linguistic elements which serve to bind the texts together. These linguistic elements and expressions are referred to as cohesive devices.

The notion that the coherence or sense of unity of a text is created by cohesion is challenged by Widdowson (1978, 1979) among others. He provides the following (invented) example to support his case.

A: That's the telephone.
B: I'm in the bath.
A: Okay.

Most people recognise the utterances in this text as somehow 'going together' even though there are no explicit cohesive links between the utterances. Widdowson suggests that we are able to create our own coherence for the sample by recognising the function that each utterance fulfils within a given context or situation. He suggests that most native speakers of English would create a domestic context in which the following functions are assigned to each utterance:

| Utterance | Function |
|---|---|
| A: That's the telephone. | Request |
| B: I'm in the bath. | Excuse |
| A: Okay. | Acceptance of excuse |

In creating a meaningful context and attributing functional intent, coherence (that is, a sense that the three utterances form a meaningful whole) is established. Widdowson suggests that as a result the missing bits of the conversation, which would make it cohesive as well as coherent, could be restored. Such a conversation might run as follows:

A: That's the telephone. Could you answer it, please?
B: No, I'm sorry, I can't answer it because I'm in the bath.
A: Okay, I'll answer it.

Edmonson (1981) also asks what distinguishes text from non-text. He points out that it is difficult to fabricate non-text because some sort of context can generally be created within which a given set of sentences can be accorded some sort of meaning. In illustrating his argument, he borrows the following text from van Dijk (who asserted that the two sentences were a non-text because there was nothing to bind them together).

We will have guests for lunch.
Calderon was a great writer.

According to Edmonson (1981: 13), any native speaker will immediately see a causal link between these two sentences. His own interpretation is as follows:

Did you know Calderon died exactly 100 years ago today? Good heavens! I'd forgotten. The occasion shall not pass unnoticed. We will have guests for lunch. Calderon was a great Spanish writer. I shall invite Professor Wilson and Señor Castellano right away . . .

It is worth noting that in order to illustrate their point, both Widdowson and Edmonson provide fictitious and very curtailed examples – three utterances in the case of one text and two in the other. It is extremely difficult to find natural texts of any duration which do not contain any form of cohesion. The other point with which one might want to take issue is Edmonson's claim that any native speaker will immediately be able to see that van Dijk's sentences are (or can be) coherent. In fact, coming up with a context such as his requires considerable ingenuity.

## 2.5 Listening purpose

Another important consideration in listening concerns the listener's purpose. Coursebooks for teaching listening sometimes seem to imply that listeners grimly focus on every word. This is, of course, simply not true. When listening to television or radio news broadcasts, we usually tune in to certain items and exclude others. The exclusion can be due to a lapse in concentration or to a lack of interest in certain topics, or to efficiency in listening.

An important factor in interactive listening is whether or not we are taking part in the interaction. Eavesdropping on a conversation is very different from actually participating in one. Because of this, it may seem a waste of time to involve learners in classroom tasks in which they are involved in listening to conversations among other people. However, such tasks can be justified on at least two grounds. In the first instance, providing the conversations are authentic (that is, they were not specifically created for the purpose of illustrating or teaching features of the language), they can provide learners with insights into ways in which conversations work. They can also provide learners with strategies for comprehending conversation outside the classroom in which they are not actively involved, but which may provide them with input to feed their learning processes.

## 2.6  What makes listening difficult?

Determining difficulty is a major problem confronting syllabus designers and curriculum specialists who choose to adopt the notion of 'task' as a central planning tool (see Nunan 1989a, for an extended discussion on this point). Fortunately, there has been considerable work done in recent years on the factors which create difficulty for listeners and speakers. (An excellent book on listening is Rost 1990.)

Brown and Yule (1983b) suggest that there are four clusters of factors which can affect the difficulty of oral language tasks: these relate to the speaker (how many there are, how quickly they speak, what types of accent they have); the listener (the role of the listener – whether a participant or eavesdropper, the level of response required, the individual interest in the subject); the content (grammar, vocabulary, information structure, background knowledge assumed); support (whether there are pictures, diagrams or other visual aids to support the text).

Anderson and Lynch (1988) present a graded language program in which they systematically varied aspects of the text which the learners heard and the tasks they were to perform. Anderson and Lynch suggest that, while a large number of factors are involved these fall into three principal categories: (1) the type of language; (2) the purpose in listening; (3) the context in which the listening takes place. We have to consider not only the number of factors involved but also the relationships between them. By holding the text constant (for example, a parliamentary debate) and varying the purpose (e.g. keeping an ear out for the end of the broadcast as opposed to making a mental note of the main points in the debate), one can alter the difficulty level of the task.

In a series of experiments Anderson and Lynch found that the difficulty of listening tasks was particularly influenced by the following:

1. The organisation of information (texts in which the order in which the information was presented matched its chronological sequence in real life were easier than texts in which the information was presented out of sequence).
2. The familiarity of the topic.
3. The explicitness and sufficiency of the information.
4. The type of referring expressions used (for example, use of pronouns rather than complete noun phrase referents made texts more difficult).
5. Whether the text described 'static' relationships (for example, geometric figures) or dynamic relationship (for example, a road accident).

The way these features were manipulated to produce texts which were similar generically but which were graded for difficulty can be illustrated by the task of 'trace the route'. In this task, students listen to a description of a journey, route or tour and have to trace this route on a map. The task designers systematically varied the type of map, the completeness of information, whether the start or end is given, the number of features and the congruence or otherwise of the information presented in the text and that displayed on the map. These variations changed the difficulty level of the task. It was found that maps which were laid out in a rectangular fashion with all roads marked were easier than those in which the roads and paths were irregular; these were in turn easier than maps consisting of natural landmarks. In terms of completeness of information, tasks became increasingly difficult according to the number of items mentioned in the text which were missing from the map. Those in which the start and end of the route were indicated on the map were easier than those in which they were omitted. As the number of features (buildings, natural landmarks, etc.) increased, so too did the difficulty. Lastly, in terms of referring expressions, it was found that reiterations were easier than synonyms. The most difficult tasks were those in which there was contradictory information in the text and on the map. In the next section we look in detail at the construction of a listening task which exploits these features.

## 2.7 Listening texts and tasks

Thus far, we have noted that successful listening involves the integration of information encoded in the message itself with broader knowledge of the world. In other words, successful listeners use both bottom-up and top-down strategies in reconstructing messages. We have also seen that listening texts and tasks differ, and can be classified in several different ways. In the first instance, we have listening tasks which involve the comprehension of aural texts in which there is only one speaker, as opposed to two or more speakers. The task of comprehending interactive language will be quite different according to whether the listener is eavesdropping or taking part in the conversation. Interactive listening can also be classified according to whether its function is primarily social or transactional. Purpose is also a crucial factor, and listening tasks will differ according to the listener's purpose. In this section, we shall look at some of the ways in which these ideas have been applied in practice. In addition to the sources cited here, Rost (1990) provides probably the best practical set of ideas on teaching listening currently available.

In pedagogical terms, it is possible to draw a distinction between bottom-up and top-down approaches to listening comprehension. Bottom-up listening activities focus learners on the individual elements and building blocks of the language. Decoding oral utterances, discriminating between individual sounds, particularly those with minimal contrasts, and identifying different stress, rhythm and intonation patterns feature prominently in the early stages of learning, and the student is only gradually moved from sound to word to sentence to text.

In a listening comprehension course which was widely used in the 1970s, the assumption that learning is a gradual, linear and additive process is evident in the way the input is staged.

> **Book 1** gives a practical introduction to the main features of pronunciation practice, with exercises in sound (phoneme) contrasts, stress and rhythm, and intonation patterns. It is divided into three parts: the first deals with individual sounds, the second with stress, rhythm and intonation, while the third contains tests.

> **Book 2** tests aural comprehension of short pieces of spoken English, longer than just a single sentence. It often uses anecdotes for this purpose, and again there are numerous exercises.

> **Book 3** contains short lectures on a variety of subjects, in styles ranging from quite formal to informal. This book exposes students to longer stretches of speech, and tests their ability both to make written notes and to reproduce these notes either orally or in writing.
> (Byrne 1973: vii)

With the development of communicative approaches to language teaching, and particularly with the increasing popularity of authentic materials, classroom activities have become more closely related to the sorts of thing learners are likely to want or need to do outside the classroom. With low-level learners, the activity rather than the listening text is modified to make the task easier. Instead of being expected to extract the full meaning of the text, the listener might only be required to determine the number of speakers or to identify the number of key words. The following shows how the activity rather than the text can be adapted.

### Tapescript

Part 1

| | |
|---|---|
| Receptionist: | Good morning. Burwood Clinic. Hold the line, please. |
| | [music] |
| | Sorry to keep you waiting. Can I help you? |
| Adam: | Yes, I'm wondering if I can make a doctor's appointment sometime today? |
| Receptionist: | Yes, certainly. With Dr Cullen? |

| Adam: | Yes, please. |
| Receptionist: | When would you like the appointment? |
| Adam: | Um, what about mid-afternoon? Would that be all right? |
| Receptionist: | Um, well, Doctor only starts his clinic at four o'clock. |
| Adam: | Four o'clock . . . Okay , well, could we make it for 4.30, please. |
| Receptionist: | Yes, certainly. What's the name, please? |
| Adam: | The name is Walker, w-a-l-k-e-r. Adam Walker. |
| Receptionist: | Okay, we'll see you then. |
| Adam: | Um, I haven't been there before. |
| Receptionist: | That's okay, I'll take all your details when you come in then. |
| Adam: | Okay, fine, bye. |
| Receptionist: | Bye. |

With low-level learners who would clearly be challenged by such input, the difficulty can be eased by letting them hear the text as often as necessary and providing a range of activities of increasing complexity. The first time they hear the text, they might be asked to identify how many speakers they hear. The second time they hear the text, they can be given a list of key words and asked to nominate how often they hear the words. Next, they can be given phrase to identify. Lastly, they can be asked to identify the number of questions they hear. These activities are exemplified below.

1. Listen to the tape. How many speakers can you hear?

2. Listen to the tape a second time. How many times can you hear these words? (Tick the column.)

Clinic

Doctor

Appointment

Surgery

Name

3. Listen again and circle the words you hear.
    1. (a) Hold the phone, please.
       (b) Hold the line, please.
    2. (a) With Dr Cullen?
       (b) With Dr Mullen?
    3. (a) What about the afternoon?
       (b) What about mid-afternoon?
    4. (a) Could we make it for four-thirty?
       (b) Could we make it for half-past four?
    5. (a) I haven't been there before.
       (b) I haven't seen him before.

4. Listen to the tape one more time. How many questions can you hear?
    □ 5 □ 6 □ 7 □ 8 □ 9

(Adapted from Nunan and Lockwood 1989)

Another technique, this time one which encourages learners to utilise both bottom-up and top-down listening strategies is the 'dictogloss'. Here, the teacher reads a passage at normal speed to learners who listen and write down as many words as they can identify. They then collaborate in small groups to reconstruct the text on the basis of the fragments which they have written down. While the technique bears a passing resemblance to the traditional dictation test, the resemblance is only superficial. In the words of the author:

> The method requires learners in the classroom to interact with each other in small groups so as to reconstruct the text as a co-operative endeavour. Learners working in self-study are required to bring their own grammatical resources into play with the notes taken during the dictation so as to create a text. Both in the classroom and in self-study, learners are actively engaged in the learning process. It is believed that through this active learner involvement students come to confront their own strengths and weaknesses in English language use. In so doing, they find out what they don't know, then they find out what they need to know and this is the process by which they improve their language skills. (Wajnryb 1986: 6)

There are four stages in the dictogloss approach.

1. **Preparation.** At this stage, teachers prepare students for the text they will be hearing by asking questions and discussing a stimulus picture, by discussing vocabulary, by ensuring that students know what they are supposed to do, and by ensuring that the students are in the appropriate groups.
2. **Dictation.** Learners hear the dictation twice. The first time, they listen only and get a general feeling for the text. The second time they take down notes, being encouraged to listen for content words which will assist them in reconstructing the text. For reasons of consistency, it is preferable that students listen to a cassette recording rather than teacher-read text.
3. **Reconstruction.** At the conclusion of the dictation, learners pool notes and produce their version of the text. During this stage it is important that the teacher does not provide any language input.
4. **Analysis and correction.** There are various ways of dealing with this stage. The small group versions can be reproduced on the board or overhead projector, the texts can be photocopied and distributed, or the students can compare their version with the original, sentence by sentence.

The dictogloss technique provides a useful bridge between bottom-up and top-down listening. In the first instance, learners are primarily concerned with identifying individual elements in the text – a bottom-up strategy. However, during the small group discussions, some or all of the following top-down strategies might be employed. In all of these, the listener will integrate background, 'inside the head' knowledge with the clues picked up during the dictation.

1. Listeners will make predictions.
2. Listeners will make inferences about things not directly stated in the text.
3. Listeners will identify the topic of the text.

4. Listeners will identify the text type (whether it is a narrative, description, anecdote etc.).
5. Listeners will identify various sorts of semantic relationships in the text.

The following texts give some idea of the length and complexity of the texts provided in the books on dictogloss. I have chosen the first text in book 1 and the final text in book 2.

### EARTHQUAKE

In 1985 there was an earthquake in Mexico City. Many thousands of people died in the disaster. People searched the city for missing relatives and friends. Rescuers worked without rest for many days. There was a great deal of suffering and enormous destruction. (Wajnryb 1986: 16)

### HATS ARE BACK

Australia has the highest rate of skin cancer in the world and moves are now under way to cut down its incidence. One means of combating skin cancer is to wear a hat. Pressured by parent committees, many schools are now introducing hats as part of the standard uniform. The committees are made up of parents who went through school when hats were rarely worn and they are the ones who have suffered badly from skin cancer. Designed by the parent committees, the hats are tested by the Cancer Council authorities before being accepted as part of the uniform. After being out of vogue for years, hats are now beginning to reappear. (Wajnryb 1988: 80)

Dictogloss exploits the principle that two heads are better than one. Students are able to pool their resources, and even low-level learners are able, through collaborative action, to 'outperform their competence'.

Anderson and Lynch (1988) have also developed a technique for making listening tasks more interactive. They have done this by changing the roles of the teacher and learners. The teacher plays a recorded text to which the students listen and complete an activity such as tracing a route on a map. The teacher pauses at certain key points, and the students are able to discuss the task. The students can also request that the teacher stop the tape at any point so they can discuss the task. The teacher only provides information on demand from the students. A number of 'problem points' are built into the task which are designed to increase the processing demands on the learners and to encourage students to interact.

The selection of problem points was guided by research into task difficulty. In the preceding section we saw that in the 'trace the route' task, in which students listen to a description and trace the route being described, the type of map, the completeness of information, whether the start or end is given, the number of features and the compatibility or otherwise of the information presented in the text and that displayed in the map can all be varied to affect the difficulty level of the task. The trace the route task is illustrated by the Tai Tu City Tour task (Illustration 1). Listeners were given the map and listened to the accompanying text.

## ILLUSTRATION 1

*Tai Tu City Tour: Introduction*
'The map you have in front of you shows part of the city centre of Tai Tu, in the Far East. As you listen, mark in the route that your tour will take. You are staying at the hotel in the centre of the map and your tour will begin and end there.

If you are not sure of the route as the guide explains it, ask for the tape to be stopped. You can then hear that part of the tape replayed, or you can ask for more information to help you.'

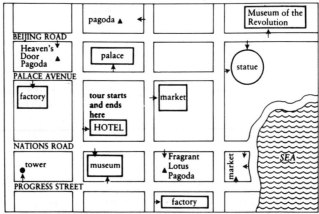

(Arrows on map indicate position of entrances to places of interest)

*Hearer's map*

*Instructions tapescript*
'right + the tour starts off from the hotel + and we go up as far as the Beijing Road + we turn into the Beijing Road + and then we take the first left and that's the first stop + the White Cloud Pagoda (*pause*) we have about half an hour or so at the pagoda + than we leave for the palace + that's down to Palace Avenue and then along (*pause*) after that we come out of the palace and go down the avenue + we go to visit the National Monument (*pause*) right + about twenty minutes there for photographs + then the bus takes us on down that road and first left to the market + and we go into the market from round the back + that's the beach side (*pause*) you'll have time to do some shopping + then back to the bus and we go along Progress Street + and the next place we visit is the Nations Museum + you'll have plenty of time for a good look round and I'll be doing a guided walk for those who want it (*pause*) and then the last stop on the tour is the silk mill + that's along Progress Street and turn right (*pause*) we have about an hour's tour at the mill + then the bus brings us back to the hotel + left into Nations Road + round the corner + and we're back at the hotel (*pause*) and that's the city tour complete'

Source:  A. Anderson and T. Lynch, *Listening* (Oxford University Press, 1988), pp. 107–108. © Oxford University Press. Reproduced by permission.

The Tai Tu City Tour is the first (and easiest) of three trace the route tasks. You will note that the roads are set out in a rectangular fashion, that it is complete (that is, all the places the tourists are to visit appear on the map) and that the start and end of the journey are indicated. There are six features in this task (some of the more challenging tasks contain ten to fifteen features.) In terms of expressions referring to these six features, one is identical, three are synonymous and two are compatible. These are the intended problem points in the task as can be seen from the following:

| **Tapescript** | **Decision** |
| --- | --- |
| we turn into the Beijing Road | turn right not left |
| the White Cloud Pagoda | identified simply as 'pagoda' |
| the National Monument | identified as 'statue' on map |
| the market | there are two markets - correct one is fish market |
| the Nations Museum | identified simply as 'museum' |

The following extracts are taken from Anderson and Lynch (1988). Students are working in small groups. The extracts illustrate the 'active listening' approach used by the authors, in which learners are encouraged to stop the tape and work collaboratively to solve the various problems associated with the task. It is worth noting that one group seems to have more success than the other, and it is instructive to note why this is so. Apart from the obvious advantages of collaborative listening, tasks such as this are an effective antidote to the 'listener as tape recorder' view of listening which learners themselves often have.

### Pre-reading task

1. What difficulties would you anticipate with a task such as this?
2. How would you prepare learners for these potential difficulties (in other words, what pre-teaching would you do)?
3. As you read the extracts, make a note of the difficulties which seem to emerge. Which group seems to be more successful?

### Classroom extract 2.1: An interactive listening task

**Group 1**

Tape:  . . . we turn into Beijing Road and then take the first left and that's the first stop, the White Cloud Pagoda.

Z:    Sorry, is this some information? Is this explain? Only a name, not Pagoda – but it is not enough to directly explain direction. Is the man enter, uh, go out of hotels. It is not enough – explain . . . I think it must explain the go out the hotel and turn the right . . . cross road and then palace behind you.

O:    If he do that . . .

Z:    . . . and then . . .

O:    . . . it will be clear.

Z:    Beijing Road . . . in Beijing Road you turn on the right.

O:    If he do that [Z] excuse me, if you do that, why you need to listen and make it – it's clear, everybody know it.
Z:    Yes, yes, you are right.
O:    That is this exercise – try to think which one.
(Adapted from Anderson and Lynch 1988: 112)

**Group 2**
Tape: . . . the silk mill + that's along Progress Street and turn right
Ss:  Stop.
F:    Where is silk mill?
B:    Silk factory?
A:    Silk factory?
B:    Maybe the factory – at the left side – in the middle.
F:    Go back?
A:    Oh no, she told to turn – they turn the first on the right
S:    On the right, yeah.
C:    The right?
A:    Yeah, so if you come . . .
S:    But this factory is on the left – the factory.
A:    No, when you come back from the museum, it's the first on the right.
F:    Go back?
J:    They turn back?
A:    I think they return and turn, but I'm not sure.
F:    Why don't we ask a question?
F:    Is it the factory on Progress Street?
(Adapted from Anderson and Lynch 1988: 113)

### Post-reading task

1. What do you see as the benefits of such a task?
2. In the light of the difficulties experienced by students, what modifications might be made to the procedure?

The authors report that students, even the weakest ones, saw the benefit of such tasks and wanted to do more of them. Students said such tasks made them more aware of:

1. The need to cope with alternative descriptions of the same thing, rather than always expecting a single term.
2. The way in which one small piece of language can affect the interpretation of a text.
3. That some native speakers (i.e. not only these materials!) are hard to understand, making it necessary to ask for something to be clarified or repeated.
(Anderson and Lynch 1988: 114)

In the next extract, the teacher has two goals, a language goal and a 'learning how to learn' goal.

### Pre-reading task

1.  As you read the text, see whether you can identify the language goal.
2.  The second, a learning-how-to-learn goal, is to get learners to group new vocabulary items according to the semantic field to which they belong, rather than alphabetically. How does the teacher attempt to do this?
3.  As you study the extract, you might like to consider whether the teacher is focusing on top-down or bottom-up processing strategies.

### Classroom extract 2.2: Listening to the news

[The teacher stands at the front of the class and addresses the students who are sitting in small groups of three to four.]

T:  Now we're going to listen to the news, and I'm going to hand out a worksheet to you all, and we're going to do as we have done before. Just listen and decide which category the news item we hear falls into. So I'll pass these around and you just read the instructions.

[She hands out the following worksheet.]

| LISTENING TASK |
| --- |
| Tick which category or categories each story belongs to. |
| CATEGORIES |
| Political/Government |
| Overseas |
| Disaster/Accidents |
| Sports |
| Art/Culture |
| Religion |
| Economics |
| Health |
| Education |
| Defence/Military |
| Judicial |

T: The first time, I'll just play the main titles or
the headlines once, and just get a general
idea. . . . Right? So don't . . . you don't have
to tick the boxes in now, you can just listen.

[She turns on a cassette player.]

Tape: This is ABC national news read by William Marga. Here're the headlines. Overseas, a
shake-up in the currency and stock markets. Syria getting ready to intervene in the
Beirut fighting; and in Moscow the death of superspy Reg Smith. On the local scene,
financial cutting expected at today's premiers' conference. Other items in the news are
student demonstrations, the cost of IVF babies, and aboriginal cricketers. The news in
detail after this break.

[The teacher stops the tape, pushes the rewind button, and turns to one of the students.]

T: What're you going to do, Irene? [She points to
the board on which are written some of the
news categories.] Next time you listen, what
will you be doing?

> S: I'm going to tick what categories they go in.
> Different items . . .

T: Good.

[She replays the news item. The students listen to the news a second time, ticking the various
categories on their handout as they do so.]

T: Now, just before we listen for the third time,
check with a partner what they've . . . how
many they've ticked on theirs and see if you've
got the same or if you can remember any of the
items.

[The students work in their small groups, comparing their handouts. The teacher gives them
three or four minutes to compare notes and then calls their attention to the front of the class.]

T: So this time listen just to confirm whether what
you heard was accurate or not.

Tape: This is ABC national news read by William Marga. Here're the headlines. Overseas, a
shake-up in the currency and stock markets.

T: Right. What did you . . . would you tick for
that?

> Ss: Overseas. Business.

T: Overseas . . . and . . .

> Ss: Business . . . business . . . business . . .
> economical.

T: Business . . . and . . . where is it? [She turns
and points at the board.]

> S: Economic.

T: Economics. 'Cause it talked about the word
. . . which word gave you that clue? Beginning
with 'C'.

> T: Stock market.

T: Stock market . . . And . . . ?

> S: Currency.

T: Currency. Good. Okay. So two there –
   overseas and economics. Let's listen to the
   next one.
[The students listen to the next items completing them successfully until they reach the last item.]
T: Medical. . . . And . . .?
                              S: And, er, economics.
T: And economics, yes, because they're talking
   about the cost of it. Good. [She plays the last
   item.]
Tape:  And aboriginal cricketers.
T: And Shaheed? [There is some confusion, and
   a number of students confer with each other.]
   What would you put it under?
                              Ss: Er, political . . . political . . . judicial.
                              S: Judicial.
T: What were the two words you heard?
                              Ss: Culture, culture.
T: I'll just rewind those words. [She plays the
   segment again.]
                              Ss: Aboriginal cricketers, cricketers, sport.
T: You changed your mind, and decided . . . ?
                              Ss: Sport, sport.
T: What sport? What was the word?
                              S: Cricket.
T: Cricketers, that's right. Cricketers, so that
   would be sport. [She consults her sheet.]
   Okay, so we'll just stop that activity for now.


## *Post-reading task*

1. The language learning goal of this task was to get learners to extract key information from an authentic listening text. Was the teacher successful in this? What, if anything, would you have done differently?
2. Is there any evidence that the task was too easy? If so, how might it be made more challenging for learners at this level?


Several interesting observations can be made about this extract. Perhaps one of the most obvious is the fact that in teaching and learning a great deal of interactive language work occurs. While this extract shows a teacher focusing on listening, there is a significant amount of talking between teacher and students and among students. Like most samples of classroom interaction, it also reveals a great deal about the teacher's purposes. It shows, for example, that the teacher has twin goals, one focusing on the development of language skills, the other focusing of the development of learning skills and strategies. She is focusing on top-down processing strategies by encouraging learners to utilise their background knowledge. Students are also learning that they can utilise resources outside the classroom to practise their listening, and that it is not necessary to understand every word for listening to be successful. Pedagogically, it could be argued that the task is too easy for the majority of the learners because they only had difficulty with one news item – that dealing with aboriginal cricketers. (Of course, we are forced to rely on the evidence from students who speak out, and it may well be that there are weaker students in the class for whom the task is at an appropriate level of difficulty.) As recently-arrived, international students in Australia, it is doubtful that these learners would have content knowledge relating to either aboriginals or cricket, and their difficulty with this particular item can therefore be neatly accounted for by a top-down theory of listening. However, in order to judge the difficulty or appropriateness of the task, we would need to know the context of the lesson as a whole, and the range of ability levels in the group.

The task is also tightly controlled by the teacher, and the students play a rather passive role. With more advanced learners, a more active role could be encouraged by getting students to choose unlikely categories and argue for these, or to rank order the categories from most to least likely. (In fact, at one stage one of the students does this by suggesting the 'death of a superspy' item could be classified under 'health'.)

## 2.8 Investigating listening comprehension

This section consists of a set of exploration tasks which are designed to encourage you to experiment with and assess the ideas on listening contained in the body of the chapter. If you are currently teaching, you will have ready access to students with whom you might explore these ideas. If not, you should endeavour to get access to a small group of non-native students who may or may not be undertaking formal instruction. If this is not practicable, you can still create some of the listening tasks, and may be able to find one or two individual non-native speakers who will agree to take part in the activities.

Where possible it is a good idea to tape record any teaching/learning activities. This makes it easier to review and evaluate the tasks.

**Task 2.1**
1. Select a text which you believe to be appropriate for a group of learners you are teaching, or to whom you have access, and develop a unit of work based on the dictogloss approach.
2. Teach the unit, and record, review and evaluate the approach.
3. Were the text and/or activities appropriate for the group?
4. What modifications would you make next time?
5. What do the students think of the technique?

## Task 2.2

Record a radio news broadcast and use it in the same way as the teacher in classroom extract 2.2. Record and review the lesson. Were the patterns of interaction similar to or different from those in extract 2.2?

## Task 2.3

1. Study the 'trace the route' task and develop a similar one of your own. Teach the task to a group of students and record the session. Review the discussion.
2. What does it tell you about the listening skills of the students?
3. What does it tell you about the appropriateness of the task?
4. Compare the discussion with those in extract 2.1.
5. What similarities and or differences are there between your students' discussion and that in extract 2.1?

## Task 2.4

Develop a parallel versions of the task using a different map and altering the difficulty of the task. You could do this by increasing the number of elements and by putting in contradictory information. Try this task on the same group of students, and record the session. Did the students have more difficulty with the task, as predicted by Anderson and Lynch?

## Task 2.5

Develop different texts for three different maps. For example, text 1 might be a tour guide explaining where the group will be going; text 2 might be a set of instructions by an hotel employee to a guest, and text 3 might be a recount by one of the tourists to a friend. Try and keep all other factors constant. (In effect, you are investigating the difficulty of different text types on listening comprehension.) Try the three tasks out on a group of students on three separate occasions, recording the group interaction as before. Review and evaluate the recordings. Is there any evidence that students had more difficulty with one text type rather than another?

## Task 2.6

Select several tasks from a listening coursebook. Analyse them and decide on their order of difficulty. Teach them over a period of time and evaluate whether your predictions were correct. What factors seemed to be most significant in determining difficulty?

## Task 2.7

Select or create a listening text which has an accompanying visual (for example, a description or set of instructions on how to make something). Write a set of comprehension questions. Administer the test to two groups of students who are at about the same level of proficiency. Let one group look at the picture, but not the other group. (Or, if you are doing the task in class, let one half of the class look at the picture but not the other half.) Evaluate the task by deciding whether the availability of the visual affected students' ability to complete the task.

## 2.9  Conclusion

In this chapter we have looked at the nature of listening comprehension. We have seen that the notion of 'listener as tape recorder' is not a tenable one: that in comprehending aural language listeners do a great deal of constructive and interpretative work in which they integrate what they hear with what they know about the world.

We also looked at some of the different ways of categorising listening texts and tasks. It was suggested that there is a basic distinction between interactive and non-interactive listening, and that interactive listening can be further categorised in various ways. In functional terms, we can distinguish between interactive listening which has the interpersonal function of establishing and maintaining social relationships, and listening which takes place in the course of transactional encounters where the primary purpose is to obtain goods and services.

We also saw how these ideas have been applied at the level of pedagogy, both in terms of teaching materials and also in terms of classroom action. From a methodological perspective, theories, ideas and research are only as good as teachers and textbook writers make them. Interesting and unexpected things happen in the classroom, and in the final analysis, principles and ideas need to be tested in practice. It is to demonstrate the operation of principles and ideas at the level of classroom action that the classroom extracts have been included.

# Chapter Three

## Speaking in a Second Language

### 3.1 Introduction

To most people, mastering the art of speaking is the single most important aspect of learning a second or foreign language, and success is measured in terms of the ability to carry out a conversation in the language. In this chapter we look at what it means to speak and interact orally in a second language, and at how data from theory and research into speaking can be translated into pedagogy. Some of the issues raised in Chapter 2 are revisited, this time from the perspective of speaking. In this chapter, I explore the following questions:

1. What are the different speaking tasks confronting learners and how might these be classified?
2. Why is the predictability–unpredictability continuum important in understanding speaking?
3. What is 'genre', and why is it an important concept in language learning and teaching?
4. What are some of the factors to consider in determining the difficulty of speaking tasks?
5. How can second language acquisition research inform the selection, development and adaptation of speaking tasks?
6. How can we stimulate oral interaction in the classroom?
7. What can we learn by recording and analysing student–student interaction in the classroom?

### 3.2 Identifying different types of speaking

In Chapter 2 we saw that listening texts and tasks can be classified in functional terms. For example, we saw that weather forecasts fulfil a different function from transactional encounters, and that this difference is reflected in the type of language which is used. Similar functional considerations help inform our analyses of texts from the perspective of the producer rather than the receiver. In his functional analysis of speaking, Bygate (1987) suggests that oral interactions can be characterised in terms of routines, which are conventional (and therefore predictable) ways of presenting information which can either focus on information or interaction. Information routines contain frequently recurring types of information structures, being either be expository (e.g. narration, description, instruction, comparison) or evaluative (e.g. explanation, justification, prediction, decision). Interaction routines can be either service (e.g. a job interview) or social (e.g. a dinner party). This distinction between information and interaction routines mirrors the distinction between the transactional and interactional (or interpersonal) functions of language discussed in the preceding chapter. According to Bygate, a further feature of oral interaction is that the participants need constantly to negotiate meaning, and generally manage the interaction in terms of who is to say what, to whom, when, and about what. His scheme is set out in Figure 3.1.

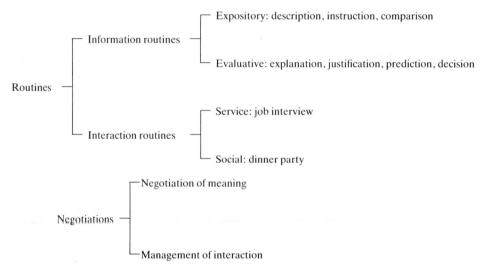

FIGURE 3.1  *Characterising oral interaction (after Bygate 1987).*

While the figure is an extremely useful typification, it may give the impression that life proceeds through sets of finite interactional routines. In fact, any interaction may contain elements of any or all of the various elements identified by Bygate. This is particularly true of negotiation, which is a characteristic of all but the most formulaic of interactions. I have therefore modified and rearranged Bygate's scheme to allow for this, the modification being set out in Table 3.1. From the table, you can see that I have created a three-dimensional grid, one dimension relating to the interactional contexts, another relating to the different functions which can be performed in these contexts, and the third relating to the management of interaction and negotiation of meaning. Such a table could be used to provide a map or profile of a given interaction. It could also be a planning device for designing a syllabus for speaking and oral interaction.

TABLE 3.1 *A planning grid for speaking and oral interaction*

| Interaction | Information | | Negotiation of meaning |
| --- | --- | --- | --- |
| | Expository | Evaluative | Management of interaction |
| | narrate describe instruct compare | explain justify predict decide | |
| S E R V I C E  Job interview<br>Booking a restaurant<br>Buying stamps<br>Enrolling in school<br>etc. | | | |
| S O C I A L  Dinner party<br>Coffee break<br>Theatre queue<br>etc. | | | |

## 3.3 Predictability and unpredictability

It is something of a truism to suggest that communication involves the reduction of uncertainty through a process of negotiation. If language were totally predictable communication would be unnecessary (i.e. if I know in advance exactly what you are going to say, then there is no point in my listening to you). If language were totally unpredictable, communication could probably not occur. I would like to suggest that most interactions can be placed on a continuum from relatively predictable to relatively unpredictable.

   Predictability will depend on a range of factors, some of which will be associated with the language itself, and some of which will be related to the context of situation, including the interlocutors and their relationships, the topic of conversation and so on. In terms of the discourse we are engaged in, predictability will depend on whether the discourse or text type contain predictable patterns, and also the extent to which we are familiar with these patterns. All other things being equal (such as shared knowledge, cultural expectations, etc.) transactional encounters of a fairly restricted kind will usually contain highly predictable patterns, while interpersonal encounters, where the focus is on the maintenance of social relationships rather than the exchange of goods and services, will be less predictable. In order to illustrate this point, consider the following texts. Text 1 is a telephone conversation I had recently with the telephone operator of a taxi company. I have had many such conversations in the past few years, and they have been virtually identical. Now and then I have tried deliberately altering the usual order of events (by, for example, trying to tell the operator at the outset that I do not want the taxi immediately but that I want to make a booking). This often has a surprisingly disconcerting effect on the operator and I can only guess that it upsets the procedures through which they enter the relevant data into their system

**Text 1**

| | |
|---|---|
| Tape: | Hold the line, please, all our operators are currently busy. [Music] |
| Operator: | Cabcharge – Account name? |
| Customer: | Macquarie University. |
| Operator: | Passenger's name? |
| Customer: | Nunan. |
| Operator: | Pick-up address? |
| Customer: | 13 Finch Avenue, East Ryde. |
| Operator: | Is that a private house or flat? |
| Customer: | Yes. |
| Operator: | Going to? |
| Customer: | The airport. |
| Operator: | How many passengers? |
| Customer: | One. |
| Operator: | Are you ready now? |
| Customer: | I'd like a cab for 2.30 pm, please. |

Operator: We'll get a car to you as close to the time as we can.
Customer: Thank you.

Text 2, in contrast, is a chat between fellow workers which takes place in the coffee break of a workplace.

**Text 2**

Gary: If I won the Lotto, I'd buy six or seven catamarans up at Noosa and sit them on the beach and hire them out and just rest there all the time.
(Everyone laughs)
Pauline: Oh yes and then you – you'd want something to do.
Gary: Yes, you would but . . .
Bronwyn: Mm no, look, even if I'd won the Lotto, I'd still have to come to work – I couldn't stand it.
Garry: No, that's right.
Bronwyn: I couldn't stand it.
Pauline: Yes, I think that um . . .
Pat: I'd buy my farm.
Bronwyn: I'd still – no, I need contact with people.
Pauline: Yes, that's right – I think I'd probably – if I'd paid off all my debts and wouldn't have that on my mind – I'd feel better – um but then I'd think I would like to work part time.
Bronwyn: Mm.
Gary: Mm.
Pauline: You know, just for . . .
Gary: Oh, I – I don't know.
Pauline: Being able to do things and then you'd still kind of . . .
Gary: I think I'd use the money a bit in investment.
(Economou 1985: 106)

For most native speakers, text 2 is less predictable than text 1. This does not mean that it has no patterns at all, just that they are less obvious. The interaction is likely to cause comprehension problems for a non-native speaker who was either eavesdropping or trying to take part in the conversation, and who was unfamiliar with coffee break chat as a cultural event. (For example, for some observers it may seem strange that Gary, a young male, is engaging in repartee with Bronwyn and Pauline who are older women).

## 3.4 The concept of genre

Within functional linguistics, the concept of genre has been proposed as a useful one for helping us to understand the nature of language in use, including the issue of predictability. We have, in fact, encountered the notion of genre, although the term itself was not used. You will recall that in Chapter 2 we looked at a number of different texts and saw that some were more alike than others. In that chapter, it was suggested that language exists to fulfil certain functions, and that these functions will determine the shape of the text which emerges as people communicate with one another. The term 'genre' refers to a purposeful, socially-constructed, communicative event. Most such events result in texts (that is, pieces of oral or written communication), for example, political speeches, nursery rhymes, church sermons, casual conversations and so on. These are all different text types, which have different communicative functions and if we saw several examples of each, we would have little trouble identifying which was which. Each has its own distinctive linguistic characteristics, and its own generic structure (that is, its own internal structure). Consider text 3, which is a personal recount.

**Text 3**
Well we had an even better time than that last week. We went up to Noosa for the weekend and stayed with Mina – spent most of the weekend on the beach, of course. On Sunday, Tony took us out in his boat. Didn't fancy that much. Pity it's such a rotten drive back.

The generic structure of this text can be characterised in the following way.

| | |
|---|---|
| Introduction | Well we had an even better time than that last week. |
| Orientation | We went up to Noosa for the weekend and stayed with Mina – |
| Event | spent most of the weekend on the beach, of course. |
| Event | On Sunday, Tony took us out in his boat. |
| Comment | Didn't fancy that much. |
| Conclusion | Pity it's such a rotten drive back. |

Grammatically, the text is characterised by the use of the simple past tense, and the use of specific reference to people and places which (we assume) are familiar to the people who are listening to the narrative. Its generic structure is characterised by a chronological sequence of events capped by an introduction, orientation, comment and conclusion. A detailed and comprehensive account of the way grammar operates as sets of options for making meaning is provided by Halliday who suggests that language structure and language function are systematically related:

Every text – that is, everything that is said or written – unfolds in some context of use; furthermore, it is the uses of language that, over tens of thousands of generations, have shaped the system. Language has evolved to satisfy human needs; and the way it is organised is functional with respect to those needs – it is not arbitrary. A functional grammar is essentially a 'natural' grammar, in the sense that everything in it can be explained, ultimately, by reference to how language is used. (Halliday 1985a: xiii)

Another point to bear in mind is the fact that genres are culturally and socially determined, and that new genres are constantly being created. This has important implications, particularly for second and foreign language teachers. In the first instance, it means that there is not a finite set of genres belonging to a culture existing 'out there' waiting to be discovered: it is not possible to say there are 364 genres in spoken English, and different members of a speech community will not necessarily agree about the number and type of genres in the language or languages spoken by that community.

Halliday and Hasan (1985) suggest that text and context can be related through a consideration of field, tenor and mode. The field of discourse refers to 'what is going on', tenor to 'who is taking part', and mode to the 'role assigned to language'. They exemplify these concepts by characterising a radio broadcast by a bishop about the nature of Christian beliefs in the twentieth century in the following manner:

Field:   Maintenance of institutionalized system of beliefs; religion (Christianity), and the members' attitude towards it; semi-technical

Tenor:   Authority (in both senses, i.e. person holding authority, and specialist) to the audience; audience unseen and unknown (like readership), but relationship institutionalized (pastor to flock)

Mode:   Written to be read aloud; public act (mass media: radio); monologue; text is whole of relevant activity
Lecture; persuasive, with rational argument

(Halliday and Hasan 1985: 14)

This view of language has a number of important implications for teaching and learning. In the first place, it suggests that we should start with whole texts or whole language events rather than discrete elements (such as words or sentences). Secondly, it would suggest that learners in class should be exposed to the types of interactional opportunity which they will encounter outside. In other words, there should be principled links between the learning opportunities presented to learners in the classroom, and the target language uses to which the language will be put. Presumably, we would not expect learners interested in developing conversational skills to develop these skills by studying monologues on the nature of Christianity by the Bishop of Woolwich. (See Nunan 1989a for a discussion of the relationship between real-world and pedagogical language use and the implications of this relationship for pedagogy.) This view of language would also suggest that we should actually provide learners with an opportunity to explore the generic structures of spoken language.

In Chapter 2 we contrasted bottom-up views of listening comprehension with top-down approaches. The bottom-up/top-down distinction can also be applied to speaking. The bottom-up view suggests that learners move from mastery of the discrete elements or building blocks of the language to a mastery of the larger components. In other words, they move from phonemes, to words, to clauses, to sentences to complete texts. Top-down approaches, such as the genre-based one outlined above, however, suggest that we work from the larger elements to the smaller. These views are contrasted by Hatch who suggests that:

In second language learning the basic assumption has been . . . that one first learns how to manipulate structures, that one gradually builds up a repertoire of structures and then, somehow, learns to put these structures to use in discourse. We would like to consider the possibility that just the reverse happens. One learns how to do conversation, one learns how to interact verbally, and out of this interaction syntactic structures are developed. (Hatch 1978: 404)

Ellis (1984) cites evidence from second language classrooms which builds on this notion. He suggests that learners can use an 'expansion strategy' to extend their messages vertically (that is, discoursally) rather than horizontally (that is, structurally). He lists three strategies through which this vertical extension may be accomplished:

1. Imitating (part of) another speaker's utterance and adding to it.
2. Building on one's own previous utterance.
3. Juxtaposing two formulaic utterances.

Bygate (1988) also argues against the notion that one moves from syntax to discourse. In fact, he demonstrates that a great deal of interactional talk consists not of complete grammatical structures, but of what he calls satellite units. Satellite units are moodless utterances which lack a finite verb or verb group. They can consist of any dependent syntactic element including noun, adjective, adverb and verb groups, prepositional phrases, pronouns and subordinate clauses. Examples from Bygate's data include the following:

Prepositional phrase:
S12: a *at the door*
S11: yes *in the same door* I think
S12: *besides the man who is leaving*
S11: *behind him*

Adjective group:
S8: aha they're very polite
S7: *polite really polite* that's er one of their characteristics

Subordinate clause:
S11: well that man I think he is a robber. a thief
S12: he might be
S11: *because he is running with a handbag*
S12: yeah
(Bygate 1988: 68)

Bygate suggests that the pedagogical implication of the view of language is that learners should be given the opportunity to practise language below the level of the clause.

In structural courses and in notional/functional courses, the units taught are clausal. Both oral and written practice focuses on finite clause units and the way they can combine. What is perhaps just as important, if not more so, is for the learner to explore the ways in which dependent units can be constituted, and thence, the way they can combine to form clauses . . . oral communication practice may offer an antidote to the 'clause-down' approach. One way it might do this is by exercising learners in the business of accessing chunks, constituting them correctly, combining them and modifying them efficiently, at a sufficiently low level of ambiguity for communication to take place. (Bygate 1988: 65)

Some SLA researchers believe that second languages are acquired through a process by which learners learn unanalysed 'chunks' of language (such as Bygate's satellite units) as formulae. Over time, they learn to break these down into their constituent elements. If this is true, it would support the top-down, discourse driven view of Bygate and others.

## 3.5 The difficulty of speaking tasks

Determining the difficulty of pedagogical tasks is one of the major challenges confronting teachers and curriculum developers who subscribe to the sorts of principle articulated above, and which have become an issue with the development of communicative language teaching. In Chapter 2 we looked at some of the factors which are implicated in the difficulty level of listening tasks, and in this section, we shall see that similar sets of factors have been identified in relation to speaking tasks.

One of the complications in determining the difficulty of speaking tasks is the so-called interlocutor effect. As we have seen, in any interactional speaking task, communication is a collaborative venture in which the interlocutors negotiate meaning in order to achieve their communicative ends. The difficulty of a task, and the success one has in achieving one's communicative goal will be partly determined by the skills of one's interlocutor(s). Interlocutor effect has to be taken into consideration by researchers investigating task difficulty, and also by those designing task-based testing procedures. In developing tests involving interactive speaking, the problem is to devise tasks in which the speaker is not disadvantaged by possible shortcomings on the part of the interlocutor.

Brown and Yule (1983b) and Brown *et al.* (1984) have carried out extensive research into the factors implicated in task difficulty. In conducting their research (which used native speaking, secondary school pupils), Brown *et al.* (1984) were confronted with a number of major problems. The first was to motivate pupils to talk while working with an unfamiliar interviewer and while being tape recorded. Their solution was to use a series of short tasks conducted under what they describe as ideal conditions and with different content and different demands to sustain the interest of the pupils. Using a wide variety of tasks created a second problem in that they did not wish to end up with 'a hotchpotch of unrelated performances from which no general description could be drawn' (p.49). They solved this problem by devising tasks which formed related groups, each group being distinguished by a particular communicative skill.

In grouping tasks according to 'communicative skill', Brown *et al.* bring together seemingly disparate real-world tasks. This can be illustrated by considering three particular tasks: (1) a diagram-drawing task; (2) a pegboard task; (3) a wiring-board task.

On the surface, these tasks appear to be very different. In one, the speaker has to tell the listener how to reproduce a coloured diagram, in the second, how to arrange different coloured pegs and elastic bands into a particular pattern on a pegboard; in the third, how to complete an electrical circuit by arranging a series of wires in the appropriate sockets. Despite their apparent differences, Brown *et al.* argue that the tasks all make similar communicative demands on the speaker. All require the speaker to provide a sequence of clear and explicit instructions, identifying and discriminating between static objects and expressing the spatial relationships between these objects. The researchers found that such tasks generated quite different types of language, patterns of interaction and communicative problems from other task types.

Whether tasks involved dynamic or abstract relationships was also important in determining task difficulty. Tasks involving dynamic relationships were more difficult than static tasks, as they required speakers to describe relationships between objects and entities which changed in the course of the task. Sample tasks included describing a car crash, recounting how a piece of equipment works, retelling a narrative based on a cartoon strip. Tasks involving abstract relationships were more difficult again than those involving the description of dynamic relationships. These tasks required the speaker to deal in abstractions such as expressing an opinion on a particular topic or justifying a course of action. Sample tasks included watching a video of a schoolteacher giving a speech in which he strongly advocates corporal punishment, and then providing an opinion on the subject.

The three task types described above all involve learners in exploiting basic information-transferring skills, and all could be rather neatly fitted onto a grid of ascending difficulty as shown in Illustration 2.

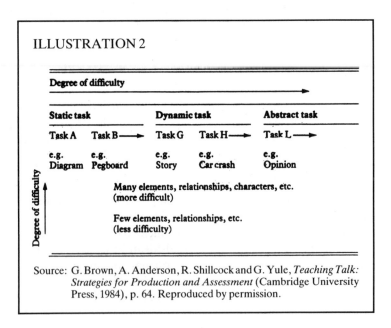

ILLUSTRATION 2

**Degree of difficulty**

| **Static task** | | **Dynamic task** | | **Abstract task** |
|---|---|---|---|---|
| Task A | Task B ➞ | Task G | Task H ➞ | Task L ➞ |
| e.g. | e.g. | e.g. | e.g. | e.g. |
| Diagram | Pegboard | Story | Car crash | Opinion |

Degree of difficulty

Many elements, relationships, characters, etc. (more difficult)

Few elements, relationships, etc. (less difficulty)

Source: G. Brown, A. Anderson, R. Shillcock and G. Yule, *Teaching Talk: Strategies for Production and Assessment* (Cambridge University Press, 1984), p. 64. Reproduced by permission.

Two other tasks identified by Brown *et al.* did not fit so neatly onto the grid. The first of these is the summary task. In such a task, the pupil has typically to give a short summary of a story presented, say, as a sequence of cartoon pictures. The researchers found that speakers had great difficulty presenting information in a condensed form, often producing 'summaries' which were as long as a complete retelling of the story.

The tasks described so far are generally one-way information gap tasks, in which the speaker has all the information which must be conveyed to the listener. They contrast with two-way tasks, in which both participants must pool their information in order to complete the task successfully. The researchers found such tasks particularly difficult to grade because of the interlocutor effect referred to above.

Brown *et al.* were interested not only in finding out which speaking tasks were easy and which difficult, but also in determining what factors helped pupils improve their performance on speaking tasks. (Pupils were judged on how successfully they managed to complete the tasks; for example, how accurately they described the spatial relationships between objects in a static task.) Contrary to expectations, the researchers found that practice did not lead to improved performance on the static tasks, although it did on the dynamic tasks. They concluded that, 'practice enables speakers to improve those aspects of the task which they had already largely mastered' (p. 123). Another condition which they investigated was the possibility that prior experience as a 'hearer' might facilitate being a speaker. This particular condition did seem to help speakers improve their performance because it helped the speaker appreciate the difficulties inherent in the task.

> Giving speakers experience in the hearer's role is more helpful than simple practice in tasks where a speaker is having real difficulties in appreciating what a particular task requires. In tasks where speakers are largely successful in meeting a particular task demand, then repeated practice may enable them to improve further their performance in this respect, and may indeed be a pleasant and motivating experience. (Brown *et al.* 1984: 123)

A further condition which enhanced performance was the opportunity to take part in a training session where tape recordings of inadequate performances were reviewed and discussed.

In conclusion, then, speaking performance was enhanced by rehearsal of the task under different conditions, and the opportunity to review and reflect on the tasks. This ability to reflect critically on one's performance as a language user is an important skill, which should be incorporated into any language programme. In Chapter 9, we look at practical ways this can be achieved through the incorporation of learning-how-to-learn tasks into teaching programmes.

## 3.6 Classroom interaction

A considerable amount of research has been conducted in recent years into learner interaction, particularly interaction which takes place through group work. In this section, we shall review some of this research, focusing on the linguistic and acquisitional aspects of interaction. Much of the research into classroom interaction among second language learners has been conducted within the discipline of second language acquisition. The theoretical point of departure for this work has been the interpretation by Long (1983) and others of the so-called comprehensible input hypothesis, which is based on the belief that opportunities for second language acquisition are maximised when learners are exposed to language which is just a little beyond their current level of competence (Krashen 1981, 1982). The central research issue here is: what classroom tasks and patterns of interaction provide learners with the greatest amount of comprehensible input? One line of research has argued that patterns of interaction in which learners are forced to make conversational adjustments promote acquisition. This view represents an indirect rather than direct relationship between environmental factors (for example, types of instruction) and language acquisition. The argument is as follows:

Step  1:  Show that (a) linguistic/conversational adjustments promote (b) comprehensible input.
Step  2:  Show that (b) comprehensible input promotes (c) acquisition.
Step  3:  Deduce that (a) linguistic/conversational adjustments promote (c) acquisition. Satisfactory evidence of the a → b → c relationships would allow the linguistic environment to be posited as an indirect causal variable in SLA. (The relationship would be indirect because of the intervening 'comprehension' variable.) (Long 1985: 378)

Numerous studies have used this theoretical framework as a point of departure. Long (1981) found that two-way information gap tasks prompted significantly more linguistic/conversational adjustments than one-way tasks. In two-way tasks, all participants have a piece of information known only to them which must be contributed to the small group discussion for the task to be completed successfully. In one-way tasks, one student has all the relevant information and must convey this to the other student(s). Duff (1986) found that convergent tasks produce more adjustments than divergent tasks. Thus, debates, which encourage divergent views and arguments, yield fewer adjustments than problem-solving tasks in which the views of all participants must 'converge' to provide the appropriate answer.

A different perspective has been provided by Swain (1985) who advances the comprehensible output hypothesis. While she accepts that comprehensible input is an important construct in understanding processes of second language acquisition, she argues, on the basis of a study involving children learning French as a second language in an immersion program, that language proficiency cannot be accounted for solely on the basis of the input received. She suggests that the role of comprehensible input on the development in particular of grammatical competence has been overstated, and that the role of comprehensible output is also significant. Output, particularly when it occurs in conversations where the learner is having to negotiate meaning, provides learner's with the opportunity to push to the limit their emerging competence. In addition to 'pushed' language use, output provides learners with the opportunity to try out hypotheses about how language works, and it may also force learners to impose syntax on their language. This latter point is particularly significant if, as Krashen (1982) suggests, learners can often extract adequate meaning from aural messages by focusing on lexis and extralinguistic information and bypassing syntactic processing.

Research has focused on other aspects of small group work besides the negotiation of meaning. For example, it has been shown that learners use considerably more language, and exploit a greater range of language functions when working in small groups as opposed to teacher-fronted tasks in which all students proceed in a lock-step fashion (Long *et al.* 1976). Bruton and Samuda (1980) found that, contrary to popular belief, learners in small groups were capable of correcting one another successfully. Porter (1983, 1986) found (also contrary to popular opinion) that learners do not produce more errors or 'learn each other's mistakes' when working together in small groups. Taken together, these studies provide a powerful rationale for the use of interactive groupwork in the classroom. However, I would add one caveat. Some of these studies have, for very good reasons, been carried out in laboratory or simulated settings. It remains to be seen whether the results hold up in genuine language classrooms, that is, classrooms constituted for the purposes of learning, not research.

## 3.7  Stimulating oral interaction in the classroom

The theory and research summarised in the preceding section suggest that learning to speak in a second or foreign language will be facilitated when learners are actively engaged in attempting to communicate. As Swain suggests: just as the research suggests that we learn to read by reading, so also do we learn to speak by speaking. This does not mean that we should never allow our learners to engage in manipulative exercises in which focus of attention is on the manipulation of linguistic form (we shall look at this aspect of language learning in Chapter 8). However, it is interesting to analyse currently available books written within a communicative language teaching paradigm, for many of these coursebooks, particularly those aimed at lower proficiency learners, consist largely of manipulative, form focused exercises. The following list of speaking exercises is a case in point. The exercises have been extracted from a coursebook whose avowed aim is to help learners use the language essential to real-life situations. The following exercises constitute the sum total of speaking practice which learners received in the course.

1. Learner listens to and reads two-line dialogue and practises with a partner.
2. Listen and repeat.
3. Listen to a model dialogue and repeat, interpolating own name.
4. Read question cue and make up question.
5. Read two line skeleton dialogue and practise with partner.
6. Listen/read a model question and ask a partner.
7. Read a model dialogue and have a similar conversation using cues provided.
8. Study a substitution table and make up sentences.

9. Study questions and answers in a model dialogue and make up similar questions using cue words.
10. Look at a picture and study model sentences. Make up similar sentences about a similar picture.
11. Listen to numbers and dates. Read numbers and dates and say them.
12. Listen to tapescript and answer written comprehension questions.
13. Listen to an interview. Ask and answer similar questions with a partner.
14. Look at diagrams of clocks. With a partner ask and answer questions about the time.
15. Listen to a model, study a map and say the route from one specified point to another.

You might consider whether this is a reasonable number of activities for low-level second language learners, and if not, what other activities might be included. Would it be a reasonable number for low-level foreign language learners? My own view is that while these exercises provide essential preparatory practice for communication, they are essentially enabling activities which do not go far enough (i.e. they give controlled practice in the grammatical and phonological building blocks of the language, but provide few opportunities for genuine communication). Even with low-level learners, it is possible to build on the fluency skills developed by such exercises, and provide learners with genuine, if limited, opportunities to engage in communicative interaction.

In the preceding section, we looked at research into classroom tasks which is aimed at identifying those tasks which prompt interactional modifications between participants. It has been suggested that two-way tasks prompt more modifications than one-way tasks, that convergent tasks prompt more modifications than divergent tasks, and so on (see, for example, Pica and Doughty 1985; Doughty and Pica 1986). Long (1989) also hypothesises that closed tasks will prompt more modified input than open tasks.

Extract 3.1 consists of two students working on three communicative tasks. In task 1, the two students are working together on a task which is more open than tasks 2 and 3. (An 'open' task is one in which there is no single correct answer. Like many concepts, the open/closed distinction represents a continuum, rather than two mutually exclusive categories. Tasks can therefore be classified as more-or-less open or closed.) They have been given a number of vocabulary items and have been asked to decide which words go together and to group them accordingly. Tasks 2 and 3 are relatively 'closed' tasks, that is, tasks to which there is a correct answer. (Tasks 2 and 3 we based on material in Hamp-Lyons and Heasley 1987.)

### Pre-reading task

1. Would you predict more negotiation in 'open' or 'closed' tasks? Why?
2. As you read the extract, identify those instances in which the learners negotiate meaning by, for example, checking whether their partner has correctly understood them, or whether they have correctly understood their partner. Do you believe

that the learners are maximising comprehensible input through negotiating meaning?
3. What factors other than the type of task influence the amount and type of talk from both speakers?

### Classroom extract 3.1: Task-based interactions

*Note: The square brackets contain interjections from the other speaker.*

**Task 1**

Two students, Hilda and Carlos, are studying the following words which have been typed onto pieces of cardboard. Their task is to group the words together in a way which makes sense to them.

GEOGRAPHY, ASTRONOMY, AGRICULTURE, ECONOMICS, COMMERCE, ENGLISH, SCIENCE, STATISTICS, BOOK, COMPUTER, PENCIL, DIARY, NEWSPAPER, MAGAZINE, THAILAND, HONG KONG, MELBOURNE, DARWIN, UNITED STATES, ASIAN, DIAGRAM, ILLUSTRATION, PICTURE, CARTOON, VIDEO, COMPETENT, LAZY, INTERESTING, SUPERIOR, UNCOMFORTABLE, REGION

[There is silence for several minutes as they study the cards.]

H: Statistic and diagram – they go together. You know diagram?

C: Yeah.

H: Diagram and statistic are family . . . but maybe, I think, statistic and diagram – you think we can put in science? Or maybe . . .

C: Science, astronomy, [yeah] and er can be agriculture.

H: Agriculture's not a science.

C: Yes, it's similar . . .

H: No. . . . er may be Darwin and science . . .

C: What's the Darwin?

H: Darwin is a man.

C: No, it's one of place in Australia.

H: Yes, but it's a man who discover something, yes, I'm sure.

C: Okay.

H: And maybe, look, yes, picture, newspaper, magazine, cartoon, book, illustration [yeah]. Maybe we can put lazy and English together. Er Hong Kong, Thailand together. Asian. Er, United States. Diary with picture, newspaper and so on. . . . Oh, I understand, look, look. Here, it's only adjective – lazy, competent, interesting and comfortable. Er, what is it? Ah yes yes. She begins to rearrange the cards.

C: Darwin

Carlos helps her to rearrange the words.

H:  Darwin . . . [take this] Together? Okay. [yes, yes]. English, Hong Kong, Thailand, United States, Darwin, Melbourne okay. Each region. Econom . . . geography, agriculture together. I think we had better to put English with the adjective – what do you think?

One of the students from an adjoining table leans across and speaks to Carlos.

S:  Maybe, maybe you can speak too.

C:  Asian . . . So we got [seven groups] seven groups. Statistic, geography, that's right [yeah]. So group 1 sta . . . statitics, statistics, diagram group 2.

H:  . . . science astronomy. . . .

C:  Yeah and er group 3 picture, newspaper, magazine, cartoon, book, diary, [illistration] illustration.

H:  Okay, group 4 lazy, competent, interesting, uncomfortable, English – because it's the adjective . . .

C:  Group 5, region, Hong Kong, Thailand, United States, Melbourne, Darwin, Asian.

H:  Okay, group 6, economics, commerce, geography, agrici . . . agriculture.

C:  So group 7, computer, pencil, video.

While this task generates considerable interaction, the relative contribution of the two speakers is rather one-sided, with Hilda, the more dominant character getting the lion's share of the speaking turns, a fact commented on by one of the other students. Data such as these underline the importance of taking social and inter-personal factors into account in grouping learners. (It is also worth noticing than in a two-way task Carlos would have had unique information to contribute. This would give him more communicative bargaining chips, and therefore more opportunity to take the floor.)

### Task 2

In this task, the students are required to read a set of instructions and draw a diagram of the apparatus described. The instructions for the task are as follows:

MAKING A PHYSIOGRAPH USING A CAMERA:

To make a physiograph, place the camera on the floor with its lens pointing directly upwards and lying immediately below the torch which has been suspended from a hook in the ceiling on a piece of string. Two other strings are hung from hooks several inches to either side of the main string to which they are connected at a point, say, three-quarters of the way down so that they form a V. The strings and torch should be so arranged that when the torch is given its first swing to set it in motion the movement of the light comes within the area of the film in the camera. Turn the torch on, turn the room light off, set the torch swinging and open the shutter. After several minutes' exposure the track made by the swinging light will have produced a delightful linear pattern on the film and this can be enlarged to make a white linear design on a black background.

H: Lie the camera on the floor – put the camera
    on the floor. But be careful, be careful. Attach
    . . . attach maybe.

                                    C: Okay . . . I fix it.

H: Below the torch . . . we have to suspend a
    torch from a hook in the ceiling — on a piece of
    string. In the studio – and, er, there's a big
    light [yes]. So, I think maybe here we can do
    like a big one, and maybe it's torch.

                                      C: Oh yes, I think you got the point.

H: You think so?

                                    C: Yes – think so

H: Very confusing you know – very. . . .

[She draws in several lines and then shows the sketch to Carlos]

H: What do you think?

                                    C: Yeah. Yes, it's good. But it's going to
                                    (inaudible) the sun – is not sun – spot.

H: Yes, better.

While this is a closed task, it does not stimulate as much interaction as the relatively more open task which precedes it. I believe that this is because it is conceptually and linguistically beyond the resources of the students, although it may also have been because the task simply did not engage their interest. Whatever the reason, the students spent relatively little time on the task, and did not complete it successfully. In selecting tasks, then, one must take into consideration the conceptual and cognitive demands as well as the learners' interests.

### Task 3*

In this task, the students are presented with a text on acidic pollution and an accompanying map (the map is shown below). There are five discrepancies between the text and the map. The students, working in pairs, are required to spot the discrepancies.

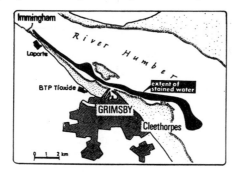

---

* From L. Hamp-Lyons and B. Heasley, *Study Writing* (Cambridge University Press, 1987). Reproduced by permission.

C: Okay. Er Immingham – I saw Immingham.
Okay Immingham [yes]. Okay, it's a problem
of pollution.

H: Yes, of course.

C: And – what? . . . And problem of wastage
from industry . . . aci . . . acidic pollution.
[Mmm] There serious acidification of local
water. [Okay]

[There is a long pause as they reread the text and study the map.]

H: I spied one, look. BTP BTB.

C: That's right.

H: Ah, one mistake. Okay. It's BTP, not BTB.
Do you agree?

C: Yes, yes, yes.

H: 'Of Grimsby and LaPorte Industry'. Where is
LaPorte? Oh, yes, . . . 'both of them on the
Humber estuary'. No, look, only one – here is
the estuary. LaPorte is not near the estuary.
Do you agree? [Yeah, yeah] Both of them, no.
They're not together in the estuary. Do you
agree? [Yes, yes.] 'Between them they
discharge more than, er . . .'

C: '60,000 cubic metres.

H: 'There is a long streak' . . . Oh look, I
understand. 'There is a long streak of stained
land along the north bank of the estuary from
Grimsby to Immingham'. It not good – it's this
one, a long . . . a long streak of stain. It is
brown, it is black. And . . . they say from
Grimsby to Cleethorpes. . . . It's not from
Grimsby to Cleethorpes, it's from Immingham
to Cleethorpes. Do you agree?

C: Mmm.

[Hilda writes down 'not from Grimsby to Cleethorpes'.]

H: Okay. 'This has a brownish-red colour from
the discharge.' It's not red colour, it's brown
col . . . er black colour. [Yeah] Black colour.
Okay, we have to find another mistake now.

C: One more?

H: Yeah.

[There is prolonged silence.]

C: . . . The Humber.

H: Excuse me? Yes? Humber, you think it's a
mistake? Maybe.

C: I don't th . . . I don't know .. what .. er, here
. . . must be Humber River.

H: Okay. And er must River Humber.

C: No, must be Humber River.

H: No, look. [She refers to the instructions.]
   They will find mistake in the text.
                                       C: Oh, yeah, yeah.
H: Okay, must be River Humber, and not
   Humber River. Okay. It means that task four
   – it's over.
[She puts down the paper.]

It seems fairly clear from this transcript that, while considerable negotiation of meaning occurs, the function of such negotiation is not to provide comprehensible input to the learners. The proficiency of both learners (post-intermediate) is sufficiently advanced to rule out such a possibility. Despite this, the tasks are valuable, not because they enable the learners to negotiate the grammatical complexity down to an assimilable level, but because they provide learners with the opportunity to produce comprehensible output with the benefits as suggested by Swain. It is also worth noting the effect of task difficulty. The second task is conceptually very difficult for these students, and in consequence they do not engage it adequately.

In preparation for the lesson from which the next interaction is extracted, the teacher has asked students to read a newspaper article on the subject of 'bad habits'. She leads a teacher-fronted discussion on the subject, and then puts learners into small groups to discuss 'bad habits'. Each small group discussion is recorded, and following the discussion the students will replay the tape, evaluate their performance and attempt to identify their errors. In comparison with the tasks in extract 3.1, this is an extremely open task.

### Pre-reading task

1. What sort of language do you think would be prompted by this task?
2. In what way(s) do you think the patterns of interaction will differ from the tasks in extract 3.1?

### Classroom extract 3.2: Group discussion

The small group from which this extract is taken consists of five women and one male student. During the interaction, the male student does not speak.

Maria: My next door neighbour . . . he make eh
   very noisy, very noisy [yeah]. I can't tell him
   because he's very good people.
[The discussion continues for several minutes.]
                                      Sylvia: . . . you don't want to say anything
                                          because you might get upset, of course. Me do
                                          the same thing because I've got neighbours in
                                          my place and always you know do something I
                                          don't like it but I don't like to say bad because I
                                          think maybe, you know, make him upset or . . .

Martha: I've got bad neighbour but I feel
embarrass . . .

Sylvia: . . . to say something, of course, like
everyone . . .

Martha: They always come in and see what I'm
doing – who's coming. [no good] [yeah, that's
no good] They want to check everything. If they
see I buy something from the market they
expect me to give them some. [oh yeah] [oh
that's not nice] But I . . . it's difficult.

Sylvia: It's a difficult, yeah, but sometime it's
difficult . . . ,

Martha: They can't understand, I bought them
and I gave money . . . [laughter] [yeah] You
know sometime difficult to the people because
sometime I can't speak the proper, the
language, and little bit hard to give to
understand . . . and that's – sometime feel
embarrass then, I can't say it, you know?

Maria: [turns to the fifth woman, who has not yet
spoken] Sarah, you tell [you tell now]

Sarah: My, er, for example, my sister-in-law she
all the time snores in her sleep [oh, yes]. And
my brother say, 'Oh, I'm sorry, we must sleep
separate' [separate beds] [laughter]. They did.
[good idea] A good idea because he couldn't
sleep.

[Laughter.]

In contrast with the interactions in extract 3.1, this extract demonstrates the different
patterns of interaction stimulated by different task types. The interaction is characterised by a relative lack of negotiation in which each learner has her set piece which
she parades for the others. At the end of the extract, there is a telling incident in
which one of the students who has not spoken is prompted to recount her anecdote.
This is not to say that such tasks are not useful. On the contrary, they provide
learners with the opportunity of taking part in more extended speaking turns. The
important point to note is that the different task types illustrated in the extracts
stimulate quite different patterns of interaction.

### Pre-reading task

1.  The next extract has been taken not from a classroom but from data collected by
    Brown *et al.* (1984) in their investigation of task difficulty. The pupils, all native
    speakers of English, are taking part in a two-way information gap task. The A role
    is the primary speaking role, while the B role is the subsidiary role. As you read
    the two extracts, decide what differences there are, if any, between the two pairs
    of speakers.

2. You will recall that Brown and her colleagues found that speakers who had prior experience as hearers performed better than those who had not had this experience. As you read the extract, you might like to consider which A speaker has had prior experience in the subsidiary B role, and what evidence there is for this in the transcript.

## *Classroom extract 3.3: An Information gap task*

FIRST PAIR
A: You start + beside the graveyard
B: Right
A: Go straight up to the volcano + turn right
B: Can you slow down?
A: Turn right
B: Right?
A: Uhu + go str- a wee bit down + you come to the giraffes + right
B: Right
A: Right you go down + turn left + and go down
B: Where to?
A: And you come to a dead tree
B: Right
A: And then you go up + then come down beside the mountains
B: Right

SECOND PAIR
A: Have you got a graveyard?
B: Yes
A: Well go over to the graveyard
B: Right
A: Go above it just a little bit
B: Right
A: Have you got a volcano?
B: Yes
A: Well go from the graveyard right up to the volcano
B: Right
A: Then + have you got giraffes?
B: Yes
A: Well go from the volcano + turn right round
B: Go right round it + over the smoking?
A: What?
B: Over the top + where the smoke is coming out?
A: No + underneath the volcano
(Adapted from Brown *et al.* 1984: 136–7)

In these extracts, it is the second A speaker who has had prior experience of being in the B position. Brown *et al.* observe that while pair 1 contains the complete task performance, the second pair only encompasses a small portion of the route on the map. In other words, when the A speaker has had prior experience as a B performer, much more language gets produced. In the second interaction, 'speaker A regularly checks that his partner has a feature before giving an instruction which uses the feature as a destination. He also gives more detailed information about the location of the route, for example by saying not just that the route goes "to the graveyard" but that it goes "above it just a little bit".' (Brown *et al.* 1984: 138).

We saw in section 3.5 that the issue of determining task difficulty was complex and relativistic, in that it was associated with the interaction of a range of factors, some related to the language with which learners were dealing, some to the complexity of the activities or procedures required of the speaker, and some to the speaker. With reference to the research carried out by Brown *et al.* (1984) and reported in section 3.2, how would you grade the following tasks from the perspective of the speaker? (In these tasks, which have been adapted from Brown and Yule (1983b), the students are working in pairs.)

**1**

Both students have photographs which are almost identical. The speaker has to describe what is in the photographs as accurately as possible in order that the listener can identify in what way his/her photograph differs from the one which the speaker is describing.

**2**

The speaker has a piece of paper on which a diagram has been drawn. The listener has a blank sheet of paper, a black pen and a red pen. The speaker has to instruct the listener to reproduce the diagram as accurately as possible on his sheet of paper. The listener has to listen carefully and to follow the speaker's instructions.

**3**

The speaker has a cartoon strip story. The listener has a set of pictures which show scenes or the characters from the story and some from different stories. The speaker has to tell the story so that the listener will be able to identify which scenes or characters fit the account he hears.

**4**

The speaker has a set of photographs depicting a sequence of events leading up to a car crash. The listener has a road layout design on which he/she has to draw the locations and movements of the cars involved in the crash.

**5**

The learners watch a short piece of video film in which a teacher expresses a fairly strong opinion that corporal punishment is necessary in school to ensure that teachers can do their work and that students can learn. Having watched the film, learners have to say what they think about the matter.

These tasks are, in fact, graded from easiest to most difficult according to whether they contain static, dynamic or abstract relationships. Tasks 1 and 2 are concerned with static relationships, tasks 3 and 4 with dynamic relationships, and task 5 with abstract relationships.

## 3.8 Investigating speaking and oral interaction

**Task 3.1**
1. Study two or three coursebooks for low-level learners and summarise the speaking tasks and exercises using the list in section 3.3 as a model.
2. What similarities and differences are there between the coursebooks?
3. What views on the nature of language and learning are implicit in the coursebooks as revealed by the tasks and exercises?
4. How adequate are the tasks and exercises in the light of the theory and research set out in section 3.2?

**Task 3.2**
1. Carry out a functional analysis of the types of speaking tasks your learners (or a group of learners with which you are familiar) will need to carry out, using the framework in section 3.2 as a guide.
2. Analyse the materials used by the learners. How adequately do these reflect the purposes for which learners require the language.

**Task 3.3**
Give several pairs of learners the three tasks used in extract 3.1. Record and analyse the language used. What similarities/differences are there? What modifications would you make to the tasks if you used them again?

**Task 3.4**
Get some students to carry out the five tasks from Brown *et al.* which are described in the preceding section. To what extent are their finding on task difficulty borne out by your experiment?

**Task 3.5**
Replicate the experiment in which Brown *et al.* investigated the effect on speakers of having prior experience as a hearer. Does this prior experience appear to improve the learners' speaking ability when carrying out information gap tasks?

**Task 3.6**
Get pairs of students to carry out one- and two-way information gap tasks. Record and analyse the language used. Do the two-way tasks appear to be more successful (for example, in prompting longer turns, more prolonged interactions, more negotiation of meaning etc.)?

## 3.9 Conclusion

Tasks and exercises for developing speaking skills should be referenced against the purposes for which learners ultimately require the language, and to this end it is useful to carry out an analysis of the materials and classroom tasks which form the basis of learners' speaking programs, and compare these with the target tasks. Another useful source of information on speaking tasks is the growing body of literature on second language acquisition. I am not suggesting the uncritical acceptance of these ideas. Rather, through the action research and application tasks suggested in the preceding section, your classrooms can become laboratories for experimenting with, contesting, and evaluating these ideas in your own context and situation.

In particular, it is worth exploring, in your own context, the claim that different task types stimulate different patterns of interaction. Here, the investigative question to pose is: is it in fact the case with my learners that different task types stimulate different patterns of interaction, or are the patterns essentially the same?

# Chapter Four

# *Reading: A Discourse Perspective*

## 4.1 Introduction

This chapter takes up some of the central themes which have been developing in the two preceding chapters and applies them to the development of reading in a second or foreign language. Some of the key theoretical and empirical perspectives on the nature of reading and learning to read are examined in the first section of the chapter. We then look at ways in which this theoretical and empirical work has found its way into the classroom through teaching materials and techniques. The key questions addressed in this chapter are:

1.  What is meant by bottom-up and top-down approaches to reading?
2.  What is meant by schema theory, and what is its influence on reading theory and practice?
3.  How does background knowledge influence the reading process?
4.  In what way can reading be said to be a social process?
5.  What are the characteristics of an effective reading lesson?

## 4.2 Bottom-up and top-down views on reading

In Chapter 2 I outlined two different views on the nature of listening: the bottom-up view, which suggests that successful listening is a matter of decoding the individual sounds we hear to derive the meaning of words and thence utterances; and the top-down view, which suggests that we use discoursal and real-world knowledge to construct and interpret aural messages. These two competing models of language processing have also had a central place in the debate on the nature of reading comprehension.

Until comparatively recently, the bottom-up approach dominated both first and second language research and theory. According to Cambourne (1979), it was the basis of the vast majority of reading schemes. Many people will recall with distaste the basic primers with their highly improbable stories which were used to develop early literacy skills. Although there is now a great deal of evidence which points to the inadequacy of the approach, it still has many adherents within the teaching profession. In addition, the 'back-to-basics' movement and introduction of 'basic' skills testing in schools indicates that the approach has a good deal of support beyond the profession itself.

The central notion behind the bottom-up approach is that reading is basically a matter of decoding a series of written symbols into their aural equivalents. Cambourne, who uses the term 'outside-in' rather than bottom-up, provides the following illustration of how the process is supposed to work:

Print → Every letter → Phonemes and graphemes → Blending → Pronunciation → Meaning
      discriminated        matched

According to this model, the reader processes each letter as it is encountered. These letters, or graphemes, are matched with the phonemes of the language, which it is assumed the reader already knows. These phonemes, the minimal units of meaning in the sound system of the language, are blended together to form words. (Phonemes are the individual units of sound in a language.) The derivation of meaning is thus the end process in which the language is translated from one form of symbolic representation to another.

One reason for the survival of this approach in the face of criticism is that it seems a reasonable and logical explanation of what happens when we read. Letters do represent sounds, and despite the fact that in English twenty-six written symbols have to represent over forty aural symbols, there is a degree of consistency. On the surface, then, it seems more logical to teach initial readers to utilise the systematic correspondences between written and spoken symbols than to teach them to recognise every letter and word they encounter by memorising its unique configuration and shape (a practice favoured by proponents of the 'whole-word' approach.)

One of the assumptions underlying this phonics approach is that once a reader has blended the sounds together to form a word, that word will then be recognised. In other words, it is assumed that the reader possesses an oral vocabulary which is extensive enough to allow decoding to proceed. This assumption is not one that can be made with second language learners for whom any form of reading instruction ought to be linked with intensive aural vocabulary development. In fact, the assumption that phonic analysis skills are all that is needed to become a successful independent reader is questionable with first as well as second language readers. Most teachers of reading have encountered children who are able to decode print after a fashion and thereby 'read' without actually extracting meaning from the text.

A number of other major criticisms have been made of the phonics approach. Much of this criticism is based on research into human memory. In the first place, with only twenty-six letters to represent over forty sounds in English, spelling-to-sound correspondences are both complex and unpredictable. It was this realisation which led to the development of primers, in which stories were composed of words which did have regular sound/symbol correspondences. Unfortunately, as many of the most common English words have irregular spellings and were therefore excluded, the stories in primers tended to be unnatural and tedious.

Research into human memory also provides counterfactual evidence. It has been shown that the serial processing of every letter in a text would slow reading up to the point where it would be very difficult for meaning to be retained. An early study by Kolers and Katzmann (1966), for example, demonstrated that it takes from a quarter to a third of a second to recognise and assign the appropriate phonemic sound to a given grapheme. At this rate, given the average length of English words, readers would only be able to process around 60 words per minute. In fact, it has been demonstrated that the average reader can read and comprehend around 250–350 words per minute. Given the fact that we can only hold in working memory about seven items at a time, readers would, under the bottom-up model, very often forget the beginning of a sentence (and perhaps even a word) before they have reached the end.

Smith (1978) has pointed out that the serial processing operations underlying the phonics approach are also contradicted by the fact that it is often impossible to make decisions about how upcoming letters and words ought to sound until the context provided by the rank above the one containing the item has been understood. Thus, in order to assign a phonemic value to a grapheme it is often necessary to know the meaning of the word containing the grapheme. If, for example, in reading a text one came across the graphemic sequence 'ho––', it would be impossible to assign a value to 'o' until one knew whether the whole word were 'house', 'horse', 'hot', 'hoot', etc. In the same way, it is impossible to assign a phonemic value to the vowel sequence in the word 'read' until it is known whether the sentence containing the word is referring to the present or the past. Additional evidence against the notion that reading proceeds through the serial processing of ever larger units of language has come from a line of research initiated by Goodman and Burke (1972). This research involved the analysis of errors made by the reader when reading aloud. Errors, termed 'miscues' by Goodman and Burke, provide evidence that something more than mechanical decoding is going on when readers process texts. They found that in many instances deviations from what was actually written on the page made sense semantically – for example, a child might read the sentence 'My father speaks Spanish' as 'My Dad speaks Spanish'. (If the child read 'My feather speaks Spanish', this would be evidence that he/she is not reading for meaning, but is decoding mechanically.)

Insights from sources such as the Reading Miscue Inventory led to the postulation of an alternative to the bottom-up, phonics approach. This has become known as the top-down or psycholinguistic approach to reading. As with the bottom-up models, there are a number of variations in this approach, but basically all agree that the reader rather than the text is at the heart of the reading process. Cambourne (1979) provides the following schematisation of the approach.

Past experience, language $\rightarrow$ Selective aspects $\rightarrow$ Meaning $\rightarrow$ Sound, pronunciation
intuitions and expectations          of print                                    if necessary

From the diagram, it can be seen that this approach emphasises the reconstruction of meaning rather than the decoding of form. The interaction of the reader and the text is central to the process, and readers bring to this interaction their knowledge of the subject at hand, knowledge of and expectations about how language works, motivation, interest and attitudes towards the content of the text. Rather than decoding each symbol, or even every word, the reader forms hypotheses about text elements and then 'samples' the text to determine whether or not the hypotheses are correct.

Oller (1979) also stresses the importance of taking into consideration psychological as well as linguistic factors in accounting how people read. He points out that the link between our knowledge of linguistic forms and our knowledge of the world is very close, and that this has a number of implications for discourse processing. Firstly, it suggests that the more predictable a sequence of linguistic elements, the more readily a text will be processed. It has been suggested that texts for initial first language readers should come close to the oral language of the reader. (The fact that phonics primers written in phonically regularised language present relatively unpredictable language at the levels of clause and text probably helps explain the difficulty many readers have with them.) Even second language learners, despite their limited knowledge of linguistic forms, should be assisted by texts which consist of more natural sequences of elements at the levels of word, clause and text. A second way of exploiting the relationship between linguistic and extralinguistic worlds is to ensure not only that linguistic elements are more predictable but also that the experiential content is more familiar and therefore more predictable. (See also Alderson and Urquhart's (1984) 'text–reader–task' structure for characterising foreign language reading.)

The significance of content familiarity for compensating limited linguistic knowledge is explored more fully in the next section. Here we should note that just as linguistic sequencing above the level of the grapheme/phoneme was unfamiliar in phonics-based primers, so also was the content, the subject matter often being remote from the experiences and interests of the readers. (For an extended discussion on linguistic and extralinguistic relationships, see Smith 1978, and Oller 1979.)

One of the shortcomings of the top-down model is that it sometimes fails to distinguish adequately between beginning readers and fluent readers. Smith, for example, advances the view that fluent readers operate by recognising words on sight. In other words, fluent reading in non-ideographic languages such as English proceeds in the same way as fluent reading in ideographic languages such as Chinese, where readers must learn to identify characters by their shape. (In ideographic languages, the characters do not represent sounds. Rather they are derived from the objects and entitites they are supposed to represent.) Of course, it does not necessarily follow that, as fluent readers proceed through sight recognition (assuming that this *is* how they read – something upon which there is by no means universal agreement), this is the way initial readers should be taught.

Stanovich (1980), in his exhaustive review of reading models, criticises the top-down notion that reading proceeds through the generation of hypotheses about upcoming text elements. He points out, for example, that the generation of hypotheses in the manner suggested by Smith would actually be more time consuming than decoding would be. In the light of the perceived deficiencies of both bottom-up and top-down models, he proposes a third which he calls an interactive–compensatory model. As the name indicates, this model suggests, that readers process texts by utilising information provided simultaneously from several different sources, and that they can compensate for deficiencies at one level by drawing on knowledge at other (either higher or lower) levels. These sources include all those looked at separately in bottom-up and top-down processes, that is, phonological, lexical, syntactic, semantic and discoursal knowledge.

Stanovich claims that his alternative model is superior because it deals with the shortcomings inherent in other models. The major deficiency of the bottom-up model is that it assumes the initiation of higher level processes, such as use of background knowledge, must await lower level decoding processes. The top-down model, on the other hand, does not allow lower level processes to direct higher level ones. The interactive–compensatory model allows for deficiencies at one level to be compensated for at another. In particular, higher level processes can compensate for deficiencies at lower levels, and this allows for the possibility that readers with poor reading skills at the levels of grapheme and word can compensate for these by using other sources of knowledge such as the syntactic class of a given word or semantic knowledge. Given deficiencies of lower level skills, poor readers may actually be more dependent on higher level processes than good readers.

## 4.3 Schema theory and reading

With the insight that there is more to comprehension that the words on the page has come an attempt to provide a theoretical model which will explain the way that our background knowledge guides comprehension processes. We have looked at aspects of this theory in Chapters 2 and 3, and here we take the ideas a little further. Much of the model-building has been carried out by researchers in the field of artificial intelligence whose ultimate aim has been to enable computers to process and produce discourse. Terms chosen by cognitive psychologists and computer specialists include 'frames', 'scripts', 'scenarios' and 'schemata'. A useful introduction and overview of this work is provided by Brown and Yule (1983a).

One of the most widely reported theories in the cognitive psychology literature is Minsky's 'frame' theory. Minsky suggests that human memory consists of sets of stereotypical situations (frames) which guide comprehension by providing a framework for making sense of new experiences. (Pearson and Johnson's 1978 view of reading comprehension as a process of relating the new to the known is based on a similar notion.)

While this theory appeals to our commonsense notions about how comprehension might work, it does have a number of problems. For example, it provides no explanation of why one script rather than another might be selected to guide comprehension. Brown and Yule see this as a major shortcoming of the theory, and they detail their major objection by inviting the reader to decide which 'frame' should guide comprehension for a reader processing a newspaper article:

> Consider the following new situation which presented itself at the beginning of a newspaper article.
>> The Cathedral congregation had watched on television monitors as Pope and Archbishop met in front of a British Caledonian helicopter, on the dewy grass of a Canterbury recreation ground. (*The Sunday Times*, 30 May 1982)
> The problem should be immediately obvious. Is a 'Cathedral' frame selected? How about a 'television-watching' frame, a 'meeting' frame, a 'helicopter' frame, a 'recreation-ground' frame? These questions are not trivial. After all, it probably is necessary to activate something like a 'recreation-ground' frame in order to account for the definite description 'the grass' mentioned in the text. (Brown and Yule 1983a: 241)

The term which has gained greater currency in the literature than any other is 'schema', a term first used by Bartlett (1932). Like frame theory, schema theory suggests that the knowledge we carry around in our head is organised into inter-related patterns. These are constructed from our previous experience of the experiential world and guide us as we make sense of new experiences. They also enable us to make predictions about what we might expect to experience in a given context. Given the fact that discourse comprehension is a process of utilising linguistic cues and background knowledge to reconstruct meaning, these schemata are extremely important, particularly to second and foreign language learners.

Widdowson (1983) has reinterpreted schema theory from an applied linguistic perspective. He postulates two levels of language: a systemic level and a schematic level. The systemic level includes the phonological, morphological and syntactic elements of the language, while the schematic level relates to our background knowledge. In Widdowson's scheme of things, this background knowledge exercises an executive function over the systemic level of language. In comprehending a given piece of language, we use what sociologists call interpretive procedures for achieving a match between our schematic knowledge and the language which is encoded systemically. Cicourel, who was one of the first to utilise the notion of interpretation in the behavioural sciences, suggested that:

> Through the use of interpretative procedures the participants supply meanings and impute underlying patterns even though the surface content will not reveal the meanings to an observer unless his model is directed to such elaborations. (Cicourel 1973: 40)

Widdowson has related this notion to the work on schema theroy. He argues that there are two types of schema operating through language. The first of these is concerned with propositional meaning, while the second relates to the functional level of language, either of which can provide textual connectivity. Thus, in Chapter 2, we saw that the connectivity of text cannot always be explained exclusively in terms of the language in the text. It also depends on our interpretive ability to make connections which do not exist in the text, but which are provided by use from our schematic knowledge of the subject in hand, or the functional purposes which the different text elements are fulfilling.

An important collection of articles on schema theory and reading is Carrell *et al.* (1988). The collection contains conceptual, position papers which provide a theoretical framework, and also a number of empirical studies showing how schema are implicated in reading comprehension.

## 4.4 Research into reading in a second language

A number of studies have been conducted into the influence of schematic knowledge on the comprehension processes of second language readers. Aslanian (1985) set out to discover what interpretive processes went on in her learners' heads as they completed a multiple choice/gap test of a reading passage. After the subjects had completed the gap test, Aslanian took them individually through the test and asked them to tell her why they had chosen one item rather than another. Transcripts of these interviews indicate that correct responses were often provided for the wrong reasons, and that incorrect responses were sometimes provided by readers who, in fact, had an adequate grasp of the passage as a whole. Aslanian's study shows that schematic knowledge structures can either facilitate or inhibit comprehension according to whether they are over- or underutilised.

> If readers rely too heavily on their knowledge and ignore the limitations imposed by the text, or vice versa, then they will not be able to comprehend the intended meaning of the writer. Whether one has understood the text or not depends very much on text variables such as sentence structure and length, vocabulary intensity, number of new concepts introduced, the difficulty and novelty of the subject matter, etc. . . . To understand the reader and the nature of the act of reading more clearly and comprehensively, one needs also to find out and describe the reader's strategies and reactions with regard to the reading tasks, and to see how the reader copes with the reading tasks and solves the problems. (Aslanian 1985: 20)

In a rather different study Nunan (1985) set out to test whether the perception of textual relationships is affected by readers' background knowledge. Subjects for the study were 100 second language, high school students who were divided into two groups. Group A consisted of longer-term learners who were orally fluent but had reading problems. Group B consisted of recently arrived immigrants. Test materials consisted of passages on familiar and unfamiliar topics from high school texts. Readability analyses showed the unfamiliar passage to be easier than the familiar passage. Both passages were analysed for the cohesively marked logical, referential and lexical relationships they contained (Halliday and Hasan 1976). Ninety-six relationships were identified which were matched across both passages, and these were used as the basis for constructing the test items. To construct the test, a modified cloze procedure was used in which the second end of the cohesive tie was deleted. The task for the reader was to identify the relationship and reinstate the deleted item.

Examples of the cohesive relationships and the way they were used to construct test items are set out below:

**Logical relationship**
Test item: Usually there would be no difficulty in deciding whether a living thing is a plant or an animal and it can be classified immediately. There are _____ some very tiny creatures which scientists know to be living, but cannot be sure whether they are plants or animals. (Deleted item: 'however'. Cohesive type: adversative conjunction).

**Referential relationship**
There is no difficulty in deciding that a bird is living and a stone is non-living, but not all things are as easy to distinguish as _____ . (Deleted item: 'these'. Cohesive type: referential demonstrative).

**Lexical relationship**
Test item: Green plants grow towards the light. This is because plants need _____ for energy. (Deleted item: 'light'. Cohesive type: lexical reiteration)

For both groups of subjects, the perception of textual relationships was significantly easier in the familiar, though syntactically more difficult, passage. Group A was also superior to group B, indicating that length of formal and informal exposure to the target language is also a significant factor in success.

As already indicated, this study was designed to test the effect of schematic knowledge on the comprehension of various types of textual relationship. Schema theory suggests that reading involves more than utilising linguistic and decoding skills; that interest, motivation and background knowledge will determine, at least in part, the success that a reader will have with a given text. This study showed that background knowledge was a more significant factor than grammatical complexity in determining the subjects' comprehension of the textual relationships in question.

This study has a number of pedagogical implications. The first of these stems from the fact that reading skills are not invariant: that is, they do not depend solely on a knowledge of the linguistic elements that make up a text. Reading is a dynamic process in which the text elements interact with other factors outside the text; in this case most particularly with the reader's knowledge of the experiential content of the text. This suggests that there is a need to relate the language being taught to the context which carries it. In instructional systems where the target language is the medium of instruction, the teaching of language ought not to be divorced from other school subjects. 'Language across the curriculum' is as important, if not more important, for second language learners as for first language readers (for suggestions on teaching language and content see Mohan 1986; Brinton *et al.* 1989). Widdowson goes so far as to suggest that foreign as well as second languages might be taught through the other subjects on the curriculum:

> A foreign language can be associated with those areas of use which are represented by the
> other subjects on the school curriculum and . . . this not only helps to ensure the link with

reality and the pupils' own experience but also provides us with the most certain means we have of teaching language as communication, as use rather than usage. (Widdowson 1978: 16)

Another study into the perception of textual relationships in a cross-cultural context is reported by Steffensen (1981). Steffensen identified relationships signalled by conjunctions in culturally significant sentences in two texts. One of these described an American wedding and the other an Indian wedding. A sentence was considered to have cultural significance if the relationship it contained could not be predicted from everyday knowledge, but which required familiarity with the culture from which it was drawn. Sample sentences from Steffensen's test passages are as follows:

American passage
(i)  Actually it was surprising that the men were in such good shape *because* they had a stag party on Thursday and didn't get in until 3 am.
(ii) The ushers seated some of the bride's friends on his side of the church *so* things wouldn't look off balance.

Indian passage
(iii) They did not create any problem in the wedding, *even though* Preema's husband is their only son.
(iv) Her husband and in-laws picked 'Uma' for her new name *since* her husband's family calls him 'Shiva'.

Steffensen had American and Indian subjects read the passages and then recall as much of the content as they could. The recall protocols were then analysed to determine whether the relationships being investigated were recalled by the subjects. This analysis revealed that Americans did better on the text containing American cultural content and Indians did better on the text containing Indian cultural content.

Steffensen concluded from her study that when readers are exposed to texts which describe aspects of a culture foreign to the reader, there will be a breakdown in the perception of textual relationships. A breakdown in relationships at the linguistic level reflects a breakdown in comprehension at the experiential level, that is, at the level of content. Her findings therefore support the contention that the process of reconstructing meaning is one of mapping the linguistic content onto extralinguistic context (see also Oller 1979). In setting out the pedagogical implications of her study, Steffensen suggests that what, at first sight, is a linguistic problem, may in fact be a problem of background knowledge. In such a case, teaching learners the facts about the customs in question would probably be more effective than drilling them in aspects of the language.

Considerable research has also been conducted into the strategies employed by good readers. This research has been selectively used to justify various proposals for pedagogical action. Walter (1982), in her book on learning to read in a second or foreign language, says that good readers utilise the following strategy when encountering a difficult text. First of all, they read the text slowly, pausing to consider what they have read. They then reread the text, looking from one part of the text to other parts in order to make connections between these different parts, and to make a mental summary of what they have read. She claims that most of the people who read in this way remember both the general points and the details of what they have read better than those who use other strategies. Her book provides numerous exercises designed for learners to search through a text and mentally organise the information it contains.

## 4.5  Reading and social context

Reading is usually conceived of as a solitary activity in which the reader interacts with the text in isolation. While not wishing to pre-empt the discussion in the section which follows, it is worth pointing out that the two language lessons we look at (classroom extracts 4.1 and 4.2) show that reading lessons are generally anything but solitary.

The social context of the second language reader is taken up by Wallace (1988), who explores in depth the circumstances in which such readers acquire and maintain literacy. She points out that learning to read is different from learning to speak, in that there is often a much stronger motivation to communicate orally than there is to communicate through reading and writing. If the use of literacy skills is a normal and accepted part of the behaviour of those with whom learners come into contact, then there is a much greater likelihood that the learners are going to want to read. In other words, learners are socialised into reading, and the motivation for learning to read is not only (or even primarily) for enjoyment or information, but because the aspiring reader wants to gain access to a 'community' of readers.

In cultural terms, reading and learning to read will mean different things to different learners. A young Polish doctor who is literate in her first language will have different expectations and views on the nature of literacy from an elderly Hmong woman with no formal schooling. This observation has obvious implications for the classroom; we must take these differences into account, not only in the texts we select, but also in the ways in which we go about teaching literacy.

The cultural, social and political implications of literacy are highlighted by Wallace in the following manner:

> Achieving literacy is seen not only as concomitant with certain social and occupational roles but in some countries goes together with political rights, such as the right to vote. Literacy is valued as part of adulthood, of full citizenship. It is clearly partly for this reason that we do not talk of children – or at least younger children – as being illiterate. Illiteracy is a stigma reserved for adulthood. Nonetheless, as teachers of reading we need from the beginning to see functional literacy as the goal; we need, that is, to show our learners that being literate, for children as well as adults, is part of day-to-day life in a personal and social sense. Children need from the beginning to see that reading is purposeful, that it helps us to achieve things. (Wallace 1988: 3)

## 4.6  Types of reading text

In Chapter 3 we looked at genre theory and its implications for language use. In this section we apply some of the insights from both genre theory and schema theory to reading. You will recall that one of the claims of genre theory is that language exists to fulfil certain functions and that these functions will largely determine the structure of the text and the language it contains. Schema theory suggests that we need to utilise information not explicitly contained in the text (i.e. 'inside the head' knowledge) to comprehend more texts adequately. As you read the following texts, consider the interpretive procedures required to understand them. What additional information does the reader have to bring to the texts in order to understand them?

### Text 1
System 816 features incredible storage capacity, the flexibility to handle a large variety of applications, and the speed to get the job done fast. And you can choose from more than 3,000 CP/M 8 or 16 bit programs as your needs grow. With the ability to expand from single to multi-user, network up to 255 systems, and upgrade as the technology advances, this equipment stands the test of time.

### Text 2
*Lemon Cream Sponge*
*Serves 6*

| | |
|---|---|
| 500 ml cream | 1 sachet gelatine |
| 500 ml milk | 3 tbs sugar |
| juice of two lemons | 1 punnet strawberries |

Melt gelatine in small quantitiy of hot water. Blend milk, cream and lemon juice together. Add gelatine mixture, stirring constantly. Chill several hours until set. Decorate with strawberries.

### Text 3
If you want to do the job right, the saying goes, make sure you use the right tool. Don't try to stop a tank with a Roach Motel. So more than in other fields, scientists are debating this question of appropriate technology as microcomputers begin to move into research facilities and R and D departments around the country.

### Text 4
New apple-fresh Cuddly Fabric Softener. A fresh new experience! New Cuddly leaves your clothes so soft and easy to iron; and now new Cuddly adds the crisp fragrance of freshly picked apples to your wash. Only new Cuddly Fabric Softener has two softening agents working together to soften your whole wash; and new Cuddly also helps eliminate static cling. Use apple-fresh Cuddly in your final rinse. Do not pour undiluted onto fabrics.

For anyone with a passing knowledge of the field, text 1 is fairly obviously about computers. However, in order to get from the text all that the author intended, one would need to utilise a certain amount of background knowledge. It is un-likely that someone with only a passing knowledge of computers will be able to say with any certainty whether the text is about micro, mini or maxi computers.

Text 2 is quite evidently a recipe, and it displays the generic structure and language of recipes. In structural terms, it consists of a title, specifications, ingredients and procedure. Linguistically, it contains language which is typical of the 'recipe genre'. Predictable function words such as articles and prepositions tend to be omitted, and the procedure usually consists of a set of imperative statements listed in chrono-logical order.

Our knowledge of text genres can, in fact, sometimes mislead us. Text 3 is a case in point. This text is extracted from an article on the use of appropriate tech-nology which was published in a popular journal. However, some people have said that it is about advertising, having been misled by the second sentence, which is couched in the language of advertisements but which is, in fact, a metaphor. (A 'Roach Motel', by the way, is an American insect trap. The insects check in, but never check out!)

## 4.7 The reading lesson

Although they are not always readily apparent, teachers' beliefs and attitudes about language, learning and teaching will have a marked influence on what they do in class and what they get their learners to do. As you read the following lesson objectives and notes from a topic-based reading programme, decide which of the insights into the nature of reading and learning to read outlined and discussed in the preceding section are evident in the lesson objectives and notes. What sorts of learner would the programme be suitable for?

TOPIC: Christmas.

GOAL: To read and write different kinds of texts around the topic of Christmas.

OBJECTIVES
To understand the purpose of Christmas cards.
To predict the likely content.
To learn to write common expressions for Christmas greeting cards.
To develop automaticity in spelling common structural words.
To develop visual memory.
To make connections between spoken and written language.
To construct a text about personal experience with appropriate staging and sequencing.
To develop reference skills.
To recognise past tense markers, to understand their function and use them appropriately in writing about themselves.

SESSION 1
Read a teacher-written book about Christmas. Discuss own experiences, attitudes.
Discuss sending Christmas cards (who to, why).
Read some messages about Christmas cards. Discuss appropriate expressions. Teacher writes and students copy.
Practise adding names, signatures, additional messages, etc., to cards.

SESSION 2
Discuss childhood Christmases. Teacher writes up useful words and expressions as they arise. Students write (however little) about their childhood Christmases. Teacher can act as a scribe if necessary. Proof read, read aloud to others, check spellings against personal spelling lists. Teacher assists with incomprehensible parts. If possible, photocopy stories and swap around class for reading. Readers check understanding with writers.

SESSION 3
Teacher writes/types up standardised version, distributes it and makes a cloze, removing selected key words, or words that cause problems. Stories can also be taped and listened to while read and to help complete cloze.
Students do word games and visual memory training activities to reinforce spelling, or matching, sequencing activities to focus on text and sentence structure.

SESSION 4
Students compare Christmases past and present. They discuss, then write about Christmases now. Teacher draws attention to contrast in tenses from past to present. As problems arise with spelling, teacher encourages students firstly to make a best attempt and then to use reference skills with dictionaries and personal spelling lists. Teacher consults with students in writing process. Students encouraged to proof read and monitor own writing. Stories are prepared for publishing in class/centre magazine.
(Nunan 1989c: 44–5)

This lesson is obviously influenced by a functional view of language. Learners are introduced to genres associated with Christmas, and their background knowledge of the genres is activated by the initial task. The teacher then provides a model of one particular genre, which is used by the learners as a basis for producing their own model.

In one of the few empirical investigations of what actually goes on in second language classrooms, as opposed to what people say, or think, goes on, Richards (1989) presents a case study of an 'effective' second language reading teacher. The bulk of the study is an ethnographic description of the teacher's class. There were four different phases to the lesson. During the first phase, students worked on material from an SRA reading kit, focusing on inferencing skills. They then worked with the rate-builder portion of the kit, focusing on developing reading fluency. The third phase of the lesson involved readers in working on exercises from the vocabulary text, and they completed the lesson by taking part in an extensive reading activity.

Richards makes the point that while it is relatively easy to describe what goes on in classrooms, moving beyond description to interpretation and evaluation is more difficult. However, as the purpose of the investigation was to identify what made the lesson an effective one, interpretation and evaluation were of central importance. From his analysis of the lesson and from interviews with the teacher, Richards concluded that the following principles capture the essence of effective instruction.

1. Instructional objectives are used to guide and organise the lessons. (The teacher formulated and conveyed to learners what the lesson was intended to accomplish.)
2. The teacher has a comprehensive theory of the nature of reading on a second language, and refers to this in planning his teaching. (The teacher used knowledge of L2 reading strategies, schema theory and the role of background knowledge rather than 'common sense' to select learning experiences.)
3. Class-time is used for learning. (Students were 'on task' for fifty of the sixty minutes.)
4. Instructional activities have a teaching rather than a testing focus. (He provided opportunities for learners to develop and improve skills and strategies rather than demonstrating mastery of such skills.)
5. Lessons have a clear structure. (The structure was outlined to students, and each activity was clearly framed.)
6. A variety of different reading activities are used during each lesson. (Variation and pacing contributed to positive attitude of students.)
7. Classroom activities give students opportunities to get feedback on their reading performance. (The teacher provided information on the kinds of strategies they were using for different tasks, and on the effectiveness of these strategies.)
8. Instructional activities relate to real-world reading purposes. (Links were provided between the SRA activities and use of learners' textbooks for learning.)
9. Instruction is learner focused. (Learners were encouraged to try and work things out for themselves.)

### Pre-reading task

Extract 4.1 contains selected extracts from the lesson analysed by Richards. As you read the extract, consider what aspects of the teaching seem to you to stand out as being characteristic of effective teaching. In particular, see whether you can identify any of the nine principles of effective teaching in action. (For the full ethnographic narrative of the lesson, you are referred to Richards 1989.)

### Classroom extract 4.1: A reading lesson

The lesson begins promptly. The teacher writes a brief outline on the board, listing the four activities which will constitute the lesson. This is to give students an awareness of what activities they are going to take part in, what will be expected of them during the lesson, and to give them a sense that they are taking part in activities that are planned and structured.

## Activity 1: Reading for understanding

Students are instructed to form pairs and work on cards from the Reading for Understanding section of the SRA Kit. Following this, they form pairs and discuss their choices.

As the activity progresses, the teacher moves about checking how the students are doing and answering any questions they may have. Selecting the right answer to the questions requires them to make inferences and deal with all the information that has been presented in the passage, or to make use of cues within the text. In responding to students' questions, however, the teacher consistently refers them to the text and draws their attention to cues they should be able to use to identify the meaning of a word or to select the correct answer. For example:

S:  What does torso mean here?

T:  [Pointing to a word in the passage] It's something to do with this word, right?

S:  With the human form?

T:  Right. It's not the head and it's not the legs.

S:  The part in between?

T:  Yeah.

In answer to another students' query about the meaning of a word, the teacher points to another word in the text and asks:

T:  What do you think it has to do with the meaning of this word?

S:  Is it the opposite?

T:  That's right.

## Activity 2: Reading for fluency

This involves the use of comprehension cards from the SRA Kit. Students choose a card which contains a text of perhaps two or three pages, followed by detailed comprehension questions. The goal is for them to try and increase their reading speed by answering the questions within a time limit.

Four possible strategies are presented to the students: A = read, questions, scan; B = questions, read, scan; C = skim, questions; D = questions, skim.

The teacher asks a few students about the text they have chosen:

T:  What passage are you going to read?

S:  Malaria.

T:  Do you know much about that topic?

S:  Not really.

T:  So what strategy are you going to choose?

S:  Strategy B.

T:  So you want to read it a little more slowly?

S:  Yes.

T:  [To another student] What's your topic?

S:  Methods of experiments in science.

T:  How do you feel about that?

S:  I'll choose A.

The teacher is trying to sensitise [students] to choosing appropriate strategies according to the kinds of material they are reading. [At the conclusion of the activity] if their score is not very good, he asks if they think a different strategy would have been better.

T:  What did you get, Maria?

S:  I got a 5. I think I misread this sentence right here.

T:  How did you read it? What strategy did you use?

S:  C

T:  So you read it pretty fast.

T:  [To another student] How did you go?

S:  Not so good.

T:  You chose B for this passage. Do you think if you had read it more slowly it would have helped?

S:  Yes, the subject is not clear, not too easy for me. The topic is about stamps.

**Activity 3: Vocabulary exercise**

The teacher announces the next activity and the time students should spend on it (about ten minutes). The teacher explains that he sets a time limit for each phase of the lesson to make sure that students work seriously on each activity and attempt to get through it in the allotted time.

As with the first activity in the lesson, although the exercise could be completed individually, the teacher asks the students to work in pairs and to negotiate and discuss their answers. Then he checks their answers by having a student read out his or her answer. Rather than confirm whether the answer is correct, the teacher asks the others to give their opinion.

**Activity 4: Extensive reading**

The last activity of the lesson is an extensive reading activity, involving reading a lengthy article from one of the class texts. The teacher explained that this is a study skills exercise dealing with how to approach something that is going to be read extensively, such as a chapter in a textbook or an article.

The following extract is taken from the reading component of a general English class for low proficiency students, and, as you will see, it is a very different lesson from the one portrayed in extract 4.1.

## Pre-reading task

1.  As you read the extract, compare it with the preceding extract, considering, in particular, the extent to which the principles identified by Richards are, or are not realised by this particular teacher.
2.  What is the pedagogical goal of the task?

## Classroom extract 4.2: Reading for factual information

The students have completed a listening comprehension exercise in which they have listened to a dialogue between two people who are about to go on a sightseeing excursion. They have also done a language exercise focusing on wh- questions for obtaining information about travel. The teacher picks up a bundle of tourist brochures.

T: Now, I'm going to give you some brochures
about Victor Harbour (a seaside resort). And
we're going to look at what the brochure tells
us – all right? It tells us . . . where it is, . . .
how to get there, . . . how long it takes, . . .
where do you catch the train, . . . and what
you can do – when you get to Victor Harbour.
Okay?

[She distributes the brochures to the students who are sitting in groups of three or four, and
asks a number of preliminary questions before initiating the following interactional routine.]

T: Now, when can you catch this train? When can
you catch the train? What does it tell you?
Have a look.

[She leans over one of the students and points to his brochure.]

T: What day's that?

S: Er, Sunday.

T: Sundays. Any other day?

S: Er, between June . . . and, er, August.

T: Yes. Yeah. And pub. . .

S: Public holiday.

T: What's a public holiday?

S: Er, Christmas.

T: Exactly, Christmas, Easter, yep. Okay. That's
right. And . . . what else?

S: Wednesday and Saturday.

T: Wednesdays and Saturdays . . .

S: School holiday.

T: Yeah, okay, when it's school holidays, . . . on
Wednesday and Saturday. Now, back to the
timetable, where do you catch the train?

S: Er, Kes-wick.

T: 'Kessick', yeah, a funny English word – not
'Kes-wick', but 'Kessick'. You catch it at
'Kessick'. All right.

[She digresses for several minutes to explain to the students where Keswick is in relation to the
centre of the city and the main suburban railway station.]

T: Remember when we were listening to the
tape, one of the people said, 'I'll go to the
tourist bureau'. You know tourist bureau?
Special office. And get . . . [She waves a
brochure.] . . . brochures, brochures.
These're brochures. What do brochures tell
you? What do brochures tell you?

[Pause.]

S: How can we, can catch the train, and . . .

T: That's right.

S: . . . how much it, er, the ticket, cost.

T:  Good. It tells you about the place, it tells you
    how to get there, where to catch the train, how
    long it takes, how much it costs. And this one
    also tells you about – eats and drinks, eats and
    drinks, okay? What you can get on the train.
    . . . Now, I would like you to work in little
    groups – just where you are. I will give you
    another brochure. Have a look at something
    you would like to do – and see what
    information you can find out. Where is it, how
    do you get there, how much it costs, what time
    it leaves . . . okay?
[She distributes new brochures to the groups.]
T:  And I'll come round and help you.
[The students begin looking at brochures together, and the teacher moves around the room,
asking the students questions and generally encouraging them.]

### Post-reading task

Imagine that the teacher has asked you for feedback on the lesson. Make a list of:
(a) the positive things you would tell her; (b) the negative points you would raise with
her.

This lesson is very tightly controlled, the teacher asking all of the questions (and
answering a good many of them as well). The aim of the lesson is to provide learners
with practice in locating key information in written texts – in this instance, tourist
brochures – which provide the learners with exposure to authentic materials even
though they are only beginners. While the lesson is ostensibly devoted to reading,
it is worth noting the amount of oral language work in which the learners are
engaged, and the amount of active listening they are required to do. Given the
quantity of teacher talk, it could be argued that the lesson involves more listening
than reading.

In observing, recording and analysing a great many reading lessons, in a range of
contexts, I have found this extract to be typical of the types of interaction which
occur. Such interactions are characterised by teacher questions which require
learners to rummage around in the text for information, and are interspersed with
lengthy teacher monologues. Even in advanced classes, there tends to be minimal
opportunities for learners to take some responsibility for their own learning. It
would not be difficult to reorganise a lesson such as this in order to increase
the opportunities for learners to do more of the work. In this lesson, learners
could have worked in pairs, one with a set of questions, the other with the timetable.
Such a simple one-way task would have provided the learners themselves with
a much more active role, at the same time as achieving the reading goals of the
lesson.

## 4.8  Investigating reading comprehension

**Task 4.1**
Select four or five reading passages from different places in a reading coursebook, randomise them and distribute them to students who have been placed in small groups. Ask the students to rank the passages from easiest to most difficult. Record and analyse the discussions. How much agreement is there among the groups? Which factors seem to be significant?

**Task 4.2**
Select four or five reading passages representing different genres, for example, a narrative, a description, an instructive text and a didactic text. Make sure that the texts are approximately the same length. Carry out the same procedure as task 4.1. Does genre seem to be a significant factor in text difficulty?

**Task 4.3**
Select an authentic reading passage which is beyond the current skills of your students. Design a series of exercises which gradually increase the processing demands on your learners. Get your learners to undertake the tasks in small groups and then discuss with them the difficulties they had. Record and analyse the discussion. What generalisations can you derive about learner perceptions on the nature of reading comprehension from the discussion?

**Task 4.4**
Administer a gap or multiple choice reading test to a number of students. Review the test with each student individually and get them to explain to you why they gave the answers they did. Record and analyse the interviews. Did you find, like Aslanian (1985), that coming up with the correct answer does not necessarily indicate adequate comprehension? Did some students who gave incorrect answers actually have an adequate overall grasp of the passage?

**Task 4.5**
Record a reading lesson or segment of a lesson and analyse it following the procedure set out by Richards. What views on the nature of reading emerge? Do you think it was a 'good' lesson? Make a list of the principles of reading which seem to underlie the lesson. To what extent do these reflect the theory and research reported in section 4.2?

**Task 4.6**
Record and analyse a reading lesson. What is the percentage of time devoted to listening, speaking and writing? What might learners be reasonably expected to learn from the lesson? Is there a mismatch between the lesson as intention (as revealed by lesson plans, materials, etc.) and the lesson which actually emerged?

## 4.9 Conclusion

While the development of reading skills involves qualitatively different processes from the development of oral language ability, both are underpinned by certain principles. In this chapter, I have tried to set out what these are. In particular, I have suggested that programmes for both oral and written language development take as their point of departure the purposes and functions to which language is put, and which determine its realisation as text.

In section 4.3 we looked at reading materials and classrooms in action, and saw, among other things, the complex relationship between oral and written language. At the level of classroom action, there is a constant interplay between listening, speaking, reading and writing, and it is clear that in a lesson which is ostensibly labelled 'reading', opportunities exist for learners to develop their other language skills as well.

# Chapter Five

## *Developing Writing Skills*

---

### 5.1 Introduction

One of the key principles from which I have taken my bearings in writing this book is that language exists to fulfil a range of communicative functions, and that these functions will be reflected in the shape of the language itself. This principle can be used to guide teaching decisions, and to inform a range of curriculum tasks, from the selection and grading of content, through to the selection of learning tasks and materials. In this chapter we see how it can provide useful insights for both the theory and practice of writing.

The chapter sets out to answer the following questions:

1. What are the differences between spoken and written language, and what are the implications of these differences for classroom practice?
2. In what ways do process-oriented views of writing contrast with product-oriented views?
3. How can knowledge of the generic structure of different text types improve writing?
4. What are the major differences between skilled and unskilled writers?
5. What is a writing conference, and how does 'conferencing' work at the level of classroom action?
6. How can learning-how-to-learn tasks be integrated into the writing lesson?

### 5.2 Comparing spoken and written language

When developing appropriate classroom activities and procedures for teaching written language, it is important to be aware of the differences between spoken and written language. In earlier chapters, we have seen that the contexts and purposes for using language are inseparable from the language itself. It therefore follows that spoken and written language, which exist to fulfil different functions, will exhibit different characteristics.

Halliday (1985b) suggests that writing has evolved in societies as a result of cultural changes creating communicative needs which cannot be readily met by the spoken language. He speculates that with the emergence of cultures based on agriculture rather than hunting and gathering, there developed a need for permanent records which could be referred to over and over again. This was the initial stimulus for the emergence of a new form of language: writing.

In the modern world, written language serves a range of functions in everyday life, including the following:

1. Primarily for action
   public signs, e.g. on roads and stations; product labels and instructions, e.g. on food, tools or toys purchased; recipes; maps; television and radio guides; bills; menus; telephone directories; ballot papers; computer manuals, monitors and printouts.
   For social contact
   personal correspondence; letters, postcards, greeting cards.
2. Primarily for information
   newspapers (news, editorials) and current affairs magazines; hobby magazines; non-fiction books, including textbooks; public notices; advertisements; political pamphlets; scholastic, medical, etc. reports; guidebooks and travel literature.
3. Primarily for entertainment
   light magazines, comic strips; fiction books; poetry and drama; newspaper features; film subtitles; games, including computer games.

(Halliday 1985b: 40–1)

These different purposes for language will be reflected in the texts through which the functions are realised: letters have different characteristics from newspaper editorials, which have different characteristics from poems, and so on. As we have seen, these differences exist within the sentence at the level of grammar, and beyond the sentence at the level of text structure.

Rather than being separate manifestations of language, it has been suggested that spoken and written language exist as a continuum, a mode continuum, and that any given text, spoken or written will exist somewhere along this continuum, depending on the extent to which it exhibits the characteristics of the different forms. Some spoken texts will be more like written texts than others, while some written texts will be more like spoken texts than others. Consider the following texts: most native speakers would recognise text 1 as being more like spoken language than text 2, even though text 1 is a written text and text 2 could conceivably be spoken.

**Text 1**
Annie,
Gone to the deli for milk. Back in a tick.
Go in and make yourself at home.
– Theo

**Text 2**

At times one's preoccupation with averages can cause one to lose sight of the fact that many of the most important workaday decisions are based on considerations of the extremes rather than on the middle of a distribution.

What are some of the features which distinguish spoken from written texts? It is sometimes suggested that spoken language is simpler than written language, that is, it is less structured. However, as Halliday has pointed out, speech is no less structured or complex than writing. Transcriptions of spoken language look less structured because they represent 'unedited' language. If we could examine all the drafts of a piece of writing, it may also look as unstructured. The two modes, in fact, represent two different kinds of complexity. Written language is complex at the level of the clause, while spoken language is complex in the way clauses are linked together. These different sorts of complexity are reflected in the lexical density of written texts (something which makes writing seem more complex). Lexical density refers to the number of lexical or content words per clause. In the following example, from Halliday, there are twelve content words in a single clause.

**Text 3**

The use of this method of control unquestionably leads to safer and faster trains running in the most adverse weather conditions.

A spoken version of text 3 might be as follows:

**Text 4**

You can control the trains this way
and if you do that
you can be quite sure
that they'll be able to run more safely and more quickly
than they would otherwise
no matter how bad the weather gets

The ten content words (control, trains, way, sure, run, safely, quickly, bad, weather, gets) are distributed between five clauses, giving a lexical density of two.

The density of written language is also reinforced by the tendency to create nouns from verbs. Examples of this process of nominalisation are as follows:

| *Spoken* | *Written* |
|---|---|
| Good writers reflect on what they write. | Reflection is a characteristic of good writers. |

Halliday calls this grammatical metaphor. He suggests that the spoken forms are in a sense more basic than the written forms, and that in writing we have altered the normal state of events. In other words, processes which in the grammatical system of English would normally be represented as verbs have been transformed into 'things' and represented as nouns. It is this transformation which prompts Halliday to use the term 'metaphor'.

Another important difference between speech and writing derives from the fact that writing is often decontextualised. In communicating a message writers are usually distant in time and place from the person(s) with whom they wish to communicate. Therefore, they have to make inferences about the relevant knowledge possessed by the reader, and decide what to include and what to omit from their text. They also need to anticipate possible difficulties that readers might have and take these into account in creating their texts. Given the lack of direct contact with the reader, they are unable to make use of feedback from the other person to adjust their message and thereby facilitate communication.

Hammond (1987) believes that it is crucial to understand the relationships between oral and written language in order to develop an effective pedagogy for teaching. She provides classroom data which shows that many children from non-English speaking backgrounds, who can produce well structured and reasonably grammatical oral texts are much less successful when it comes to writing. This may partly be accounted for by the fact that the children she investigated had been learning oral language longer than written language. There is also the physical effort which is needed to produce written texts. More important, however, is the fact that children are frequently asked to write a story such as a narrative or a recount after they have already produced an oral version for the teacher and the class. Because the two modes of oral and written language exist to fulfil different functions, asking children to produce a written version of a story which has already been adequately told is inappropriate. 'Writing a recount, immediately following an oral recount of the same event, is not an adequate purpose for writing, as the two texts are doing the same job. They are fulfilling precisely the same purpose, and hence the effort required to produce an effective written text is simply not worth while' (Hammond 1987: 15).

## 5.3  Writing as process and writing as product

There is a perennial tension in most aspects of language learning and teaching between language as process and writing as product. Traditionally, in curriculum practice, a distinction has been drawn between the activities of the syllabus designer, which have been focused on products, and the activities of the methodologist, which have been focused on processes. However, in recent years this oversimplistic division has become difficult to sustain (Nunan 1989a). Broadly speaking, a product-oriented approach, as the title indicates, focuses on the end result of the learning process – what it is that the learner is expected to be able to do as a fluent and competent user of the language. Process approaches, on the other hand, focus more on the various classroom activities which are believed to promote the development of skilled language use.

Product-oriented approaches to the development of writing favour classroom activities in which the learner is engaged in imitating, copying and transforming models of correct language. This usually occurs at the level of the sentence. In coursebooks produced in the 1960s and 1970s, there is the belief that before students can be expected to write coherent paragraphs they should have mastered the language at the level of the sentence. Writing classes should therefore be devoted in the first instance to sentence formation and grammar exercises.

While the notion of learning by imitating appropriate (or what was thought to be appropriate) written sentences fitted in well with the sentence-level view of structuralist linguistics, and the bottom-up approach to language processing and production, it did not marry so happily with more contemporary views of language and learning which concentrated more on language at the level of discourse. In addition, instead of looking at completed texts, teachers of writing became much more interested in the processes writers go through in composing texts. It was recognised that competent writers do not produce final texts at their first attempt, but that writing is a long and often painful process, in which the final text emerges through successive drafts.

Methodologically, these ideas found their way into practice in the process approach to writing. In this approach, the focus in the first instance is on quantity rather than quality, and beginning writers are encouraged to get their ideas on paper in any shape or form without worrying too much about formal correctness. The approach also encourages collaborative group work between learners as a way of enhancing motivation and developing positive attitudes towards writing. In addition, and more controversially, attention to grammar is played down.

A number of interesting classroom techniques, including 'conferencing', emerged from the process approach to writing. The aim of conferencing is to encourage young writers to talk about their initial drafts with the teacher or with fellow students. The technique draws on principles of discovery learning, as well as the notion of linking reading with writing. In the next section, we shall look at how a conferencing session between a teacher and pupil develops.

While process writing added a valuable new dimension to language classrooms, it has also attracted criticism. One such criticism is that the process approach confines children largely to narrative forms and that this represents a serious limitation on their ability to master text types such as reports, expositions and arguments which are essential for academic success at school and beyond. Martin (1985) argues that these forms of factual writing encourage the development of critical thinking skills which in turn encourage individuals to explore and challenge social reality, and that learners who are denied the opportunity of developing factual writing skills are also denied the tools which would help them to challenge their social reality.

In his critique of process writing, Rodrigues claims that:

> The unfettered writing process approach has been just as artificial as the traditional high school research paper. Writing without structure accomplishes as little as writing a mock structure . . . [Students] need structure, they need models to practise, they need to improve even mechanical skills, and they still need time to think through their ideas, to revise them, and to write for real audiences and real purposes. (Rodrigues 1985: 26–7)

Horowitz (1986), looking at the writing demands made on second language learners at university, has similar criticisms. He claims that process writing fails to prepare students to write examination essays. The approach is also based on an inductive approach to learning which only suits some learners. (See the discussion on inductive versus deductive learning in Chapter 8, and the discussion on learning style preferences in Chapter 9.) Other criticisms by Horowitz include the fact that process writing gives a false impression of how university writing will be evaluated, and that choice of topic, an important process-writing principle, is irrelevant in most university contexts.

In her analysis of recent research into the teaching of writing, Zamel (1987) claims that, despite insights into the complexities of the composing process revealed by process-oriented studies, most writing classes are still based on mechanistic, product-oriented exercises and drills which research has largely discredited. She cites studies which purport to show that learners get few opportunities actually to write. When ESL students do get to write, teachers tend to view the resulting texts as final products to evaluate, which conveys to students the message that the function of writing is to produce texts for teachers to evaluate, not to communicate meaningfully with another person.

According to Zamel, the writing class should take into account the learners' purposes for writing which transcend that of producing texts for teacher evaluation. Writing skills can develop rapidly when students' concerns and interests are acknowledged, when they are given numerous opportunities to write, and when they are encouraged to become participants in a community of writers. Lastly, she suggests that teachers should themselves become action researchers in their own classrooms, and that by engaging in the types of inquiry and investigation she advocates, they can apply insights from what they have learned in the most 'profound' way. She, along with numerous others, has encouraged teachers to investigate their own practices, and the effects of those practices on their students, and has found it to be an excellent way of bridging the gap between theory and practice.

Unfortunately, like many educational debates, proponents of process and product approaches present and preserve distinctions which are more ostensible than real. There is no principled reason why process writing cannot be integrated with the practice of studying and even imitating written models in the classroom. In fact, modelling can be seen as a text-level written equivalent of the practice of providing learners with formulaic oral language at an early stage of development. The claim that such modelling constricts the learner's creative freedom remains to be demonstrated. Creativity, and creative freedom can only exist within certain boundaries and conventions if communication is to be effective, and a major task confronting the learner of a second or foreign language is to identify the boundaries of his or her new language.

## 5.4  The generic structure of written texts

In the preceding three chapters, we have looked at the importance of context, purpose and audience to language learning and use. We have seen that these have an important bearing on the shape of a text. In the previous chapter, for instance, we saw that cooking recipes as texts exhibit certain characteristics which distinguish them from advertisements or newspaper editorials. It was further suggested learning to read can be enhanced if readers are sensitised to the internal shape, or generic structure, of the texts they are reading. These principles, drawn from systemic–functional linguistics, can also assist beginning writers.

Hammond (1989) demonstrates that an analysis of the generic structure of children's writing can provide valuable insights into what makes good and poor writing. The following two texts were written in normal classroom writing sessions by two different children who were provided with the lead sentence: 'When I walked out of school, the dog limped up to me', which was followed by a ten minute discussion session.

**Text 5**
1. When I walked out of school
2. the dog limped up to me.
3. He was grey with white spots.
4. He had very floppy ears indeed.
7. I took him to my house.
8. and bandaged his leg.
9. Then I knew what was wrong with him.
10. He was in a dog fight.
11. I got my dog's chain.
12. I put it on him.
13. I took him for a walk.
14. Then the owner of the dog saw the dog and I
15. I took (the) chain off the dog
16. and went home.

**Text 6**
   The Dog
1. It was crying
2. so I took it home.
3. As soon as my mother came home from work
4. she gave it a name.
5. We named it Kelly.
6. I bandaged its leg.
7. I had great fun with Kelly.

The generic structure of both texts shows why text 5 works better than text 6. In the first place, it has a complete narrative structure of orientation–complication–

resolution. The fact that the complication precedes the orientation quite satisfactorily shows that the writer has a good control of the narrative form. In contrast, text 6 has no orientation at all.

> The writer has ignored the given opening sentence and substituted a related complication as an opening. There is a resolution to this complication, but then a second resolution to an implied complication (that the dog did not have a name) appears next. An aspect of the first resolution reappears and then there is a sort of coda at the end. In all, the structure of the text is incomplete and rather messy. (Hammond 1989: 17)

There are several practical implications of this research into children's writing. In the first place, young writers (and readers) need to be exposed to a range of different types of text. However, in addition to this, they need to be shown how the different text types are characterised by different generic structures (in the case of narratives, the orientation–complication–resolution structure). They should also be given the opportunity to compare different versions of a text, and helped to see how the way in which information is organised within a text will partly determine its effectiveness.

## 5.5  Differences between skilled and unskilled writers

Studying the differences between skilled and unskilled writers provides information which can be transformed into pedagogy. In a review of research on writing, Zamel (1982) cites studies which show that less skilled writers tend to focus on the mechanics of writing and are inhibited by their concern for formal correctness. They are also less able to anticipate the likely problems of the reader. In process terms, skilled writers are much more aware of writing as a recursive activity involving revisions of successive drafts of one's texts, during which one's ideas might change, necessitating the rewriting of whole chunks of text. Unskilled writers, on the other hand, tend to limit themselves to teacher-generated rules and modifications of lexis. In an investigation of the composing process of eight proficient ESL writers, Zamel discovered that only one composed in her first language and then translated into English.

Similar findings are reported by Lapp (1984), cited in Richards (1990). At the pre-writing stage, skilled writers spend time planning the task, while unskilled writers spend little time planning and, in consequence, are confused when they begin. At the drafting stage, skilled writers write quickly and fluently, spend time reviewing what they write, and do most of their reviewing at the sentence and paragraph level. Un-skilled writers spend little time reviewing what they have written, review only short segments of text, and are concerned principally with vocabulary and sentence formation. Finally, at the revision stage, skilled writers revise at all levels of lexis, sentence and discourse, review and revise throughout the composing process, and use revisions to clarify meaning, while unskilled writers do not make major revisions in the direction or focus of the text, make most revisions only during the first draft and focus primarily on the mechanics of grammar, spelling, punctuation and vocabulary.

## 5.6  Writing classrooms and materials

The following extracts are taken from two recently published coursebooks on writing in a second language. The introductions to coursebooks can be very revealing. These two samples reflect clearly the authors' ideologies, and echo some of the current theoretical and empirical issues discussed in the preceding section. In particular, they emphasise the interaction between process and product, focusing on the need to revise and polish one's initial efforts. The significance of one's audience, the importance of one's purpose and the links between the classroom and the real world are also underlined. It is interesting to see the way these principles are reflected in the tasks and exercises developed by the authors.

> Writing is clearly a complex process, and competent writing is frequently accepted as being the last language skill to be acquired. . . . Few people write spontaneously, and few feel comfortable with a formal writing task intended for the eyes of someone else. When the 'someone else' is a teacher, whose eye may be critical, and who indeed may assign a formal assessment to the written product, most people feel uncomfortable. It makes sense then, that the atmosphere of the writing classroom should be warm and supportive, and non-threatening. It helps if teachers show willingness to write too, and to offer their attempts for class discussion along with those of the students; it helps if students can work together, assisting each other, pointing out strengths and weaknesses without taking or giving offence. Many of our tasks suggest working with a partner or in groups, and we see this work as very important; not only does it make the task livelier and more enjoyable, but it makes sure that students see that writing really is co-operative, a relationship between writer and reader. Usually the writer has to imagine a reader, but co-operative writing provides each writer with a reader and makes the writing task more realistic and more interactive. . . . Writing is commonly seen as a three-stage process: pre-writing, writing and rewriting. Although this is very much an oversimplification, it is a helpful one. In the past teachers concentrated on the end of the second stage, i.e. after the writing had been done. They did not see how they could intervene at the pre-writing and writing stages, as rewriting was seen only as 'correcting the mistakes'. We now understand the importance of all three stages as part of the writing process, and try to help students master the process by participating in it with them, rather than contenting ourselves with criticising the product, i.e. the composition, without knowing much about how it was arrived at. (Hamp-Lyons and Heasley 1987: 2–3)

> This book . . . provides non-threatening guided opportunities to practise (or rehearse) the very sort of writing tasks that are required in real life. Secondly, it provides guidance and practice in the aspects of language and form so important to effective writing. So, you find models of different types of texts with explanations and discussion points. You find exercises which deal, for example, with organisation and ordering of ideas, paragraphing, linking ideas, appropriate word choice, economy of phrasing, layout, spelling and punctuation. . . . Thirdly, the book emphasises that the demands of writing vary considerably depending on the proposed reader, the purpose, the content and the writing situation. Students are urged to think about the relationship between the four determinant factors and the features of written language above. For example, there are exercises on

appropriate wording to achieve results in letters of protest or complaint, exercises on economic use of words to keep down costs in advertisements and so on. Lastly, it reflects throughout that writing is a process which always, but to varying extents and in various ways, requires preparation, drafting and revising. The exercises help students to be more aware of this process and thereby to improve the effectiveness of their writing. . . . The book does not aim to teach items of vocabulary or grammar, except where such items seem to be specific enough to the writing context and important enough to the successful completion of the tasks being set to warrant special guidance and practice. (Brown and Hood 1989: 3–4)

I have extracted these introductory paragraphs from two recent writing course-books because they illustrate the key points which have have emerged in the chapter so far. Both sets of authors share similar attitudes. They emphasise the need to integrate both process and product in the writing classroom, and suggest that writing is minimally a three-stage process of pre-writing, writing and revision. Purposes and audiences are also seen as important. In addition, Hamp-Lyons and Heasley argue for a collaborative approach to writing, while Brown and Hood stress the importance of providing models for the learners and allowing them opportunities in class to rehearse those things they will need in the real world beyond the classroom.

Some of the points on conferencing are also illustrated in classroom extract 5.1, which shows conferencing sessions with a number of individual students. Analysing such conferencing sessions can reveal as much about teachers' beliefs about the nature of learning to write as introductions to coursebooks tell us about writers' attitudes and beliefs.

### Pre-reading task

1. What do the following extracts reveal about the teacher's attitudes towards the mechanics of writing, the content of the text, and the writing process?
2. As you read the extracts, make a note of the different messages about the nature of writing and the writing process which the different learners are receiving from the teacher. Divide these into messages which are explicit and those which are implicit.

### Classroom extract 5.1: A writing conference

**Conference with Daniella**

T:  Right Daniella, which story is this one, I've
     forgotten.
                              D:  When I went to Melbourne.
T:  When you went to Melbourne. You just tell
     me a little bit about it before I read it. What's it
     going to be about?
                              D:  It's about . . . we played . . . [inaudible]

T: Yes, . . . Which is the final draft? Right, well
how come we still . . . , you haven't rewritten
it yet, you haven't done it yet, finished it? Are
you going to have this finished or not?

D: Yes.

T: You are going to publish it. Right, I think I've
seen this before, haven't I?

D: Yes.

T: I'm just checking the last things, am I, the
spellings and stuff, right? Right, when I went
to Melbourne. Just make that a capital W for a
title. Right. You read it to me.

D: When I went to Melbourne . . .

T: When I went to Melbourne, right.

D: . . . Melbourne for a week, it was freezing,
and we had to stay inside all day.

T: Right. See this one 'inside' – we'll just make
that one word. Can we squash it together?
i-n-s-i-d-e is one word, right?

In this first conference, the teacher focuses principally on the mechanics of the writing process, because he has already worked on the content in a previous conference. He checks the spelling and punctuation and encourages the pupil to get the piece right before going on to another piece.

**Conference with Alex who has written a piece on the topic of 'tools'**

T: What's it called?

A: Tools.

T: Tools. What's it going to be about? Can you
tell me about it in your own words?

A: I, I wanna do a second draft with that one, and
this one's done.

T: That is the second draft?

A: No, this is a different one.

T: A different story. Well, let's work on one of
them first. Which one are you going to work
on? Which one would you like to bring to the
publishing . . .

A: This one

T: That one. So really, that's your first draft, is it?

A: That's my second draft.

T: Well, come over here and let's see what this is.
You reckon you've changed it, you've fixed up
spelling and sentences and things?

A: I was reading – I was reading this one to
Vlatko.

T: You've conferenced with a friend?

A: Yes.

T: And you've written it out, and now you want
to conference with me. Well, I'll believe you.
It's a shame you've lost other parts, though.
Read it to me, please.

A: 'Tools. Tools can help us use – to make houses
or buildings and to fix things if they break.
You need to make boats and cars and things.
Cars and machines have' – supposed to be –
'lots of different things'.

T: Good. Fix it up then. Please don't disturb
Daniella, as she is writing out her final copy.
Try to write very quickly, Daniella, so it can
go to the typist today. . . . I think the word
'different' we've used lots of times. . . .
Spelling mistake! Go and fix it up.

A: Another spelling mistake.

In this conferencing session, the teacher focuses on both content and form. There is some dispute as to whether the text they are working on is a first or second draft. At the beginning of the conference the teacher asks the pupil to retell the story in his own words, but this does not happen, and eventually the pupil reads the text. When Alex says that he had read the story to Vlatko, the teacher reformulates this as, 'You've conferenced with a friend?' The bulk of the conference is taken up with the teacher pushing the pupil to come up with additional content suggestions, although it is worth noting that the pupil's contributions are minimal, and that it is the teacher who does most of the talking.

### Conference with Leila

T: Who is it next? I think it is Leila. Would you
bring me your two drafts, please. Right, what
story is it, Leila?

L: Fred and Barney.

T: Fred and Barney. Could you tell me a bit about
it in your own words – a retelling.

[Leila tells the story, and then reads out what she has written until the teacher intervenes.]

T: Oh, right. Is it making sense to you? Or are
there some parts where it doesn't make . . .

L: I . . . I made some mistakes . . .

T: Can you see where they are?

L: Yes.

T: Let's try and fix them up then. Fred and
Barney were old friends 'til the old days.

L: Days.

T: Do you mean they were friends in the old
days?

L:  Yes.

T: Right, so what you're saying here is Fred and
Barney were old friends in the old days, and
Barney . . .

L:  Said . . .

T: To Fred. I think we'll say, and Barney told
Fred to go . . . to go to his friend's house and
call them, isn't it? You said 'them for dinner'.
Fred went to tell them to come for dinner.
Barney had made the food, but he made it too
hard, and when he was trying to cut the
chicken, he could not cut, or eat?

L:  Eat.

T: Eat the chicken. Shall we say . . .

L:  Cut and eat the chicken.

T: Shall we say cut and eat . . . Cut and eat the
'chicken'? Or eat 'it'?

L:  Eat, eat it.

T: Yeah, I think eat 'it', don't you? Because
we've already said the 'chickens', haven't we?
Eat it, full stop. Fred and Barney's . . . friends
went home and had lunch at their house. It's
that one . . . the only one?

L:  Their.

T: Fred and Barney packed up – I want you to
find the spelling of that – and went to a
restaurant to eat. That's good. Where did you
get that word from?

L:  I looked it in the dictionary.

T: Good. . . . Fred and Barney went home and
went to sleep, and the next day they did not go
anywhere . . . they stayed home. Why?

L:  'Cause there's nothing to do.

T: Right. Do you think that ending's sort of a
good ending for this story?

L:  Yes, you know Mr Mercurio, you know, beans
has to be a 's' at the end.

T: Good. But beans is spelt wrong.

L:  Oh.

T: . . . Beans is not up there, but how do you
think it might be? It's not the double e, what
might it be?

L:  e-a-n.

T: Right. That's right. So we'll fix that up for you.

In this final conference, the teacher does allow the pupil to do a retelling. He also uses metalanguage: 'a retelling', 'a creative story', although he does not dwell on these. After Leila has read her story, the teacher tries to get her to identify her mistakes. He does not have much success with this, however, and ends up pointing out most of these himself.

### Post-reading task

Review the conferencing sessions. Does one stand out as being more effective/less effective than the others? Why is this?
[I am indebted to Jenny Hammond for providing me with the data from which these conferencing sessions have been extracted.]

### Learning skills and the writing process

In recent years, the value of teaching students about learning as well as about language has been recognised. Studies into learning strategies and learning how to learn are finding their way into the literature in increasing numbers. Evidence suggests that it is beneficial for learners to reflect on their own learning strategies and preferences (see Chapter 9). In their book on learning how to learn, Ellis and Sinclair (1989) outline a seven-step process designed to encourage learners to reflect on the strategies which might assist them in becoming more effective writers. They do this by providing a series of exercises designed to encourage learners to reflect on the following questions:

Step 1: How do you feel about writing English?
Step 2: What do you know about writing English?
Step 3: How well are you doing?
Step 4: What do you need to do next?
Step 5: How do you prefer to practise your writing?
Step 6: Do you need to build your confidence?
Step 7: How do you organise your writing practice?

The following tasks from Ellis and Sinclair (1989) help learners to explore these questions. It is interesting to note how the purposes are reflected in the tasks. In using tasks such as these, which have a twin focus on learning as well as language, it is important to establish a link for the students between the task and its rationale, otherwise the learning-how-to-learn dimension will be lost.

**1**
(a) If possible, bring to class an example of writing by a native speaker of English. Try to bring the type of writing you need to want to be able to do, for example:
  a business letter
  a telex
  a poem

(b) Work with another class member who has brought in a different type of written text. Compare your examples and make a note of the specific characteristics that make them different from each other, for example:

　layout
　style of language
　length
　organisation of ideas, etc.

(c) Compare your findings with the rest of the class and make notes under the following headings:

　*Type of written text*
　*Specific characteristics*

**2**

Read Javier's suggestion for testing himself.

> *I take a business letter, for example, and read it and make notes on the content. Then I try to reconstruct the letter from my notes. I compare my version with the original letter to see how well I've done.*
> Javier, Argentina

Do you know of any other good ways of testing yourself?

**3**

Read what Mazharuddin says about assessing himself.

> *I'm studying medicine in London and I do a lot of practice examinations. I always give myself plenty of time to read everything I've written very carefully. I check spelling, grammar and pronunciation.*
> Mazharuddin, India

Think of a real-life situation you have been in recently where you needed to write English. How well do you think you wrote?

**4**

Here are some examples of how Javier and Mazharuddin set themselves short-term aims.

Name: Javier

| What? | How? | When | How long | Done |
|---|---|---|---|---|
| Improve spelling | Copy out three times and test myself | 15.8.88 | 10 mins. | √ |

.......................................

Name: Mazharuddin

| What? | How? | When | How long | Done |
|---|---|---|---|---|
| Improve use of<br>– connectors<br>– sequencers | Write notes first and organise them.<br>Add connectors and sequencers.<br>Then write out in full. | 15.8.88 | 1 hour | √ |

[Use the blank chart on page 115 to do your own self-assessment.]

**5**

You have been asked to produce a brief guide for new students joining your class next term. (a) Decide what information you think a new student would want to know. (b) Decide how you are going to present it. (c) Produce the first draft. Compare your drafts in class and make decisions about the final version.

**6**

Your teacher will dictate part of a text to you and then ask you to continue writing the text on your own. You should try to develop the topic further and use the same style. When you have finished, read your text to the class.

I have included these extracts because they show very clearly how learning-how-to-learn goals can be integrated with language goals, and realised at the level of pedagogy. The best of these tasks simultaneously develop learners' language skills and learning skills.

## 5.7 Investigating writing development

**Task 5.1**
Collect sample statements from learners about how they go about learning English. Construct some writing tasks similar to those devised by Ellis and Sinclair. Administer them to a group of students. Discuss the tasks with the students. Record and evaluate the discussion. Did the tasks seem to 'work' for the students? Why, or why not?

**Task 5.2**
Teach some of the tasks in Ellis and Sinclair. Discuss these with the students, focusing in particular on the strategies underlying the diffferent tasks. Do different students have different strategy preferences? Do they agree on the strategies underlying the different tasks?

**Task 5.3**
Record and analyse a conferencing session between a teacher and two or three students. Does the teacher tend to focus on a limited number of problems (e.g. the mechanics of the writing process)? Does he/she elicit contributions from the students, or tell them what he/she thinks is correct? Do different students receive different or similar treatment?

**Task 5.4**
Analyse a number of writing coursebooks, or the writing exercises from a general coursebook. How varied are the exercises? What do they reveal about the author's views on the writing process?

**Task 5.5**

If possible, obtain samples of several students' writing over an extended period such as a semester or a year. Analyse the samples. What evidence is there that the students' writing skills have developed? Is the improvement at the level of lexis, grammar, text structure, or is there evidence of improvement at all levels?

## 5.8 Conclusion

Learning to write coherently, and in a way which is appropriate for one's purpose and audience, is something which many people never manage in their first language, despite the fact that a substantial part of the educational process is devoted to the development of such skills. The process is every bit as difficult in a second language. In this chapter we have looked at some of the current issues and concerns in the teaching of writing. We have seen that written language has its own characteristics which reflect the purposes for which it has evolved, but that it is more useful to think in terms of a 'mode continuum', from 'more like spoken language' to 'more like written language', rather than in terms of discrete categories. We also looked at the controversy over writing as process and writing as product, and some of the pedagogical implications of the process/product distinction, as well as the different characteristics of skilled and unskilled writers.

# Chapter Six

## *Mastering the Sounds of the Language*

### 6.1 Introduction

The teaching of pronunciation has always been dealt with from a rather different perspective from other language skills. The influence of the first language seems to be much greater in relation to pronunciation in contrast with the acquisition of morphology and syntax. In addition, gifted learners who attain native speaker mastery of other aspects of their second language rarely master the phonological system as effectively if they begin learning the language after puberty.

At the level of classroom action, efforts to teach pronunciation have sometimes resulted in practices which range from the mildly eccentric to the bizarre, including rhythmic chants and dances designed to get learners to integrate their bodily movements and gestures with their attempts at articulating the new language. The popularity of such practices has persisted despite the fact that there is little empirical evidence that they are significantly more effective than more traditional exercises.

In this chapter we look at some of the theoretical positions which have been taken in the teaching of pronunciation. Recent research into the acquisition of L2 pronunciation which provides insights into ways of teaching pronunciation effectively is also reviewed. The second part of the chapter is devoted to an examination of pronunciation materials. We also look at extracts from two pronunciation lessons.

The chapter sets out to answer the following questions:

1. What is meant by 'contrastive phonology', and how has it influenced the teaching of pronunciation?
2. What is the difference between 'segmental' and 'supra-segmental' features of pronunciation, and how can these be taught?
3. How can pronunciation be taught from a communicative perspective?
4. How can a learning-how-to-learn perspective be added to the teaching of pronunciation?

## 6.2  Contrastive phonology

Mastering the sound system of a second language presents great difficulties for learners. Most learners who begin learning the second language after the onset of puberty never manage to acquire native-like mastery of the sound system, although they may develop native-like skills in grammar and vocabulary. Brown, among others, suggests that the problem of acquiring a flawless pronunciation after puberty supports the notion of a critical period for language acquisition. The critical period is

> a biologically determined period of life when language can be acquired more easily and beyond which time language is increasingly difficult to acquire. The critical period hypothesis claims that there is such a biological timetable. Initially the notion of a critical period was connected only to first language acquisition. Pathological studies of children who failed to acquire their first language, or aspects thereof, became fuel for arguments of biologically determined predispositions, timed for release, which would wane if the correct environmental stimuli were not present at the crucial stage. (Brown 1987: 42)

Whether or not the critical period hypothesis is supported by subsequent research, the problems of acquiring the phonology of a second language present a formidable challenge to any theory of second language acquisition. In his book on language transfer, Odlin (1989) highlights the powerful influence of the first language on the efforts of learners to master the sound system of a second language. In studying cross-linguistic influences of a first on a second language, he suggests that attention needs to be paid to both phonetic and phonemic differences. Phonetic analysis compares the two languages in terms of the physical differences between their respective sound systems, dealing, in particular, with the ways in which sounds are produced and perceived. Phonemics contrasts the sound systems of the languages in terms of their minimum meaningful units. For example, in English, the sounds represented by /p/ and /b/ provide a phonemic contrast because words which differ only in these sounds, 'pin'–'bin', have different meanings.

The potential utility of a contrastive analysis of learners' native and target languages is captured in the following description:

> A study by Scholes (1968) of the perception of vowels by native and non-native speakers of English indicates that non-native speakers are likely to categorize foreign language sounds largely in terms of the phonemic inventory of the native language (cf. Liberman *et al.*, 1957). In Scholes's study, native speakers distinguished between the vowels /e/ and /æ/ (as in the words *rain* and *ran*), whereas speakers of Russian and Greek did not. In contrast to other non-native speakers of English, speakers of Persian, which, like English, has a phonemic contrast between /e/ and /æ/, did distinguish between the two vowel sounds. (Odlin 1989: 114)

Swan and Smith (1987) outline some of the problems for second language learners of English which can be attributed to first language interference. Examples of contrasts between English and a range of languages are provided below:

*Spanish*
While the Spanish and English consonant systems show many similarities, the vowel systems and sentence stress are very different, and these can cause great difficulty for Spanish-speaking learners of English. (p. 72)

*Russian*
The two major features which distinguish the Russian sound system from English are the absence of the short–long vowel differentiation and the absence of diphthongs. English rhythm and stress patterns are also hard for Russians to master. (p. 117)
[Diphthongs are units of two vowels pronounced as a single syllable, e.g. 'bout'.]

*Arabic*
The Arabic and English phonological systems are very different, not only in the range of sounds used, but in the emphasis placed on vowels and consonants in expressing meanings. While English has twenty-two vowels and diphthongs to twenty-four consonants, Arabic has only eight vowels and diphthongs to thirty-two consonants. (pp. 142–3)

*Japanese*
Japanese has a rather limited phonetic inventory, both in number of sounds and their distribution. There are only five vowels, though these may be distinctively long or short. Syllable structure is very simple (generally 'vowel + consonant', or vowel alone). There are few consonant clusters. Japanese learners therefore find the more complex sounds of English very hard to pronounce, and they may have even greater difficulty in perceiving accurately what is said. (p. 213)

*Chinese*
The phonological system of Chinese is very different from that of English. Some English phonemes do not have Chinese counterparts and are hard to learn. Others resemble Chinese phonemes but are not identical to them in pronunciation, and thus cause confusion. Stress, intonation and juncture are all areas of difficulty. In general, Chinese speakers find English hard to pronounce, and have trouble learning to understand the spoken language. (pp. 224–5)

The consensus of opinion, then, is that all learners regardless of their first language background find English difficult to understand and pronounce (not a particularly surprising conclusion to reach), and that learners from different L1 backgrounds will have different problems, reflecting the contrasts between the first and second languages. The problem for teachers with a range of L1 speakers in their class is how to deal with this heterogeneity, because what is difficult for a speaker from one first language background will not necessarily be difficult for a speaker from a different background.

During the years when audio-lingualism dominated language teaching, a great deal of effort was expended in getting learners to perceive and produce word contrasts such as 'rain' 'ran' which differed only in a single sound. The most common form of activity was the 'minimal pair exercise' (see section 6.4 for examples of these). With the emergence of communicative approaches to language teaching, these exercises became somewhat less popular among textbook writers. It was pointed out that, for example, while native speakers of Japanese might have a great deal of difficulty perceiving the difference between 'lice' and 'rice' when these words are produced in isolation, in communicative tasks, the second language speaker can use the situational and linguistic context to determine the meaning of the word.

In teaching and learning the sound system of a second or foreign language, a basic distinction is drawn between the study of individual sound differences of the type we have already discussed, and the study of rhythm, stress and intonation. It has been argued that these so-called supra-segmental features of the language are more important for comprehensible production than the individual sounds. Supra-segmental contrasts are particularly important when moving from a non-tonal language such as English, in which such changes mark attitudinal and emotional meaning, to a tonal language such as Thai in which changes in intonation and pitch mark phonemic differences (for example, the Thai word 'haa' said with a falling intonation means 'five' whereas the same word said with a rising intonation means 'to look for'). Learners moving between tonal and non-tonal languages have great difficulty with these intonation and pitch contrasts. (Rost 1990 provides an excellent treatment of these issues; see, in particular, chapter 2, on auditory perception and linguistic processing.)

In discussing the pedagogical implications of pronunciation features, Byrne and Walsh (1973) argue that the supra-segmentsal features of stress, rhythm and intonation are much more important for intelligible pronunciation than producing native-like vowels and consonants. However, they also point out that the supra-segmentals are much more difficult to learn, to teach and to use because native speakers will vary the patterns with which they use these features 'according to circumstances' (Byrne and Walsh 1973: 159). What they mean by this is that native speakers will vary their stress, rhythm and intonation to signal differences of attitude, degrees of politeness and deference and other interpersonal aspects of communication, and that it is therefore difficult to teach these differences. Since the time that they were writing, however, we have learned a lot more about these features of language and how to teach them.

Odlin cites research which suggests that similarities beween the supra-segmental patterns of two languages can facilitate acquisition. Japanese children learning English appear to be facilitated in their acquisition of questions by the similar intonation patterns between the two languages. Finnish first language speakers, on the other hand, seem to be delayed in their acquisition of English question patterns, and this delay may be due to the absence of rising intonation in yes/no questions in Finnish. (See also Brown 1990 for a detailed treatment of these issues, which, although dealt with from the perspective of listening comprehension, are also particularly pertinent to pronunciation.)

## 6.3 Recent theory and research

In Chapter 9 we look at language teaching methodology from the learner's perspective, focusing in particular on research into learning styles and strategies. In relation to pronunciation, research into the learning strategy preferences of students has consistently shown that mastery of the sounds and pronunciation of the target language is a high priority for most learners. In his large scale study involving 517 learners, Willing (1988) found that this aspect received the highest rating overall, with 62 per cent of respondents giving it their highest overall rating, and these results held across groups with widely different first language backgrounds (see Chapter 9, for details of this study). For example, 70 per cent of Vietnamese L1 speakers, 77 per cent of Arabic speakers, 69 per cent of South Americans, and 62 per cent of Polish speakers gave this their highest rating. Similar findings are reported in Nunan (1988b). Stevick also provides anecdotal evidence to support the view that learners are particularly concerned with the pronunciation of the target language which manifests itself in demands by the learners for pronunciation drills.

> At first I explained this to myself by saying that these students had been brainwashed by audio-lingual teachers in their secondary schools, or that they had some personal craving to be dominated or that they were intellectually lazy and found that drills made fewer demands on their imagination or ingenuity. Over the years, however, these explanations have not convinced me. Maybe there is more to this kind of drilling than I had thought. If there is, what might it be? (Stevick 1982: 51–2)

He goes on to suggest three reasons for the persistent demands of students for pronunciation drills. In the first place, drills provide the emotional security which comes from engaging in a narrowly defined task. Secondly, it is relatively easy, when engaged in pronunciation drills, to 'spot the difference' between one's own production and that of a native-speaking model. Attending to such differences is much more difficult when one is engaged in communicative tasks. The third and final reason advanced by Stevick is that the highly predictable nature of repetitive drills provide learners with a breathing space during which they can conserve their mental energy. Another reason (though not one advanced by Stevick) might simply be that drills 'work'. Anecdotal evidence suggests that it is difficult to master phonological aspects of a language without some form of repetitive drilling – although this need not necessarily take the form of prolonged exercises in mimicry.

Stevick suggests that, when working on establishing fluency and rhythm, teachers can use variations to maintain interest. Some of the variations he suggests are:

1. Repetition by the whole class versus repetition by groups or rows versus individual repetition.
2. Calling on students (or groups) in fixed order versus calling on them in random order.
3. Students' books closed versus students' books open.
4. Two or three repetitions per student (or group) versus only one repetition before going on to the next student (or group).
5. Slow tempo versus fast tempo.
6. Tone of voice: neutral versus mysterious or mischievous versus triumphant or emphatic.
7. Loudness: barely audible versus normal versus oratorical.

Stevick points out that here we have:

> 3×2×3×2×2×3×3 alternatives. The arithmetical product is 648. A few combinations are
> self contradictory, of course. For example, 'choral repetition by the whole class' cannot go
> along with 'random versus fixed order of recitation'. Even so, we are left with some
> hundreds of perfectly workable combinations. Let me emphasise once more that coming up
> with such a large number is not just a sterile *tour de force* on my part. (Stevick 1982: 55–6)

There have been a number of recent investigations of the acquisition of phonology
by second language learners. Much of this research has evolved from work by Labov
(1972) who studied variations in the pronunciation of native speakers, and who
sought to account for these variations in terms of socio-linguistic factors. Tarone
(1982, 1983) applied some of this work to second language acquisition and came to
the conclusion that different types of communicative task will elicit different types of
language. For example, spontaneous speech will contain different language from
oral reading or language which has been elicited by a researcher.

In a similar tradition, Sato (1985) carried out a longitudinal investigation of the
phonological development of an adolescent Vietnamese learner of English. She
found that some phonological features were affected by the type of communicative
task in which the learner was engaged while others were not, and that some features
varied over time while others did not. She also found evidence of first language
interference on production, noting in particular that learners have great difficulty
with final consonant clusters, which do not exist in Vietnamese.

> It seems reasonable to argue that if clusters are extremely difficult for Vietnamese learners
> of English, in the early stages of acquisition they may not be able to alter their performance
> very much, whatever the communicative task they are engaged in and however much
> attention they pay to articulation. (Sato 1985: 194)

In Chapter 8 we see that certain grammatical features of the target language seem
to be impervious to instruction. In other words, learners master these features in an
order which seems to be determined by an inbuilt syllabus rather than by the syllabus
of the course the learner undertakes. Research such as that of Sato suggests that
certain features of phonology might also be resistant to instruction, though not
necessarily for the same reasons as those which hold for the grammar. It may well be
that production of these items (such as final consonant clusters for Vietnamese
speakers) cannot and should not be forced by instruction.

In one of the few survey articles to have been published on pronunciation,
Pennington and Richards (1986) evaluate the current status of research into the
teaching of pronunciation from the perspective of communicative language teaching.
They point to the uncertain status of pronunciation in a model of language predicated
on a notion of communicative rather than purely linguistic competence. They suggest
that accuracy at the segmental level is no longer the basic aim of pronunciation
teaching and that 'teaching isolated forms of sounds and words fails to address the
fact that in communication, many aspects of pronunciation are determined by the
positioning of elements within long stretches of speech'. Their article contains the
following recommendations for teaching pronunciation:

1. The teaching of pronunciation must focus on longer-term goals; short-term objectives must be developed with reference to long-term goals.
2. The goals of any explicit training in pronunciation should be to bring learners gradually from controlled, cognitively based performance to automatic skill-based performance.
3. Teaching should aim toward gradually reducing the amount of native language influence on segmental, voice-setting, and prosodic features but should not necessarily seek to eradicate totally the influence of the native language on the speaker's pronunciation in the second language.
4. Pronunciation should be taught as an integral part of oral language use, as part of the means for creating both referential and interactional meaning, not merely as an aspect of the oral production of words and sentences.
5. Pronunciation forms a natural link to other aspects of language use, such as listening, vocabulary, and grammar; ways of highlighting this interdependence in teaching need to be explored.

(Pennington and Richards 1986: 219)

The research and theory presented so far suggests that the learner's first language will have a strong influence on L2 pronunciation, but that there may also be developmental sequences akin to those for morphosyntax which may be impervious to instruction. (We look in detail at the issue of developmental sequences and teachability in Chapter 8.) In integrating pronunciation instruction into our programs, we need to distinguish between segmental and supra-segmental features, paying particular attention to the latter. In addition, we should concentrate on those errors which interfere with successful communication, rather than isolating, for pedagogical purposes, those phonological forms which, while they may make the learner sound 'foreign', do not impede comprehension. (It is also worth looking at Brown and Yule's (1983b) ideas on the development of a speaking syllabus.)

Kenworthy (1987), who provides a balanced treatment of theory and practice, identifies six principal factors affecting pronunciation learning. These are as follows:

1. **The native language.** We have already looked in some detail at the influence of the first language on the sound system of a second.
2. **The age factor.** Kenworthy refers to the commonly held belief that there is a strong relationship between second language pronunciation ability and age. The question of whether there is an age-related limit on the mastery of pronunciation has been well researched, but like many other areas in language teaching, the results are rather mixed, and it is too early to state that there is a simple and straightforward link between age and pronunciation ability.
3. **Amount of exposure.** Once again, there are problems with this factor, not the least of which involves quantifying 'amount of exposure'. Many people living in the target country hear little of the target language, while others living in their own native country may have significant exposure to a foreign language. Kenworthy concludes that while amount of exposure is a contributory factor, it is not a necessary factor in the development of pronunciation.
4. **Phonetic ability.** 'Phonetic ability' refers to whether someone has an 'ear' for a foreign language, and tests have been developed to measure this factor (which is

generally referred to as 'phonetic coding ability' or 'auditory discrimination ability'. There is some evidence that good discriminators are able to benefit from pronunciation drills, while poor discriminators are not. Kenworthy points out that this is an ability which the learner brings to the learning situation, and claims that as a result it is beyond the control of the teacher (although this is something with which many would disagree).

5. **Attitude and identity.** The ability to adopt and develop a foreign pronunciation has also been linked with the extent to which the learner wants to identify with the target culture. This factor may be cross-related to other factors such as age and length of residence in the target country.

6. **Motivation and concern for good pronunciation.** This final factor is probably also related to personality. Some students seem unconcerned about making mistakes, be they grammatical or phonological, just so long as they are communicating effectively. Others are very concerned about correctness, which may stem from a desire to identify with the target culture, or because they have a natural inclination to speak correctly.

Kenworthy concludes her review of theory and research by identifying three ways in which a teacher can influence learners. The first of these is to persuade learners that good pronunciation can greatly facilitate comprehension. Secondly, the teacher should stress that intelligibility and communicative effectiveness, not native-speaking mastery, will be the goals. Lastly, the teacher can demonstrate ongoing concern for the learners' progress in developing intelligible and acceptable pronunciation. A major problem confronting many teachers is the so-called fossilised or stabilised learner. This is the learner who reaches a particular level of proficiency and is unable to progress beyond this point. Pronunciation seems to be particularly vulnerable to fossilisation with many learners who have progressed beyond an intermediate level of proficiency. For an extremely useful article on ways of changing fossilised pronunciation, see Acton (1984).

These comments provide a convenient bridge into the next section of the chapter where we look at pronunciation in practice. For a more detailed and yet extremely accessible introduction to the English sound system, see Knowles (1987).

## 6.4 Pronunciation in practice

During the 1960s and 1970s, minimal pair exercises such as the following were extremely popular in pronunciation classes. These exercises generally focused learners on perception in the first instance, and only required production as a second stage.

Ask the students whether the words in each pair are 'S' (the same) or 'D' (different). (Hide your lips so that their shape will not show the class which sounds you are making.)

| west–vest | worse–worse | vet–wet | wine–vine |
|-----------|-------------|---------|-----------|
| wane–wane | wheel–veal | wane–vane | vane–wane |
| verse–worse | vane–vane | vine–wine | veal–wheel |
| veal–veal | vest–west | wet–wet | vest–vest |
| wet–vet | verse–verse | wheel–veal | wine–wine |

(Byrne and Walsh 1973: 83)

The instruction to teachers to hide their lips is interesting. Proponents of communicative language teaching would probably argue that teachers should be helping students to exploit such things as lip shape and mouth movement to help them distinguish between minimal sound contrasts.

Exercises such as these have become less popular with the emergence of communicative language teaching for reasons already outlined. These days the focus is much more on supra-segmental features of the language, and this is reflected in most recently published coursebooks. Here are two examples:

> *East–West* Book 1 (Graves and Rein 1988)
> *Yes–no* and *wh-* question intonation
> -s as /s/, /z/, or /əz/
> Intonation of *or* questions
> Can/can't
> -d as /t/, /d/or /əd/
> Question intonation
> Contrastive stress in numbers ending in *-teen* and *-ty*
> Sentence stress
> Series intonation
> Stress in noun–noun and adjective–noun combinations
> Sentence stress
> Word stress
> Sentence stress

> *The Australian English Course* (Nunan and Lockwood 1989)
> Identifying stressed syllables in words
> Identifying reduced forms of subject + be, e.g. I'm, he's, she's
> Distinguishing between teens and tens e.g. thirteen/thirty
> Identifying the number of syllables in one, two and three syllable words
> Different ways of asking questions
> Distinguishing between voiced and devoiced initial consonants
> Use of stress and intonation to indicate surprise
> Identifying polite or rude utterances from intonation
> Identifying most important words in sentences by stress
> Identifying stressed words in a short message
> Recording and comparing own pronunciation with taped model
> Identifying stressed and unstressed present/past forms of 'be'
> Distinguishing between stressed and unstressed vowels

There are numerous ways in which you can give a communicative orientation to pronunciation work. If you are using commercial materials, you should, where possible, augment these with taped samples of authentic language from native speakers, because the specially scripted and acted tapes which accompany many commercial materials differ from authentic speech. (Increasingly, contemporary coursebooks are including authentic and simulated materials.) You should also provide learners with plenty of examples of ways in which shifts in intonation signal attitudinal shifts. In the following examples (all from Nunan and Lockwood 1989), exercises 1 and 2 illustrate the use of authentic data, while exercise 3 demonstrates to learners the use of stress and intonation to signal surprise.

**Pronunciation exercise 1**
*Aim*: To identify reduced forms of 'be'.
*Exercise*: Listen to the tape:

| Unstressed | Stressed |
|---|---|
| I'm | I am |
| she's | she is |
| they're | they are |
| he was | he was |
| we were | we were |

Now read these sentences. Do you think the words in quotation marks are stressed or unstressed? Put a circle around the stressed words.

A: It 'was' a very nice restaurant we went to the other day.
B: 'Were' the Barlows there?
A: Yes, they 'were'. Peter 'was' there too, but Anne 'wasn't.'
B: 'Is' it still open for lunch?
A: Yes, it 'is', although we were there for lunch, of course.
    We might go again next week. 'Are' you interested in coming?
B: Yes, I 'am' as a matter of fact.

Now listen to the dialogue and make any corrections you like.
Compare your dialogue with a friend's.

**Pronunciation exercise 2**
*Aim*: To identify the stressed words in a short message.
*Exercise*: Listen to this part of the tape again and underline the stressed words. You may listen to the tape as often as you like.

Head to Circular Quay and discover Sydney with a famous explorer. You can join Urban Transport's big red explorer bus for unlimited one-day travel around 20 of Sydney's most popular sightseeing attractions on an 18 kilometre circuit around the city from 9.30 am to 5 pm seven days a week. Travel at your own pace. Get on and off as often as you like during the day.
Now compare your work with a partner. Discuss it with the teacher.

**Pronunciation exercise 3**
*Aim*: To identify the use of stress and intonation to indicate surprise.
*Exercise*: We can use stress and intonation to show how we feel. For example, we can ask questions in different ways. Listen to this dialogue.

Interviewer:  When do you watch television?
Viewer:        Oh, usually early in the morning, before Mum and Dad are awake.
Interviewer:  When do you watch television?

In the first question, the interviewer is seeking information. In the second question, the interviewer is expressing surprise.
Listen to questions on the tape. Write I next to the questions seeking information and S next to the questions indicating surprise.

1  How much is the television set?  _____
2  When was the programme shown?  _____
3  Where did you say he got it?  _____
4  What do you like watching?  _____
5  Why do you like *Inspector Gadget*?  _____

Extract 6.1 is from a pronunciation lesson in which students are working in small groups with a language master, which enables them to replay short stretches of speech. Their task is to transcribe the sentences they hear, and represent visually the stress and intonation patterns. In the first part of the extract, the students are working collaboratively. Half way through the activity, the teacher enters and takes charge.

### Pre-reading task

1. What problems would you anticipate a small group encountering in working on a pronunciation task without a teacher?
2. The learners spend most of their time listening intensively to the tape. Do you think that listening is important to the development of pronunciation? Why or why not?

### Classroom extract 6.1: A small group pronunciation practice task

The teacher is working with a large group of newly arrived immigrants. The students are split into small groups. The group we focus on comprises four students using a language master. It is obvious that they have used the language master before as they know precisely what to do. One student operates the language master card. Students hear the question: 'How much experience have you had as a motor mechanic?' They are required to decode what they hear, write it on the board, underline the stressed words, and link together words that are pronounced as a single unit.

S: I write on the board?
                              S: No, you write on the board please because
                                 you're taller.
S: [Reads as the sentence is written on the board.]
   How . . . how much experience have you had
   as a motor mechanic?
                              Ss: Have you had.
[They repeat the sentence several times, and listen to the language master again. The students work together to identify the stress and link words as they repeatedly play the master sentence.]

Ss: How much experience have you had as a
motor mechanic?'

S: As a motor . . . ?

S: Yeah, motor . . . motor mechanic.

[The students come up with the following representation of the question: How much experience *have* you *had* as a motor mechanic? They then work together to identify the tense. One student nominates the past tense. They finally settle on the present perfect, and one student draws a time line to explain to the other students.]

S: Go on.

[They play the language master: 'Let's start from the beginning. . . . When'd you do your training? Let's start from the beginning. When'd you do your training?' The group scribe writes on the board 'let's'.]

S: Capital L

[They listen repeatedly to the tape and the scribe writes: Let's start from the beginning. When did you do your training?]

S: When did you do training?

S: Your training.

S: 'Your' no.

[The students are not certain about 'your', and the scribe crosses it out. One student objects but the erasure stands. 'From' and 'beginning' are linked, and then 'when', 'did' and 'do' are linked. After further discussion, this is rubbed out, and 'when' and 'do' are linked instead. The students are still unsure about 'your'. They listen to the tape another dozen times, repeating parts of the sentences. The schwa symbol is written above 'did'. There is further discussion on whether or not 'your' is there. One woman student insists that it is, so 'your' is reinstated. The students decide that they have satisfactorily completed this segment of the task, and go on to the next sentence. 'I did my apprenticeship as a motor mechanic in Hong Kong.']

S: I did as motor mechanic in Hong Kong.

[Laughter. They play the tape several more times, and attempt to repeat the sentence. Most students have difficulty with the word 'apprenticeship'. They go back to the beginning of the exercise, and as each card is replayed, the students practise by saying and writing down what they think the sentence could be. At this point, the teacher comes up and checks the work.]

T: It's very difficult, isn't it? 'When did you do
your training?' What . . . what kind of answer
would you give to 'When did you do your
training?' What would the answer be? What
kind of answer? Would it be 'In Paramatta'?
Or would it be 'In 1960'? or . . .

S: Er, the time . . . when I do. . . er my training.

T: The time when I *did* my training. Right, so did
you, did you understand, Steve?

S: Yes.

T: Yeah, so 'when' – it'll be a time. Okay?

[The last card is replayed. 'I did my apprenticeship as a motor mechanic in Hong Kong.']

T: It's very fast. [Laughter]

S: I did my 'prenticeship . . .

T: Apprenticeship. Repeat.

S: Apprenticeship.

[She then writes the sentence on the board and links 'as' and 'a' after two more listenings to the card. She puts the stress on 'apprenticeship' and then links 'I' and 'did'.]

T:  Do you know what an apprenticeship is?
     Steve? [Yeah] Do you remember that one?
     . . . What about clapping? No, together – let's
     help each other.

[She then gets the students to clap out the intonation of the sentence as they repeat it word by word.]

### Post-reading task

Review the extract. Do you think the teacher's intervention is helpful or not?

The extract demonstrates the importance of perceptual salience to successful pronunciation. The students work hard to understand the sentence on the tape, and it is by no means certain that the teacher's intervention is advantageous. At the end of the extract the teacher moves from a focus on perception to production through rhythmic clapping and repetition.

In the small group phase, the students are actively involved in the task, and in interactional terms it works, even if there are questions over whether it is improving the perceptual salience of the phonological features being studied.

Extract 6.2 is another pronunciation task with a rather more advanced group of learners. In extract 6.1, the students are directly engaged in the perception and production of the language, whereas in this extract the students are involved in language awareness activities.

### Pre-reading task

The extract illustrates one way in which it is possible to have a twin focus on both language and learning in a pronunciation lesson with more advanced learners. As you read the extract, see whether you can identify the 'hidden' message in the task.

### Classroom extract 6.2: Learning how to learn pronunciation

T:  I want to tell you about a friend of mine. Her
     name's Ying, and she really feels she has
     problems with her pronunciation. She can't go
     to class 'cause she's at home with a young
     baby. She has got a cassette recorder at home,
     and she asked me the other night what could
     she do to improve her pronunciation. Have
     you got any advice we could give her? Kim?

                              S:  Yes, we can tell him – tell her, how to . . . to
                                  start to learn the English at home. [Mmm] Just
                                  as we learn from the school so we can tell her to

start to learn with the cassette . . . [right] and maybe look at the mirror to look at how to move her tongue and lip.

T: Right, to practise the different sounds. Right, so that would be good, for practising sounds, then, she could listen to the cassette and use a mirror. What else could she do? Irene, have you got any other tips?

S: She could read some books for her child, and tape those.

T: Yes, that would be excellent. Reading stories for her child and taping them, yes. And also now you can get children's stories on cassette, that you can get from the library. So she could be playing those, and, erm, playing them to her children, at the same time listening.

S: Or, she could go to the creche, when she takes her child and try to ask the other mums there if they could meet in her place or one week in someone's else place and get together with the English speaking mums [yes] . . . Then she could learn. And ask them if they would help her – every time she says the word wrong [Mmm] would they please correct her.

T: Mmm, yes that's an excell . . . and, um, that way she's making friends, too. And if she was very keen and had the time . . . if she had a small tape recorder, you could actually tape record conversations, yes? And then replay them at home and then listen and practise responding to them or repeating. Good.

S: And she could have the radio on, when she's home, have the radio on when she does the dishes or whatever she's doing . . . the cooking – have the radio on and listen. And sometime there might be some words which when she has heard before and that's how she might get interested.

T: Right, yes, if she's heard them before and you listen again and you say 'ah yes, that's great. I know that word' and you've got all the meaning. Christoph, have you got any other suggestions?

S: If, er, she has very problem with, er, pronunciation, she can borrow tapes from library, and listen to these tapes and repeat words – again, again [mmm, that's right]. This could be very helpful for pronunciation.

T:  Good. Oh, well, I'll . . . when I see her
    tomorrow night, I'll give her some of that extra
    advice.

### Post-reading task

Do you think this task is successful? If not, what modifications would you make to it?

The task protrayed in this extract is designed to get students thinking about the learning process in relation to pronunciation rather than simply practising the sounds of the target language. It is particularly designed to get students thinking about ways of practising pronunciation outside the classroom; in other words, it has a learning-how-to-learn orientation. It also stimulates an interactional pattern in which each learner is encouraged to give a rather longer extemporised presentation than is usual in classes of this type. The 'hidden' message is that it is important to activate one's language use outside the classroom whenever possible.

## 6.5 Investigating pronunciation

**Task 6.1**
1.  Record a short interview with learners from a number of different first language backgrounds (for example, Spanish, Chinese and Arabic). Analyse their pronunciation in terms of segmental and suprasegmental features.
2.  What differences can you find which can be attributed to the different first languages of the speakers?
3.  Make a list of the aspects of pronunciation which cause difficulty in comprehension.
4.  How might these be dealt with in developing a program for these learners?

**Task 6.2**
Analyse a number of coursebooks and list the different pronunciation exercises. How varied are these? Is there any attempt to integrate them with the other content in the book? Is the focus on segmental or supra-segmental aspects of pronunciation?

**Task 6.3**
Survey a class of learners individually and ask them: (a) how important pronunciation is to them; (b) how they like to practise their pronunciation. Do they seem to prefer mechanical drilling or meaningful communication? What are the implications of their responses for classroom practice?

**Task 6.4**
Record and analyse a lesson or lesson segment devoted to the teaching of pronunciation. What beliefs about the nature of pronunciation emerge from the lesson? What modifications would you make to the lesson/lesson segment?

## 6.6 Conclusion

Pronunciation is a neglected skill in many classrooms, despite the obvious importance attached to it by learners. In this chapter we have seen that pronunciation work can be integrated in communicative language work, and that, while it requires repetitive language work, this need not be boring. The classroom extracts illustrated two quite different ways in which pronunciation work can be carried out within a communicative context, the first involving collaborative problem-solving, and the second language awareness.

The major theoretical shift which has occurred with the development of communicative approaches to language teaching has been from segmental work to a focus on supra-segmental features of rhythm, stress and intonation. In terms of teaching goals, the shift has been to focus on the development of communicative effectiveness and intelligibility, rather than on the development of native-like pronunciation.

# Chapter Seven

# *Teaching Vocabulary*

## 7.1 Introduction

The status of vocabulary within the curriculum has varied considerably over the years. It suffered significant neglect during the 1950s and 1960s when audio-lingualism had a dominant influence on methodology, but made something of a comeback during the 1970s under the influence of communicative language teaching. In this chapter we look at the influence of language learning theories on approaches to the teaching of vocabulary. At the level of classroom action, we also look at techniques and classroom exercises and activities for teaching vocabulary.

In their collection of articles on the teaching of vocabulary, Carter and McCarthy suggest that the following questions are constantly asked by teachers and students:

1. How many words provide a working vocabulary in a foreign language?
2. What are the best words to learn first?
3. In the early stages of learning a second or foreign language, are some words more useful to the learner than others?
4. Are some words more difficult to learn than others? Can words be graded for ease of learning?
5. What are the best means of retaining new words?
6. Is it most practical to learn words as single items in a list, in pairs (for example, as translation equivalents) or in context?
7. What about words which have [several] different meanings? Should they be avoided? If not, should some meanings be isolated for learning first?
8. Are some words more likely to be encountered in spoken rather than written discourse? If so, do we know what they are?

(Carter and McCarthy 1988: 1–2)

In this chapter we look at what theory, research and practice have to say about these questions and the issues which underlie them. In particular, the chapter concerns itself with the following questions:

1. What is the relationship between vocabulary and grammar in the language curriculum?
2. On what principled bases can vocabulary be selected and sequenced?

3. How can learners use context to comprehend new words?
4. What does second language acquisition research have to tell us about the acquisition of vocabulary?
5. What are semantic networks, and how can they be used to teach vocabulary?
6. What part does memory play in the development of vocabulary?

## 7.2  The status of vocabulary in the curriculum

For much of this century, the principal focus of language teaching has been on the grammar of the language. While grammar translation approaches to the teaching of language provided a balanced diet of grammar and vocabulary, audio-lingualists suggested that the emphasis should be strongly on the acquisition of the basic grammatical patterns of the language. It was believed that if learners were able to internalise these basic patterns, then building a large vocabulary could come later. This emphasis on grammar and, to a certain extent, pronunciation, at the expense of vocabulary reflected a tradition going back to the nineteenth century when the International Phonetic Association published its six principles of language teaching. These principles, which were later reflected in audio-lingualism, advocated the inductive teaching of grammar, a focus on the spoken language of everyday life and an emphasis on the direct teaching of the target language rather than translation. Hockett (1958), one of the most influential structural linguists of the day, went so far as to argue that vocabulary was the easiest aspect of a second language to learn and that it hardly required formal attention in the classroom.

Since then, however, the status of vocabulary has been considerably enhanced. This has come about partly as a result of the development of communicative approaches to language teaching, and partly through the stimulus of comprehension-based methods such as the Natural Approach (Krashen and Terrell 1983). Proponents of these methods point out that in the early stages of learning and using a second language one is better served by vocabulary than grammar, and that one can, in effect, 'bypass' grammar in going for meaning if one has a reasonable vocabulary base. (More recently it has been argued that while one can bypass grammar to a certain extent in comprehending a language, this does not also hold for speaking and writing, where one needs to mobilise grammatical knowledge in order to convey even the most rudimentary ideas. See, for example, Swain 1985.)

Rivers (1983: 125) has also argued that the acquisition of an adequate vocabulary is essential for successful second language use because, without an extensive vocabulary, we will be unable to use the structures and functions we may have learned for comprehensible communication. Also, in contrast with the development of other aspects of a second language, particularly pronunciation, vocabulary acquisition does not seem to be slowed down by age. In fact, Rivers argues that vocabulary augmentation seems to become easier as one matures, probably because one has a richer knowledge of the world on which to draw. In addition, the more one's vocabulary develops, the easier it is to add new words – the first ten words are probably the most difficult to learn.

These days, then, the consensus of opinion seems to be that the development of a rich vocabulary is an important element in the acquisition of a second language. Certainly, contemporary coursebooks are as carefully structured lexically as they are syntactically. A key issue for coursebook writers and curriculum developers concerns the basis on which one selects and sequences vocabulary. 'Frequency' is one often invoked criterion, and in the next section we look at the use of frequency counts in the generation of lexical lists.

## 7.3  Word lists and frequency counts

Considerable attention has been paid to the issue of a minimum adequate vocabulary. West (1960) published a list of 1,200 words based on a frequency count of the 2,000 most frequent words in English which he argued provided learners with a 'minimum adequate speech vocabulary'. According to West, these words would enable learners to express practically any idea they wanted to. Fox (1979) argues that 'minimum adequate vocabularies' might be adequate for productive purposes, but that they leave learners seriously under-equipped to deal with authentic language. He provides a graphic illustration to support his contention. In the following paragraph, Fox has substituted nonsense words for all the words in the original paragraph not included in West's original list.

> Many persons who 'talk' with their hands are blunk. They have doubts about what they are saying, so they try to cover up by drolling a false parn of excitement and urgency. These same people are usually very gruk and may be overtalkative and speak too loudly. Hurbish feelings are belave by the person who tries to keep all leeds to a monton; such a person is nep, porded, and lacking in self-ruck. Slussion is frequently trunded by a veeling wurd, zornish eye, and an inability to face other people directly. Blunkness and codision are shown in a number of leeds. A man may run his hand through his hair or over the top of his head if he is dork; a man or woman may frung the back of the neck. They are trying to tell themselves to galump. Jalup in kanted by a rantid loercion with one's modical abdurance. The woman or man who nardles with hair or keeps polluking clothing is arbushed and socially incrup. A woman may smooth out feluciary argles or blum at her skirt, and a man may blum at his tie or snickle his farn.

According to Fox, the reader who only possesses West's 2,000 words will find the text practically incomprehensible, and he argues that learners who want to comprehend such material need a much more extensive receptive vocabulary. 'Receptive' words are those which readers understand but which they do not necessarily use.

Lists such as West's, which are based on frequency counts, assume that teaching learners the words they are most likely to encounter frequently is the most cost effective way of building a functional vocabulary. Many years ago Ogden and Richards (Ogden 1930; Richards 1943) put forward a proposal for Basic English which was predicated on similar assumptions. They devised a list of basic vocabulary containing 850 words which, they claimed, would allow the learner to communicate complex ideas. However, as Carter and McCarthy (1988) point out, these 850 vocabulary items have more than 850 meanings. (In fact, they cite Nation who has calculated that they have 12,425 meanings). The question faced by teachers is: which of these multiple meanings should be taught and in what order?

In his critique of word lists generated on the basis of frequency, J. Richards (1974) points out that frequency does not necessarily equate with usefulness or relevance to learner needs. Coverage, or the range of contexts in which the words are encountered, may also be more important than frequency. The ease with which words may be learned is another factor to be taken into consideration, and here we need to determine whether abstract, high frequency items are more difficult to learn than low frequency concrete items. Richards also suggests that 'familiarity', a concept incorporating frequency, meaningfulness and concreteness, needs to be taken into consideration. Richards' article is an important one, suggesting as it does that we may need differentiated vocabulary lists for different learners, and that the lists should reflect the communicative needs of the learners. In a sense it is a precursor to the debate over the relative claims of general and specific purpose English which emerged later in the decade and which is ongoing. Proponents of general purpose English would argue that learners should be taught a 'common core' of high frequency items rather than items specific to a particular discourse domain.

The most recent lexicon for second language teaching has been derived from the multi-million word Birmingham Corpus (Renouf 1984). Only with the advent of computer technology it has become feasible to analyse such vast corpora of data. The analysis has been able to show the different functions performed by the words and the frequency of occurrence of these functions. This has enabled the researchers to point up the very different patterns of usage of different forms of a base word. The morphological pair *certain* and *certainly* are cited as an example.

**certain**
Function 1. (60% of occurrences) Determiner as in:
/a certain number of students/in certain circles/
Function 2. (18% of occurrences) Adjective as in:
/I'm not awfully certain about . . . /We've got to make certain/
Function 3. (11% of occurrences) Adjective, in phrase 'A + *certain* + noun', as in:
/. . . has a certain classy ring/there is a certain evil in all lying/

**certainly**
Function 1. (98% of occurrences) as in:
/it will certainly be interesting/He will almost certainly launch into a little lecture . . ./
(Sinclair and Renouf 1988: 147–8)

The 200 most frequent word forms in the Birmingham Corpus are reproduced in Illustration 3. According to the authors, the list generally reflects the intuitions of language teachers about which words should be in a language course.

ILLUSTRATION 3

*First 200 word forms in the Birmingham Corpus, ranked in order of frequency of occurrence:*

| | | | | |
|---|---|---|---|---|
| 1 the | 41 what | 81 because | 121 come | 161 last |
| 2 of | 42 their | 82 two | 122 work | 162 great |
| 3 and | 43 if | 83 over | 123 made | 163 always |
| 4 to | 44 would | 84 don't | 124 never | 164 away |
| 5 a | 45 about | 85 get | 125 things | 165 look |
| 6 in | 46 no | 86 see | 126 such | 166 mean |
| 7 that | 47 said | 87 any | 127 make | 167 men |
| 8 I | 48 up | 88 much | 128 still | 168 each |
| 9 it | 49 when | 89 these | 129 something | 169 three |
| 10 was | 50 been | 90 way | 130 being | 170 why |
| 11 is | 51 out | 91 how | 131 also | 171 didn't |
| 12 he | 52 them | 92 down | 132 that's | 172 though |
| 13 for | 53 do | 93 even | 133 should | 173 fact |
| 14 you | 54 my | 94 first | 134 really | 174 Mr |
| 15 on | 55 more | 95 did | 135 here | 175 once |
| 16 with | 56 who | 96 back | 136 long | 176 find |
| 17 as | 57 me | 97 got | 137 I'm | 177 house |
| 18 be | 58 like | 98 our | 138 old | 178 rather |
| 19 had | 59 very | 99 new | 139 world | 179 few |
| 20 but | 60 can | 100 go | 140 thing | 180 both |
| 21 they | 61 has | 101 most | 141 must | 181 kind |
| 22 at | 62 him | 102 where | 142 day | 182 while |
| 23 his | 63 some | 103 after | 143 children | 183 year |
| 24 have | 64 into | 104 your | 144 oh | 184 every |
| 25 not | 65 then | 105 say | 145 off | 185 under |
| 26 this | 66 now | 106 man | 146 quite | 186 place |
| 27 are | 67 think | 107 er | 147 same | 187 home |
| 28 or | 68 well | 108 little | 148 take | 188 does |
| 29 by | 69 know | 109 too | 149 again | 189 sort |
| 30 we | 70 time | 110 many | 150 life | 190 perhaps |
| 31 she | 71 could | 111 good | 151 another | 191 against |
| 32 from | 72 people | 112 going | 152 came | 192 far |
| 33 one | 73 its | 113 through | 153 course | 193 left |
| 34 all | 74 other | 114 years | 154 between | 194 around |
| 35 there | 75 only | 115 before | 155 might | 195 nothing |
| 36 her | 76 it's | 116 own | 156 thought | 196 without |
| 37 were | 77 will | 117 us | 157 want | 197 end |
| 38 which | 78 than | 118 may | 158 says | 198 part |
| 39 an | 79 yes | 119 those | 159 went | 199 looked |
| 40 so | 80 just | 120 right | 160 put | 200 used |

Source: J. McH. Sinclair and A. Renouf, 'A lexical syllabus for language learning', in R. Carter and M. McCarthy, *Vocabulary and Language Teaching* (London: Longman, 1988), p. 149. Reproduced by permission.

An issue of central importance to the selection and grading of vocabulary concerns the relationship between the frequency of lexical items in corpora derived from native speakers, and the learnability of such items for second language learners. It is often naively assumed that there will be a close correspondence between frequency and learnability. However, as we see in section 7.5, this is not the case at all.

## 7.4 Vocabulary and context

One of the central themes of this book is that language reflects the contexts in which it is used and the purposes to which it is put. If we assume that language is also best encountered and learned in context, then this has particular implications for practice. In the first place, it would argue against the learning of lists of decontextualised vocabulary items. Rather, the focus in class will be on encouraging learners to develop strategies for inferring the meaning of new words from the context in which they occur, and teaching them to use a range of cues, both verbal and non-verbal (e.g. pictures and diagrams in written texts) to determine meaning.

Kruse makes five suggestions for teaching written vocabulary in context:

1. *Word elements such as prefixes, suffixes and roots.* The ability to recognise component parts of words, word families, and so on is probably the single most important vocabulary skill a student of reading in EFL can have. It substantially reduces the number of completely new words he will encounter and increases his control of the English lexicon.
2. *Pictures, diagrams and charts.* These clues, so obvious to the native speaker, must often be pointed out to the EFL student. He may not connect the illustration with the item that is giving him difficulty. He may also be unable to read charts and graphs in English.
3. *Clues of definition.* The student must be taught to notice the many types of highly useful definition clues. Among these are:
   (a) Parentheses or footnotes, which are the most obvious definition clues. The student can be taught to recognise the physical characteristics of the clue.
   (b) Synonyms and antonyms usually occur along with other clues: *that is*, *is* clauses, explanations in parentheses, and so on.
      (1) *is* and *that is* (X is Y; X, that is Y) are easily recognisable signal words giving definition clues.
      (2) appositival clause constructions set off by commas, *which*, *or*, or dashes (X, Y,; X – Y – ; X, which is Y,; X, or Y) are also physically recognisable clues.
4. *Inference clues from discourse*, which are usually not confined to one sentence:
   (a) Example clues, where the meaning for the word can be inferred from an example, often use physical clues such as *i.e.*, *e.g.*, and *for example*.
   (b) Summary clues: from the sum of the information in a sentence or paragraph, the student can understand the word.
   (c) Experience clues: the reader can get a meaning from a word by recalling a similar situation he has experienced and making the appropriate inference.
5. *General aids*, which usually do not help the student with specific meaning, narrow the possibilities. These include the function of the word in question, i.e. noun, adjective, etc. and the subject being discussed.

(Kruse 1979: 209)

In one of the few recent empirical investigations of vocabulary development, Palmberg (1988) uses a computer game to provide a context for an experiment into vocabulary acquisition. He also takes language needs and interests as his point of departure in an experiment to test the effects of playing with computer games on the learning of vocabulary by young children. The game *Pirate Cove* was selected for its appeal to the age and interests of the two subjects, who were nine and eleven years old. The target vocabulary of the game consisted of 118 words, only 3 of which ('eight', 'list' and 'old') had been taught to the eleven year old child. The experiment was carried out in three phases. In phase one, the children played the game with the aid of the experimenter, who acted as an interpreter, providing Swedish equivalents to the words as they appeared on the screen. Phase two, which occurred a month later involved the children in replaying the game and providing the experimenter with Swedish translations or equivalents of the words and text appearing on the screen. Phase three, took place a month after phase two. The subjects were given a list of 50 concrete nouns from the target vocabulary and asked either to give the Swedish translation of the words or to nominate associations triggered off by the words.

Palmberg found that the learners had a great deal of success in completing the test task in phase three. Seventy per cent of the words were assigned correct translation equivalents, the subjects were partly successful with a further 20 per cent of the words, and had no success with the remaining 10 per cent. Palmberg concluded from this that his subjects were greatly assisted by the cognates which exist between Swedish and English, but he also suggested that the results were noteworthy because the subjects were quite young, and also that they were able to transfer their context-bound learning of the vocabulary items in phases one and two to the context-free test situation in phase three. The experiment suggests that when teaching new vocabulary, we should begin by teaching the new items in context, but that at a later stage learners should be given the opportunity of dealing with the words out of context.

Honeyfield (1977) also stresses the importance of context in the teaching of vocabulary. He points out that even with a functional vocabulary of the three thousand most frequently occurring items in English, learners will still not know around 20 per cent of the items they will encounter in an unsimplified text. The problem confronting both teacher and learners is that no course can provide learners with anything like the vocabulary they will need to comprehend authentic texts. It is therefore important to provide learners with strategies for inferring the meaning of unknown vocabulary from the context in which it occurs (rather than getting them to undertake the time-consuming task of memorising long lists of words, or looking up unknown words in a dictionary which would make the reading process unbearably slow and tedious, and which would probably contribute little to the actual learning of vocabulary). Honeyfield makes a number of suggestions for helping learners develop their skills in inferring meaning from context. These include the familiar cloze or gap exercise in which words are deleted from a text, words-in-context exercises, and context enrichment exercises. Words-in-context exercises are those in which learners encounter target vocabulary items in the meaningful context of a continuous text, and use the surrounding context to arrive at the meaning through focused discussion. Context enrichment exercises take learners through several stages in which progressively more context is provided. They are designed to show learners how the more context one takes into account, the greater are the chances of guessing an unknown word.

Examples of these procedures are provided below. As you look at them, you might like to think which might be most, and which least helpful in actually teaching learners strategies for dealing with unknown vocabulary.

## Cloze exercise

---

*Instructions*: Some words have been taken out of this piece of English. Try to guess all the words and write them in the correct places. If you are not sure of a word, just guess.

DESERT PLANTS
Many desert plants are able to turn their leaves to avoid the direct rays of the sun. Some leaves protect themselves from the great heat by not (1) _____ flat in their normal position but by curling up until the (2) _____ when it is cooler. Some plants have leaves that are covered with (3) _____ thin hairs that can draw moisture from the (4) _____ . Others have hard or shiny surfaces that prevent loss of (5) _____ .

Most cactus plants are covered with (6) _____ points known as 'thorns', that protect them from being (7) _____ . Other plants produce poison substances that (8) _____ hungry animals away. (From Hollon 1968: 7)

---

## Words-in-context exercise

---

*Instructions*: Work in small groups to find the meaning of the words in italics by completing the questions and exercises.

THE FORCE OF CIRCUMSTANCES
She was sitting on the verandah waiting for her husband to come in for luncheon. The Malay boy had *drawn* the *blinds* when the morning lost its freshness, but she had partly raised one of them so that she could look at the river. Under the *breathless* sun of midday it had the white *pallor* of death. A native was *paddling* along in a *dug-out* so small that it hardly showed above the surface of the water. The colours of the day were *ashy* and *wan*. They were *but* the various *tones* of the heat. (From Maugham 1969: 46)

1. Multiple choice questions type 1
   In the story a blind is:
   (a) a drawing
   (b) a set of double doors
   (c) a plant in a pot
   (d) a covering for a verandah

2. Multiple choice questions type 2
   Which of these pieces of information help you to guess the meaning of *pallor*?

---

(a)  A native was paddling a dug-out in the river.
(b)  It is midday.
(c)  The colours of the day were ashy and wan.
(d)  The river had pallor.
(e)  Pallor is related to death.
(f)  In the story, pallor is white.

## Context enrichment exercise

*Instructions*: This exercise will help to direct your attention to the kind of information that a context may give you. In the exercise, there are three sentences, each one adding a little more information. Each sentence has three possible definitions of the italicised word. On the basis of information in the sentence, decide if the definition is improbable, possible, or probable. Write one of these words on the line for each definition.

1.  We had a *whoosis*.
    (a)  a tropical fish          _____
    (b)  an egg beater            _____
    (c)  a leather suitcase        _____
2.  We had a *whoosis* but the handle broke.
    (a)  a tropical fish          _____
    (b)  an egg beater            _____
    (c)  a leather suitcase        _____
3.  We had a *whoosis*, but the handle broke, so we had to beat the egg with a fork.
    (a)  a tropical fish          _____
    (b)  an egg beater            _____
    (c)  a leather suitcase        _____

(Yorkey 1970: 67)

As I have pointed out in preceding chapters, our understanding of language learning and teaching can be greatly informed by observing and analysing interactions between participants in the learning process, and brief portraits of teachers and learners in action have been included in the book to illustrate this point. In the following class-room extract a small group of students is involved in the context enrichment exercise. It can be seen that the task stimulates a great deal of interactive language work, particularly as the students try to determine what is required of them. In a follow-up discussion, the students said they found the exercise particularly useful in helping them see the importance of using context for arriving at the meaning of unknown words.

### Pre-reading task

Before you read the extract, study the context enrichment exercise above. How would you introduce this to a group of students who have not done such a task before? As you read the extract, compare what you would have done with what the teacher does.

## *Classroom extract 7.1: Deriving meaning from context*

T: This exercise is basically looking at how you
can use context to find the meaning of a word.
And what I want you to do is discuss among
yourselves and decide – if you look down at the
first exercise I want you to decide which of
these might be a definition for this – whether
it's improbable, possible, probable. Okay?

S: Oh, we have to put here, after the a. b. c . . .
[yeah] which one is improbable, which one is
possible or is probable?

T: Yeah. What you've got here is a nonsense
word – a nonsense word. Imagine it's a word
you don't know in English. You just discuss
among yourselves.

S: Okay, we had a – what is this . . . a tropical fish
. . . an egg beater . . . a leather suitcase.

S: Okay, I'm sure the c., a leather suitcase, is
improbable.

T: Why?

S: Doesn't have anything to do with that name.

T: If you had a sentence 'We had a leather
suitcase'. Is that possible?

S: What? We had a . . . ?

T: We had a leather suitcase. Is that, is that good
English? Does that make sense?

S: Yes. Yes.

S: [We have . . . *whoosis*] that means . . . is
improbable [but if] is improbable and
impossible is more or less the same?

T: Improbable . . .

S: and impossible

T: Improbable and probable . . .

S: No . . .

T: . . . but possible . . .

S: And impossible. Means improbable is more or
less like impossible?

T: [Pause] Yes. . . . unlikely, unlikely, unlikely.

S: For me . . . for me . . . I don't know for you
. . . leather suitcase doesn't have anything to
do with with this word.

[The students begin working by themselves. There is considerable negotiation as they attempt simultaneously to work out what they are supposed to be doing, and at the same time actually doing the task.]

S1: But for me put here improbable.

S2: But it . . . the . . . the instruction, the

instruction say something different . . . we
have to . . . we have to change this word and
and make sentence with a, b and c. For
instance, 'We had a leather suitcase', 'We had
an egg beater', and 'We had a tropical fish.'
[Is that it?] That's the instruction. [Mmm]
Okay. So we have to decide if, if this sentence
is . . . if those sentence are good English or
not. [You mean each one?] Uhuh.

S1: What sentence? We had a . . .
S2: We had a tropical fish.
S3: Yes. Possible. [Yes]
S1: Improbable, I think. [Why not? Why not?]
S2: We had, er, a tropical fish.
S3: We had an egg beater.
S2: We had an egg beater.
S1: That's, that's probable [Yes].
S2: Is it probable, why not? [Possible, probable]
S1: We had a leather suitcase. Yes, possible. I
    think all of them's possible. Why not?
S3: All synonym [?]
S2: Why not probable?
S1: Okay, the first one, it's possible, but not
    probable, no?
S2: You can't prove that.
S1: Okay, the first one is possible – write possible,
    no? [I think so.]

### Post-reading task

1. Did you find the teacher's instructions helpful or not?
2. How effective was the task in stimulating the learners to interact with one
   another?

This extract shows the considerable negotiation which went on between the learners
as they attempted to complete the task before clarifying exactly what they were
required to do. The teacher, who wanted the students to work things out for themselves and who tried to keep out of the way, should probably have spent more time
setting up the exercise, particularly as this was the first time the students had undertaken a task of this sort. The major source of difficulty for the students was the lack
of context in the first part of the task and the lack of clarity about precisely what was
required of them. With increasing context, the task became progressively easier, and
they completed the third part relatively quickly. In the beginning, the students seem
to want to provide their own situational context until one of them says, 'The thing is,
we don't we don't worry about the meaning, just the you know, the sentence is all
right?'

Many activities such as these are aimed at weaning learners away from an over-reliance on the use of dictionaries, particularly when dealing with extended texts. An article of faith of the communicative language teaching movement is that one need not understand every word in a spoken or written text for communication to be successful. However, it could be argued that the pendulum has swung too far, and that it is time to reassert the value of dictionary work in extending vocabulary.

The arguments in favour of dictionary use have been put by Summers, who claims that in recent years teachers have 'actively discouraged the use of dictionaries', and who criticises the view that the meanings of new words should only be arrived at through contextual clues.

> In reality, unknown words within texts – whether in the form of a repetition, an encapsulation, a superordinate or subordinate term – are very often not deducible from contextual clues . . . many of us would like to believe that teaching words in some systematic way could be helpful – whether in semantic sets, by collocational or semantic feature matrices, even by linking them via their etymology, morphology or phonology – but naturally occurring language is not easily systematised. Trying to deduce the meaning of an unknown word from the text is one valuable strategy in understanding language, and so is dictionary use, but it is only by repeated exposures that a word can enter a person's active vocabulary, whether in first or subsequent language acquisition. (Summers 1988: 112)

Summers suggests that dictionaries provide learners with a powerful analytic tool, not only for finding out meanings and checking spellings, but also for gaining insights into the grammatical aspects of the item in question. The dictionary can also overcome one of the limitations of contextual exercises, in that, in contrast to the context bound meaning of the word (which may be idiosyncratic or peripheral to its core meaning), the dictionary presents the prototypical meanings of the word. Also the activity of matching the dictionary definition of the word to its use in context helps to create deeper links within the student's mind. (See the discussion on 'depth of processing' in the section on vocabulary and memorisation.)

One current initiative of note is in the development of dictionaries for second language learners which incorporate principles of learnability and learner-centredness. One such initiative is the *Macquarie Learner's Dictionary* (Candlin and Hennessy 1990) which adopts an inductive approach vocabulary development. The aim of the authors is to produce a tool for learning, not simply a reference work. It also incorporates socio-cultural information into the data entries.

The relative merits of context as opposed to the use of dictionaries is evident in the approach taken by textbook writers. The authors of *East–West* come down firmly on the side of context, as is evident in the following extract from their introduction.

> In deciding how to teach a vocabulary item, consider how you can get the meaning across most clearly and most quickly. Many new words can be understood through the context in which they appear or through the accompanying illustrations. Draw students' attention to the aids wherever they exist. Concrete visual examples are usually best. If the student's book does not provide relevant illustrations, use classroom realia, the clothes the students are wearing that day, mime, stick-figure drawings on the board, or pictures from a magazine or a picture dictionary such as the *New Oxford Picture Dictionary*. Where

illustration is not possible, use synonyms or paraphrased verbal explanations, provided you can keep your language simple. As you speak, write on the board to ensure that students follow your explanation. Certain vocabulary items are best understood in a larger context and may require that you act out a situation to convey meaning. . . . Where there is no other efficient way to teach a vocabulary item, have students use a bilingual dictionary, or you or a student can offer a translation; but consider the use of native language a last resort. Dependence on bilingual dictionaries encourages students to see English in terms of their native language and to translate word for word. More seriously, it prevents them from relying on context and other clues essential to effective language learning. (Graves and Rein, 1988: xi)

Some of the writing on vocabulary instruction gives the impression that the use of dictionaries on the one hand and context strategies on the other are mutually exclusive. This is not the case, and learners need both skills. The difficulty is in showing learners when it is more cost effective in terms of time to infer meaning from context, and when it is worth consulting a dictionary. I have found that it often takes considerable time and effort to convince learners that they need not understand every word they encounter.

## 7.5 Vocabulary development and second language acquisition

Research into second language acquisition has largely confined itself to the areas of morphology and syntax, and, to a certain extent, phonology. The acquisition of pragmatic, strategic and lexical competence have been generally overlooked (although there are a few exceptions – see, for example the papers in Wolfson and Judd 1983). A major investigation by Johnston (1985) into the acquisition of syntax and morphology of adult immigrants generated a great deal of data on the acquisition of lexis to which Johnston makes passing reference. His report contains lexical lists of the words used (and presumably acquired) by learners at different levels of proficiency. At the time his report was published, Johnston had had little opportunity to analyse the lexical data. However, he does note a number of regularities in the lexical behaviour of the learners he studied. One phenomenon he observed was the tendency of learners to use only one member of a lexical pair such as *good/bad*. With post-beginner to low-intermediate learners, 'good' occurred fifty times, while 'bad' was only produced once. With intermediate level learners, 'easy' was only half as frequent in the data as 'hard'. This tendency only to use one member of a lexical pair can be explained by the use of negation (e.g. 'not good', 'not hard') as a substitute for the under-used member of the pair. Johnston claims that this phenomenon is important because, pedagogically, it is often assumed that the two pairs should be taught together. The result of this is often confusion. 'It seems to be the case that learners have limited memory space for lexical processing and have a greater than normal tendency to recall the wrong word if a lexical pair is vying for the one slot' (Johnston 1985: 366).

If one assumes that the frequency with which learners use particular words reflects their order of acquisition (which may well be a dangerous assumption to make), then Johnston's lexical frequency counts make interesting reading. Consider the following frequency counts for prepositions and pronouns by pre-intermediate learners for example (the numbers in brackets indicate the instances of use). It is interesting to compare this order with the order in which the items are taught in coursebooks.

**Prepositions**

| | | | |
|---|---|---|---|
| *in* (506) | *at* (57) | *by* (16) | *behind* (1) |
| *to* (203) | *from* (29) | *until* (5) | *between* (1) |
| *for* (153) | *of* (23) | *over* (4) | *into* (1) |
| *about* (75) | *on* (19) | *inside* (3) | *since* (1) |
| *with* (63) | *near* (18) | *under* (2) | |

**Pronouns**

| | | | |
|---|---|---|---|
| *I* (1154) | *she* (81) | *your* (20) | *mine* (3) |
| *my* (432) | *we* (72) | *us* (17) | *its* (1) |
| *you* (311) | *it* (45) | *her* (12) | *itself* (1) |
| *he* (231) | *him* (31) | *their* (5) | *our* (1) |
| *they* (194) | *his* (23) | *myself* (4) | |
| *me* (157) | *them* (23) | *himself* (3) | |

While the frequency counts do not indicate whether or not the items have been used correctly by the learners, they make interesting reading. Most noteworthy is how infrequently some items which are taught very early in standard coursebooks are actually used by learners: for example, one popular coursebook introduces the rarely used prepositions 'between' and 'below' in Unit 2, and 'our' in Unit 3. (See my earlier comment on the relationship between frequency and learnability.)

Johnston derives a number of pedagogical principles from his research. The following observations are made on the teaching of vocabulary:

1. As learners have great difficulty learning at one time sets of items that are closely related (such as pronouns), do not teach these as paradigms.
2. In the same way, lexical opposites such as *narrow/broad* should not be introduced in the same lesson or even the same unit of work.
3. As learners tend to equate a single form with a single function, words that have more than one function should not be introduced at the same time (for example, the word 'there' which can act as either an existential subject or a demonstrative).

In her discussion of L2 vocabulary acquisition, Channell (1988) makes passing reference to Krashen's acquisition/learning distinction (we look in detail at this distinction in the next chapter), suggesting that learning is the process and acquisition the end result of vocabulary development (thereby, by inference, rejecting Krashen's early position that learning cannot lead to acquisition). She suggests that a new vocabulary item is acquired when the learner can identify its meaning in and out of context and it can be used naturally and appropriately. In other words, we can only talk about acquisition when learners have both productive as well as receptive control of the new item.

Drawing on work in error analysis, Channell compares research into the speech errors of native speakers with that of second language learners. This research suggests that a learner's first and second vocabulary knowledge are linked together in their mental lexicon phonologically, semantically and associationally, and that learners can make conscious the links between them. However, she also points out that much more research is needed, particularly into the errors made by learners in naturally occurring speech. Her paper concludes with the following implications for classroom practice:

1. Since the lexicon appears to be an independent entity in processing, there is justification for teaching approaches which make vocabulary work a separate learning activity. It is not essential always to integrate vocabulary with general communication.
2. Presentation of vocabulary should pay specific attention to pronunciation, in particular word stress. So visual presentation and reading may not be the best ways to introduce new vocabulary.
3. Learners should be encouraged to make their own lexical associations when they are learning new vocabulary. (However, at present we do not know which kinds of association are the most useful in aiding retention.) [See the discussion on memory in this section.]
4. Semantic links play an important role in production. This suggests the use of semantic field based presentation methods [see the next section on semantic networks].

(Channell 1988: 94)

The research discussed in this section makes numerous suggestions for pedagogy, some of which run counter to conventional wisdom. In evaluating such research, it is important for teachers to experiment with these suggestions, in an informed way, with their own learners in their own teaching situations. It may be that some of the suggestions do lead to more effective learning outcomes. On the other hand, they may not. A great deal of research on vocabulary acquisition and use is carried out in laboratory or simulated settings, and the results may not usefully translate to the classroom.

## 7.6 Semantic networks and features

The principle of avoiding items that are semantically related in some ways runs counter to the notion of using semantic networks or fields in teaching vocabulary. A semantic network consists of words which share certain semantic features or components. A componential analysis can show, in diagrammatic form, what relates and differentiates members of a particular semantic network. Illustration 4 (from Rudzka *et al.* 1981) provides a componential analysis for words which indicate different kinds of spatial limit.

ILLUSTRATION 4

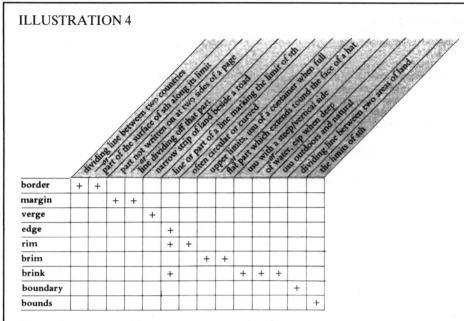

| | dividing line between two countries | part of the surface of sth along its limit | part not written on at two sides of a page | line dividing off that part | narrow strip of land beside a road | line or part of a line marking the limit of sth | often circular or curved | upper limits, usu of a container when full | flat part which extends round the face of a hat | usu with a steep/vertical side | of water, esp when deep | usu outdoors and natural | dividing line between two areas of land | the limits of sth |
|---|---|---|---|---|---|---|---|---|---|---|---|---|---|---|
| **border** | + | + | | | | | | | | | | | | |
| **margin** | | | + | + | | | | | | | | | | |
| **verge** | | | | + | | | | | | | | | | |
| **edge** | | | | | + | | | | | | | | | |
| **rim** | | | | | + | + | | | | | | | | |
| **brim** | | | | | | | + | + | | | | | | |
| **brink** | | | | | + | | | | + | + | + | | | |
| **boundary** | | | | | | | | | | | | + | | |
| **bounds** | | | | | | | | | | | | | | + |

Source: B. Rudzka, J. Channell, Y. Putseys and P. Ostyn, *The Words You Need* (London: Macmillan, 1981), p. 186. Reproduced by permission.

Tasks such as 'spot the odd one out' are designed to develop learners' sensitivity to semantic networks. Classroom extract 7.2 illustrates the way in which such tasks can be carried out collaboratively. They are often extremely revealing of learners' lexical knowledge. In the extract, a small group of students is engaged in spotting the odd word out in each group. They are supposed to be working in a teacherless group with the following worksheet, although the teacher intrudes from time to time to help.

---

HANDOUT

SPOT THE ODD WORDS OUT
EXAMPLE:

radio      *computer*      video      television

Discuss the following words. Put a circle around the odd word out and say why it is the odd word.

| | | | |
|---|---|---|---|
| tourist | visitor | traveller | student |
| investigate | determine | explore | enquire |
| elderly | intelligent | stupidly | talkative |
| utilize | uncover | reveal | disclose |

### Pre-reading task

1. What language would you predict the learners might need in order to complete the task?
2. What role does the teacher play in this task? Is he helpful to the students or not?

### Classroom extract 7.2: Spot the odd word out task

S1  Tourist visitor traveller student.

S2: Student [Yeah] – must be that one, yeah.

T:  Why d'you think, why is student the odd one out?

S2: Oh, tourist, visitor, traveller – they are moving [yeah]

S1: They are going . . .

S2: They have something in common, no?

T:  Yeah, yeah. But I'd like you to say what it is they have in common, you know? How would you describe it?

S3: Okay, second·investigate, determine, explore, enquire. I think, determine [determine] yeah, because investigate, explore, enquire is [synonymous, synonymous] . . . means . . . to know something. Mmm Okay.

S1: Third elderly, intelligent, stupidly, and talkative. Intelligently, and stupidly, you know, I think have er some relations between because there is the opposite meanings.

S3: How about, er, elderly and talkative?

S2: Talkative – what means talkative?

S1: Yeah, too much.

S2: Talkative . . .

S1: How about the elderly? [Adjective] Had a more experience and they get the more . . . [yeah].

S3: Intelligent, stupidly maybe that's the part of the human being . . . which is, I think . . . Okay. Oh [wait, wait a minute].

S1: Okay, this is this is different ad . . . kind of adjective that the [inaudible]

S2: Okay, all right.

T: So which one did you decide?

Ss: Elderly, elderly.

T: Why's that?

> S2: Because er its quite different this, because this match with your age, with your age, and the other one is with your, kind of person that you are

T: Personality. [Personality, yeah]

S1: Er, utilise, uncover, reveal, disclose. Yeah, this is utilise. Uncover, reveal, disclose – all of them the same meaning. Uncover, reveal, disclose.

> S2: Uncover? What's uncover?

S1: You know, cover and uncover. [Gestures]

> S2: Oh. Reveal, okay [good]

T: But how would you define, how would you define those three words? What is, would be the dictionary definition of those three words?

> S3: You mean the uncover and reveal?

T: Reveal and disclose. What is the . . . what is the meaning that they share?

> S2: To find [to find] something, and to [uncover, revealed]
>
> S3: And the other one doesn't have anything with find. The other one means the opposite of doing something.

Athough this is intended basically as a collaborative small group task, the teacher plays an important role in pushing the students to articulate the underlying semantic relationships between the words which belong together. Such relationships can be extremely subtle, and it is not always easy, even for native speakers, to spell them out. From the extract, we can see how much more useful are collaborative discussions based on semantic networks in sorting out relationships between words, than say, individualised, dictionary-based memorisation tasks.

## 7.7 Memory and vocabulary development

A great deal has been written about the role of memory in the development of a second language lexicon, and techniques for memorisation receive relatively generous treatment compared with its use in other aspects of second language development such as the acquisition of syntax and morphology. Stevick (1976) summarises some of the classic research into memory which has been carried out by cognitive psychologists and relates this to language teaching. This research has demonstrated that in order for new items to enter long-term memory, some form of active involvement on the part of the learner is desirable. In other words, a learner who has activated this knowledge through use will be more likely to retain it than a learner who has simply heard or read the item and seen a translation. The research also shows that regular revision is important, and that revision which is distributed over a period of time is more effective than 'massed practice'. In the learning of a list of vocabulary items, for example, six 10-minute sessions over the course of a week will result in more effective learning than a single 60-minute session.

Stevick makes a great deal of the notion of 'depth', by which he means the amount of intellectual and emotional effort which the learner invests in the learning process. He reports his own lack of success in improving his knowledge of Swahili by listening to Swahili news broadcasts and repeating aloud as he listened.

> When I put this plan into practice, however, I was disappointed. I was indeed able to repeat along with the tape fairly well, but the experience produced only fatigue, with no perceptible improvement in my Swahili. The words were going into my ear and out my mouth all right, but they were not disturbing anything in between: in the metaphor of 'depth', the words were flowing over my mind so fast that they had no time to sink in. They remained instead on the surface, and evaporated almost immediately. (Stevick 1976: 35)

One rather idiosyncratic method based on the notion that the more active the learning the more effective it is likely to be is Asher's Total Physical Response. Asher (1977) attempted to recreate in foreign language classrooms conditions which he hypothesised underlie successful first language acquisition. He claimed that children received their initial input in the form of instructions couched in the imperative which required them to make physical responses. 'Pick up the blue ball!', 'Put your dolly in the box!' He suggested that initial foreign language instruction should follow the same procedure, learners carrying out commands in the target language, and thereby utilising their whole bodies as they processed words and short utterances. He claimed some startling feats of memory and retention in experiments carried out to put the Total Physical Response to the empirical test. (In Chapter 12, we look in some detail at this and other methods.) It remains to be seen whether these claims can be substantiated in relation to the teaching of vocabulary.

In his analysis of current trends in vocabulary teaching, Nattinger (1988) presents a number of classroom techniques for vocabulary development. He separates these into techniques for comprehension (understanding and storing words), and production (retrieving and using these words). Techniques for comprehension include utilising context clues, word morphology, mnemonic devices, loci, paired associates and key words, Total Physical Response, cognitive depth, formal grouping, word families, historical, orthographical similarities, and collocations. Techniques for production include pidginisation, situational sets, semantic sets, metaphor sets, and collocations. These are briefly described below.

**Comprehension**
*Context clues.* Techniques for guessing vocabulary from context include activating background knowledge from the topic of a text, obtaining clues from grammatical structure, pronunciation and punctuation, and using the natural redundancy of surrounding words. For example, the reader should be able to guess the meaning of 'workaholic' in the following sentence: 'My father was a *workaholic*, he worked so long and so hard that we rarely saw him.'

## Word morphology
Learners can be taught to extend their vocabulary by mixing and matching word stems, suffixes and affixes.

## Mnemonic devices
These are tricks for committing words to memory. Nattinger points out that there is resistance to the use of such devices by many teachers.

## Loci
These are a form of mnemonic in which a list of words to be learned are associated with a familiar visual image such as a room or a well known tourist spot. Each word is associated in some way with one of the items in the visual image, and the image is used to assist in the recall of the words.

## Paired associates
In this technique, which is similar to the use of loci, words in the first and second language which have some similarity of sound and meaning are associated. Nattinger cites Curren's example of the German word *schwarz* which means black and which could be associated with the English word 'swarthy'.

## Key words
Here the target vocabulary item is paired with its native language equivalent in an idiosyncratic way. 'For example, in learning that the Spanish word *perro* means "dog", one might notice that the first syllable of the new word sounds like "pear" and would then visualize a large pear-shaped dog waddling down the street' (Nattinger 1988: 66).

## Total Physical Response
In this technique, the target vocabulary items are paired with relevant physical actions. (See the discussion on the previous page, and Chapter 12.)

## Cognitive depth
This technique was developed by Craik and Lockhart (1972). Students are asked one of the following questions in relation to each word.
1. Is there a word present?
2. Is the word printed in capitals or in lower case letters?
3. Does it ryhme with . . . ?
4. Is it a member of . . . category?
5. Does it fit into the following sentence?
Each question forces successively deeper levels of processing, and Craik and Lockhart found that there was superior retention and recall when words were related to questions 4 or 5 than 1 or 2. (See also Stevick's discussion of 'depth of processing' on the previous page.)

## Formal groupings
Certain vocabulary items can be memorised by teaching students to recognise basic forms of words and how they combine with certain affixes. For example, students

could be taught the meanings of words such as *tele* (far, distant), *phone* (sound), *photo* (light) *graph* (write, mark) and then given lists of vocabulary items containing these words and asked to guess the meanings of these compound words.

**Word families**

This is an extension of the formal grouping technique. Exercises can be developed to show how word 'families' are developed from a single root. (Nattinger provides the following example: part, partition, partly, partner, participant, particular, particle.)

**Historical, orthographical similarities**

This involves the development of associations based on historical, orthographical similarities between cognate language. For example, there are many words in languages such as Spanish and Italian, or English and German, which share common or closely related meanings and which can be exploited to assist learners to expand their target vocabulary.

**Collocation**

Collocations are words which are commonly associated. Nattinger suggests that exercises to develop and strengthen these associations can greatly facilitate learning. The following sample collocational exercise is from Brown (1974: 9).

> Choose the items that collocate most usefully with each verb. The number of lines left after each verb is a guide to the number of useful collocations possible.
> 1. To appeal .............................   the slow student
>    ...........................................   against the judge's decision
>    ...........................................   to my friend for help
>    ...........................................   him to learn from his
> 2. to encourage ..........................   mistakes
>    ...........................................   etc.
>    ...........................................

At various points in the book, we have seen the importance of teaching students strategies for independent learning. Illustrations 5–7, which have been extracted from Ellis and Sinclair (1989), are designed to sensitise learners to the learning processes, including memorisation strategies for building and maintaining an adequate vocabulary in a second language.

ILLUSTRATION 5

*Activity: Common features*

a) Here are some words which have been sorted into groups. Can you see what each group has in common?

Group 1: shoe  shop  shout  shine  sheep
Group 2: greenhouse  breadboard  penknife
Group 3: biology  geology  psychology
Group 4: run  jump  hop  sprint  jog

b) Sort the following words into groups. When you have finished, find out if another learner can discover what your groups have in common.

walnut  melon  currant  tomato  blackberry  raspberry  chicken  banana  chestnut  peach  gooseberry  grapefruit  thyme  hazelnut  lemon  pear  turkey  strawberry  kitchen

How many different ways of grouping these words did your class use?

c) Can you think of any other ways of grouping the words in (b) that could help you to remember them? What are they?

Source:  G. Ellis and B. Sinclair, *Learning to Learn English* (Cambridge University Press, 1989), p. 35. Reproduced by permission.

## ILLUSTRATION 6

a) Choose a topic, for example 'politics'. Write it in the middle of a blank sheet of paper.

b) What is the first word that comes into your mind which is connected in some way with it? (If the word is in your language, find out the English for it.) Write the English word anywhere you like on the paper and join it to the first word.

c) Continue in this way, adding new words as you think of them.

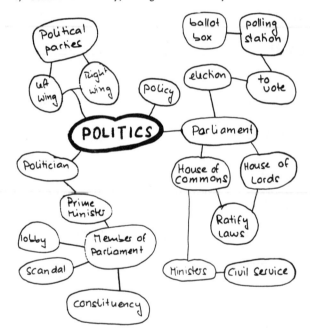

Source: Ellis and Sinclair, 1989, p. 36. Reproduced by permission.

# ILLUSTRATION 7

*Activity: Word tour*

a) Think of a town or city you know well. Imagine that you are organising a sightseeing tour for tourists.

b) Think of five places you would include on your tour and write down the order in which the tourists will visit them.

c) Learn your tour off by heart so that you can picture it in your mind.

d) Whenever you have five new English words to learn, imagine these words are the tourists on your tour and picture the words in the places on your tour, like this:

| *Tour:* Trafalgar Square | *Words to learn:* apron |
|---|---|
| Buckingham Palace | dustpan |
| Houses of Parliament | vacuum cleaner |
| Westminster Abbey | feather duster |
| Downing Street | broom |

– Imagine Nelson (on his column in Trafalgar Square) wearing an apron.
– Imagine the Queen brushing the floor in Buckingham Palace and using a dustpan.
– Imagine a Member of Parliament vacuuming the corridors in the Houses of Parliament.
   Can you imagine pictures for the other words?

*Activity: Word clip*

For words that are difficult to picture in your mind, make up a story, like a video clip, in your mind. Imagine famous people acting in your video clip and doing or saying the words you want to remember.

Source: Ellis and Sinclair, 1989, p. 38. Reproduced by permission.

## 7.8 Investigating the teaching and learning of vocabulary

**Task 7.1**
Record some of your learners having a casual conversation (for example, in a coffee break) and do a lexical analysis of their language. What items seem to be frequently used? Are there any surprises?

**Task 7.2**
Compare the order in which you teach prepositions and pronouns with the frequency orders revealed by Johnston's research. What similarities and differences are there in the orders?

**Task 7.3**
The following statements were made by second language learners when asked to describe their approaches to learning vocabulary. Ask a group of learners to write A (agree) or D (disagree) next to the statements.

1. I think learning new words,is the most important part of learning another language. I don't care if I get the grammar wrong, as long as I have the words I need.
2. I try to learn five new words each day. I make lists and stick them up around my room. Every evening I spend a little time memorising the new words and revising the ones I have learned.
3. I read a lot and use a dictionary. Every time I find a word I don't understand, I look it up.
4. You don't really need a big vocabulary. When I'm talking to people, I can usually find a way to get my message across, even if I don't have the exact word.
5. English and German share lots of words, so I try to find similarities between the languages to help me remember.
6. I try to avoid having translations. I put new words into a sentence and then memorise the words in context.

Now get the students to write a statement summarising their own attitude toward the learning of the vocabulary.

Get the students to compare and discuss their responses. Tape the discussion and make a summary of the issues which emerge. What attitudes and beliefs about the learning of vocabulary are implicit in the discussion? Are you happy with these? Would you like to encourage learners to develop different/more flexible approaches? Suggest some strategies for doing this.

**Task 7.4**
The following task is from Nunan and Lockwood (1989). Which of the two word lists do you think might be easier to memorise and why?

*Work in small groups (3–4 students). Half of the groups study Word List A. The other half study Word List B. Study the list for 5 minutes, then cover it and write down all the words you can remember.*

*Word List A*
licence, money, traffic, coat, run, shoes, lounge, read, driver, Bankcard, dress, permit, bedroom, talk, kitchen, teller, toilet, socks, bank, walk, laundry, parking, write, shirt, cheque

*Word List B*

| licence | bank | bedroom | coat | talk |
|---------|------|---------|------|------|
| driver | cheque | kitchen | shoes | run |
| traffic | money | lounge | dress | walk |
| permit | Bankcard | laundry | socks | write |
| parking | teller | toilet | shirt | read |

*Discussion: Which word list was easier to remember? Why?*

Get two groups of students to complete the task. Which group was the more successful? Does this bear out your prediction? Why or why not?

## Task 7.5

Record a group of students completing the following task (you may substitute your own words if you wish). What sort of discussion does the task generate? Compare it with classroom extract 7.2. What are the similarities/differences between the discussions? Give the task to groups of students at different proficiency levels. Is there an 'optimum' level for the task?

SPOT THE ODD WORDS OUT

| tourist | visitor | traveller | student |
|---------|---------|-----------|---------|
| Barrier Reef | Brisbane | Ayers Rock | Kakadu Park |
| bus | car | train | plane |
| engagement | passenger | booking | reservation |
| swimming | sailing | diving | trekking |
| tourist | holiday | vacation | trip |

(From Nunan and Lockwood 1989)

## Task 7.6

Give the Birmingham 200 word frequency list to a group of students and ask them to select and rank the 30 most useful/important words. Do these reflect the frequency order as identified in the Birmingham corpus?

# 7.9 Conclusion

For a number of years, the teaching of vocabulary was neglected in language classrooms, despite the importance that learners attach to the task of building and maintaining an adequate vocabulary. It could be argued that in a second, as opposed to foreign language context, the initial stages of language learning should be devoted almost entirely to vocabulary work. On those occasions when I have lived and worked in a foreign country, I have found more communicative value for effort in focusing, in the first instances, on developing a survival vocabulary to the comparative neglect of other aspects of the target language.

The development of communicative approaches to language teaching has done much to enhance the status of vocabulary, and some interesting empirical and practical work is currently being undertaken in the area. Theoretical and empirical issues currently being investigated include work on word lists and frequency counts, the importance of context to vocabulary acquisition, lexicography and the role of the dictionary, semantic networks and features, and cognitive processes, particularly lexical search processsses and memorisation. On a practical level, an indication of the enhanced status of vocabulary is the recent publication of a major coursebook based on a lexical syllabus. (For a good introduction to lexical syllabuses see Willis 1990.)

As vocabulary teaching regains an important place in the language classroom, the issues, principles and practices reviewed in this chapter will become increasingly useful and significant. It is hoped that the chapter has provided insights which teachers can test in their own classroom. It is also to be hoped that some of the issues may find their way into an enhanced research agenda, for, despite the renewed interest, the amount of published research in the area remains disappointingly small.

# Chapter Eight

# *Focus on Form: The Role of Grammar*

## 8.1 Introduction

Lay persons, language learners, and many teachers themselves would probably see the central pedagogical role of the language teacher as the teaching of grammar, and the correcting of learners' errors. However, the place of grammar in the language classroom is currently rather uncertain. This uncertainty has been brought about with the development of communicative approaches to language teaching, along with theoretical and empirical insights from second language acquisition research. In this chapter we review this research and explore its implications for the classroom, focusing in particular on the following questions:

1. What is the 'contrastive' hypothesis, and what are the implications of the hypothesis for teaching grammar?
2. What were the 'morpheme order studies' and what were the methodological implications of these studies?
3. How can we account for the fact that certain grammatical items seem to appear in predetermined sequences?
4. What is 'grammatical consciousness-raising' and how does it differ from traditional grammatical instruction?
5. What is the contribution of systemic–functional linguistics to the teaching of grammar?
6. What are pedagogical grammars and how can they be used in the classroom?
7. What is the difference between inductive and deductive approaches to the teaching of grammar?

## 8.2 The 'traditional' language classroom

Traditionally, the language classroom was a place where learners received systematic instruction in the grammar, vocabulary and pronunciation of the language, and were provided with opportunities for practising the new features of the language as these were introduced. Methodology training focused on the most effective ways for teachers to present and provide practice in the target grammar.

For many curriculum specialists, the 'contrastive' hypothesis provided an important guide to the selection and sequencing of items for instruction (see, for example, James 1980). This hypothesis claims that a learner's first language will have an important influence on the acquisition of a second. It predicts that where first language rules conflict with second language rules, then errors reflecting the first language will occur as learners try to use the second language – in other words, the first language will 'interfere' with the second. For example, it predicts that Spanish first language learners will tend, when learning English, to place the adjective after the noun, rather than before it, as this is the way it is done in Spanish. Such an error is the result of 'negative transfer' of the first language rule to the second language. 'Positive transfer', on the other hand, occurs when the rules of the two languages coincide, and learners can thus exploit their first language knowledge in learning the second language. A third possibility is where a linguistic feature of the target language does not exist in the first language (as is the case with the English system of articles for Chinese learners, or the existence of nominal classifiers in Thai for learners whose first language is English).

The contrastive hypothesis holds, firstly, that learners' difficulties in learning a second language can be predicted on the basis of a systematic comparison of the two languages, and secondly that learners from different first language backgrounds (say Chinese and Spanish) will experience different difficulties when attempting to learn a common second language (such as English), and that they will master different aspects of the grammar at different times. As we see in the next section, it was the strong claims of contrastive analysis which ultimately got it into trouble, for when researchers actually analysed the errors that learners made, and the difficulty they had with different features of the target language, they were unable to sustain many of the claims made by the contrastivists.

## 8.3 Second language acquisition research and its influence on practice

During the early 1970s a series of empirical investigations into learner language were carried out. These became known as the 'morpheme order' studies, and their principal aim was to find out whether there is a 'natural' sequence in the order in which second language learners acquire the grammar of the target language. The studies followed on from a pioneering piece of research by Brown (1973), who discovered that children learning English as a first language passed through strikingly similar stages in acquiring fourteen grammatical structures and that, contrary to expectations, there was no relationship between the order in which items were acquired and the frequency with which they were used by the parents.

Dulay and Burt (1973, 1974a, b) found that, like their first language counterparts, children acquiring a second language appeared to follow a predetermined order which could not be accounted for in terms of the frequency with which learners heard the language items. Moreover, children from very different first language backgrounds (Spanish and Chinese) acquired a number of morphemes in virtually the same order. However, the order differed from that of the first language learners investigated by Brown. Bailey *et al.* (1974) replicated the studies with adult learners and came up with strikingly similar results.

As a result of these and other investigations, it was concluded that in neither child nor adult second language performance could the majority of errors be attributed to the learners' first languages, that learners in fact made many errors in areas of grammar that are comparable in both the first and second language, errors which the contrastive hypothesis predicted would not occur. The researchers concluded from these investigations that a universal order of acquisition existed which was driven by an innate learning process. It also appeared that the nature of the target language, rather than contrasts between the first and second language, drove the acquisition process.

Krashen (1981, 1982) and Dulay *et al.* (1982) set out a number of principles for practice which they claim are derived from the morpheme studies as well as other SLA research reported in the literature (see, for example, Hatch 1978). These claims, are, in fact, either highly contentious, or self-evident, as can be seen from the following examples, which are extracted from Dulay *et al.* (1982: 261–3). I have also provided a gloss/comment on each claim. (As you read these principles, you should bear in mind the fact that many of these claims go well beyond the research findings themselves.)

1. There appear to be innate processes which guide L2 acquisition.
   [The finding that learners, regardless of their first language, appear to learn a second language in the same order prompted the notion that an internal mental mechanism 'triggered' the acquisition process.]
2. Exposure to natural communication in the target language is necessary for the subconscious processes to work well. The richer the learner's exposure to the target language, the more rapid and comprehensive learning is likely to be.
   [The fact that conscious, explicit instruction was unable to alter the order of acquisition led to the suggestion that the processes responsible for second language acquisition must be largely subconscious.]
3. The learner needs to comprehend the content of natural communication in the new language.
   [The largely commonsensical notion that we cannot acquire what we do not comprehend, and the limited success of oral drills, led to a focus on comprehension as the key to acquiring a second language.]
4. A silent phase at the beginning of language learning (when the student is not required to produce the new language) has proven useful for most students in cutting down on interlingual errors and enhancing pronunciation.
   [This point is derived not from the morpheme studies, but from a series of case studies carried out in the early 1970s and reported in Hatch (1978).]

5. The learner's motives, emotions, and attitudes screen what is presented in the language classroom, or outside it.
   [Proponents of a comprehension-driven methodology had to account for the failure of some learners to acquire. They did this by postulating an emotional 'filter' which blocks the target language.]
6. The influence of the learner's first language is negligible in grammar.
   [This point stems directly from the finding that learners tend to make similar mistakes regardless of their first language. However, it should be noted that even in the days before criticism of the morpheme studies became widespread there was controversy over the actual percentage of errors which could be attributed to first language interference.]

The net effect of these recommendations was to play down the role of grammar in the classroom. The efficacy of grammatically structured syllabuses was questioned, as was grammatical instruction, and the role of error correction. The role of grammar, as traditionally conceived, was thus seriously undermined. Whether or not such prescriptions actually had any effect on teachers' classroom practice is another matter, which could be settled only by looking at what teachers actually do; however, they certainly gained widespread currency in the literature.

The morpheme order studies have come in for severe criticism in the years since their appearance. Major criticisms have been made of the way in which the data were collected and analysed, and of the elicitation instrument used by the researchers – the Bilingual Syntax Measure (BSM), a sequence of cartoon-style pictures which are meant to elicit the target morphemes. It has been suggested that the results obtained by the BSM may be an artifact of the instrument itself, and that data collected by other means may have resulted in different orders (for a discussion of this, see Larsen-Freeman 1975, 1976; Nunan 1987b; Larsen-Freeman and Long 1991. The scoring procedure, in which subjects were said to have 'acquired' a structure if they used it correctly 90 per cent of the time has also been criticised. There seems to be no principled reason why 90 per cent, rather than, say, 80 per cent or 100 per cent should have been selected. Additionally, it is important to collect information on incorrect as well as correct usage, as this sheds light on the developmental process.

Other criticisms include the fact that there is no principled relationship between the different items selected for investigation; that items which behave quite differently are grouped together (the definite and indefinite article were grouped together, although we now know they behave quite differently (Pica 1985)). In a detailed critique of the studies, Johnston criticised the fact that linguistic forms are studied in isolation from their communicative functions (Johnston 1985). It is also claimed by Pienemann and Johnston (1987) that the morpheme order researchers fail to offer a theoretical rationale for the findings. By this they mean that the researchers are unable to say why the items appear in the order they do, or to make predictions about the likely acquisition orders of items which have not been investigated. Breen (1985) has also criticised the failure of SLA researchers to take the social context within which learning takes place into consideration in the design and implementation of their research.

In an important study conducted in the 1970s, Larsen-Freeman (1975) used a range of tasks for eliciting morpheme orders in adult subjects over a six month period. The tasks included the Bilingual Syntax Measure, a sentence repetition task, a listening comprehension test, a cloze test and a writing test. While the morpheme accuracy orders on some tasks were similar to those of Dulay and Burt, they differed on other tasks. This raises the possibility that the order in which items appear to be acquired is determined in part by the type of instrument employed. In a follow-up investigation, Larsen-Freeman (1976) found that frequency of input might be one factor influencing acquisition orders.

Despite criticisms of the early morpheme studies, subsequent research has provided substantial evidence that certain grammatical items appear in predetermined sequences, and that these predetermined sequences do not appear to be alterable by instruction (see, for example, Cancino *et al.* 1978; Hyltenstam and Pienemann 1985). For example, all learners, regardless of whether they are learning in a second or foreign language context, and regardless of whether they are receiving instruction, appear to go through the following four stages in the acquisition of negation:

| | |
|---|---|
| Stage 1: 'no + verb' | No work/No understand. |
| Stage 2: 'don't + verb' | I don't like/He don't can swim. |
| Stage 3: 'auxiliary + negative' | She can't go./He don't stay. |
| Stage 4: analysed don't | He didn't stay. |

The most elegant hypothesis on the development of acquisition orders is one first developed for German as a second language by Meisel, Clahsen and Pienemann in Germany, and later applied to English. These researchers claim that we can explain and predict the order in which grammatical items are acquired by what are called speech processing constraints which limit the amount of language we can hold in short-term memory. In developing our competence in a second language we pass through a series of stages. Each stage is more complex than the one before it, complexity being defined in terms of the limits on short-term memory.

According to this hypothesis, learning a second language is basically a matter of mastering a series of mental operations. In order to speak a language fluently, these must become largely automatic, in the same way as the physical operations in breathing, walking, running and driving a car must become automatic for us to carry out these actions competently. Because speech processing operations are very complex, and also because the time available for speaking or comprehending is limited, it is only possible to focus on a limited part of the whole speech processing operation at any one time. Learning a language, then, is a matter of gaining automatic control of these complex mental routines and subroutines.

In learning English, we first learn isolated words and phrases. The next stage is the 'standard' word order of subject + verb + object, for example: 'I like rice', 'I go home', 'I can swim'. Then comes a stage in which the learner adds an element to the 'core' structure, for example 'yesterday, I go home'. After this comes a sequence of stages in which the learner develops the ability to rearrange internally words from the core structure, for example 'can you swim?'. Here 'can' is moved from the middle of the structure to the front. At the next stage, learners would be able to carry out more complex rearrangements, producing structures such as 'where are you going tonight?'.

You can see from these examples that each stage builds on the one preceding it, and makes progressively more demands on memory. I have grossly oversimplified the hypothesis here to give you some idea of the logic behind it. For a more detailed and comprehensive account see Johnston (1985) and Pienemann and Johnston (1987).

There have been a number of different, even contradictory responses to the finding that some grammatical items are impervious to instruction (in other words, that instruction cannot change the order in which the items are acquired). As we have already seen, one suggestion made as a result of the morpheme order studies was that we should abandon all attempts to grade syllabuses grammatically and to teach grammar systematically. Rather, learners should be immersed in communicative activities in which the focus is firmly on meaning rather than form. An alternative suggestion is that syllabuses should still be grammatically sequenced but that the sequencing should follow the 'natural order'. These conflicting suggestions underline the fact that research is often neutral as to its implications for practice and that we need to test these ideas in the classroom to determine their effects on acquisition.

There are, in fact, a number of problems which emerge when one attempts to apply the results of this research. If one is to follow a natural order of instruction one must have classes consisting of learners who are all at the same developmental stage. It is also necessary for these learners all to progress at the same rate. While these conditions might obtain in some foreign language contexts (for example, with total beginners), they are problematic in second language contexts. Additionally, in second language contexts, we need to consider the possibility that learners may need to learn some language items (such as question forms) as formulae to enable them to communicate at early stages of their second language development. Another factor which needs to be considered is the long-term effect of instruction. It may well be that even though learners are incapable of reproducing a particular item at the time it is taught, systematic exposure over a period of time will speed up acquisition in the long run. This is certainly one of the implications we can derive from Long's (1983) literature review which demonstrated that instruction speeds up the rate at which learners learn in contrast with those who try and pick the language up naturalistically, without formal instruction.

Lastly, there is a problem in assuming that the learning of a language occurs in a linear sequence. We know, in fact, that language learning is an organic process characterised by backsliding, leaps in competence, interaction between grammatical elements, etc. This organic rather than linear nature of language development is due in part to the fact that structures are not learned in isolation, but that they interact with each other. Eisenstein *et al.* (1982) investigated the development of progressive and simple forms and came to the conclusion that the problem of learning closely related verb structures is that while each has its own job to perform, it is also interconnected with other structures. This makes it difficult for the learner to determine where the boundaries are, and therefore, to know when it is appropriate to use one structure rather than another. Eisenstein *et al.* point out that ultimately the challenge of learning closely related verb structures is probably that they have to be integrated into the semantic and grammatical system in such a way that each marks off its own meaning domain, i.e. in the case of verbs, its own portion of time.

In summary, SLA research has done a great deal to advance our knowledge of language learning processes and outcomes. Above all else, it has demonstrated the complexity of the processes involved in learning a second language. We now have data which show that it takes much longer than was once thought to move from one developmental stage to another. The research also supports something which learners have been telling us for years: that, if anything, we tend to overload them in the classroom. Other pedagogical outcomes are less certain. There seems to be little support for an approach in which all explicit grammatical instruction is eschewed. However, the questions of when, how, and how much focus to place on grammar has not been settled. Ultimately, claims made by SLA researchers outside the classroom can be settled only by validating studies inside the classroom. Recent work on grammatical consciousness-raising has attempted to marry SLA research with pedagogy, and it is to such work that we now turn.

## 8.4 Grammatical consciousness-raising

The 'organic' view of language learning presented at the end of the preceding section is consonant with the notion of grammatical instruction as consciousness-raising (CR). The clearest and most perceptive introductions to grammatical CR are contained in Rutherford (1987) and Rutherford and Sharwood-Smith (1988).

CR rejects the split between conscious learning and subconscious acquisiton. However, it also contrasts with traditional grammatical instruction in a number of important respects. In the first place, there is much greater attention paid to form–function relationships. It also attempts to situate the grammatical structures and elements in question with a broader discoursal context. In addition, it takes an organic rather than linear view of learning, and therefore rejects the rather naive notion that once something has been taught it will of necessity have been learned. Rutherford (1987), in building his case for consciousness raising, explicitly rejects the 'traditional' beliefs that language is constructed out of discrete entities and that language learning consists of the gradual accumulation of these entities. He also rejects the notion that grammatical rules can be directly imparted to the learner through teaching because of the complexity of many rules, and because of the interrelationships between them. For this reason, he sees classroom activities as being basically inductive rather than deductive (see section 8.6 below). These activities are meant to facilitate the learning process by providing data through which learners may form and test hypotheses, and also by helping learners link the new with what they already know. Unlike traditional approaches to teaching grammar, then, grammatical CR fulfils a process rather than product role: it is a facilitator, a means to an end rather than an end in itself. It has been argued that for language-to-language development to occur, learners must 'notice the gap between their own production and that of native speakers (Schmidt and Frota 1986). One function for CR is to assist learners to 'notice this gap'.

Sharwood-Smith (1988) take a rather different line from Rutherford, arguing that 'traditional' instruction is one type of consciousness-raising. He draws attention to the distinction between 'explicit' knowledge and 'implicit' (the former denoting a conscious, analytical awareness of the formal features of the language, the latter referring to an intuitive feeling for what is correct), and suggests that CR can be both highly explicit or largely implicit. (For a detailed treatment of the role of implicit and explicit knowledge in language learning, see Bialystock 1981, 1982.)

The following examples of grammatical consciousness-raising exercises have been taken from Rutherford (1987) and Nunan and Lockwood (1989). While some of them bear a superficial resemblance to 'traditional' grammar exercises, they have quite a different purpose. In the first place, they are derived from genuine interactions and authentic texts, not ones which were designed for pedagogical purposes. In the second place, the pedagogical context from which they have been extracted is basically communicative in nature. Additionally, the exercises 'recycle' language points over several units of work, allowing learners to reformulate their understanding of the structures over time. Lastly, they invite learners, inductively, to develop hypotheses about the target feature of the language.

> Look at a map of the city.
> Find the suburb where you live.
> Imagine you are having a party at your place this Saturday night.
> What would be the easiest way to get from the city to your place by public transport?
> Now write instructions on a piece of paper for a friend.
>
> Look at this conversation skeleton.
>
> A: Coming?
> B: Where?
> A: Ayers Rock.
> B: Why?
> A: Holiday.
> B: When?
> A: Next week.
> B: Sorry.
> A: Why?
> B: Work.
>
> Now expand it into a complete conversation.
>
> A: ............ coming ............?
> B: Where ............?
> A: ............ Ayers Rock.
> B: Why ............?

A: ............ holiday.
B: When ............?
A: Next week.
B: ............ sorry ............
A: Why ............?
B: ............ work.

When we are surprised by a statement, we can show our surprise by asking a question, and putting the stress on the question word. For example:

The weather looks okay.    → *Does* it?
The wood's wet.    → *Is* it?

What questions would we ask to show surprise at these questions?

That is Yoshi over there.    →
Alice likes white wine    →
I live next door.    →
Tomoko is from Japan.    →
Alex lives across the road.    →
The wine is cold.    →

What do the italicised referents in the following text refer to?

After *they* saved a little money, Howard and Ellen wanted to buy a house. So they *did*. The floor plan was almost exactly the same as *that* of Ellen's parents home where *she* was reared. Buying *it* was not easy *for the young couple*, but Ellen was determined to go through with *it*. *She* could not stand living in their small apartment any longer. She wanted the kind of space *that* she had always lived with. Howard couldn't quite understand *his* wife's insistence on moving to more spacious quarters. *Their* small apartment was big enough for *him*. In fact *it* was almost like *the one* he had lived in as a child. But he could remember *his* mother saying almost daily, 'If only *I* had more room'.

(Rutherford 1987: 160–1)

Grammatical consciousness-raising, as discussed in this section, and illustrated by the above examples, can be realised in many different ways, and there are numerous creative techniques for sensitising learners to grammatical principles within a communicative context. The different examples show quite clearly that there are many ways of teaching grammar, and it is wrong to imply that teachers are confronted with two mutually exclusive choices when it comes to teaching grammar: either avoiding the teaching of grammar altogether, or returning to a 'traditional' form-focused approach.

## 8.5 Systemic functional linguistics and pedagogical grammars

One of the major models of language informing this book is that of systemic functional linguistics. This approach argues that language exists in context, and that the context and purposes for which language is used will determine the ways in which language is realised at the levels of text and grammar. While there is no one-to-one relationship between form and function (otherwise we should not be able to communicate to a very sophisticated degree at all), the relationships between the two are not arbitrary. The fact that there are principled links between form and function has been eloquently argued by Halliday (1985a, b).

Recent work in systemics has also addressed the issue of grammar, and the debate over whether or not grammar should be taught. Like most contemporary views of grammatical consciousness-raising, this approach advocates explicit grammatical instruction, though not a return to 'traditional' grammar teaching. Not surprisingly, given the general approach to language as summarised above, the approach is a top-down one which begins with whole texts and works down, rather than beginning with individual grammatical items and working up (usually, only as far as the sentence). In other words, when the teacher wants to focus on a particular grammatical item, that item is introduced within a particular context, and learners work from context to text to sentence and clause, rather than from clause/sentence to text. (For examples of how this is done see Butt 1989.) The pedagogical approach derived from this model of linguistics also seeks to show learners how language differs according to the context in which it is produced, the purposes for which it is produced, and the audience to which it is addressed.

Within the context of literacy development, Hammond suggests that the teaching of grammar from a systemic functional perspective, in which learners are taught how language actually works at the level of text, has a number of major benefits. Principal among these is the fact that it can contribute to learners' literacy awareness. It also provides teachers and learners with a shared vocabulary for talking about language and the way it works. This, she claims, contributes significantly to successful literacy development.

> A teacher who, as part of the regular language sessions, talks about, analyzes, compares, contrasts and reflects on written texts, whether they be published texts or the students' own writing, not only promotes an interest in written texts, but provides the students with a language that enables them to reflect on and analyze written texts themselves. It enables the students to remove themselves from the process of creating a written text, to objectively analyze it and to develop an insight into what makes one text successful and another unsuccessful. (Hammond 1989: 19)

No one seriously interested in the development of second and foreign language has ever suggested that learners do not need to master the grammatical system of the target language: the debate has been over how learners can best acquire the target grammar (see Widdowson 1990 for an incisive discussion on the relationship between grammar and meaning). Wilkins, one of the principal architects of communicative approaches to language teaching, argues for a notional syllabus, that is, one in which the basic building blocks are the meanings and concepts expressed through the language, not the grammatical elements. However, he also points out that acquiring the grammatical system of the target language is of central importance, because an inadequate knowledge of grammar would severely constrain linguistic creativity and limit the capacity for communication. 'A notional syllabus, no less than a grammatical syllabus, must seek to ensure that the grammatical system is properly assimilated by the learner' (Wilkins 1976: 66). More recently Swain (1985) has added empirical weight to this claim, showing that exposure to the target language in meaningful contexts is insufficient for most learners to develop a sophisticated working knowledge of grammar. Such a working knowledge is important because learners' ability to express themselves is constrained by the extent to which they can encode their meanings grammatically.

In other words, grammar exists to enable us to 'mean', and without grammar it is impossible to communicate beyond a very rudimentary level. In terms of methodology, the debate, as we have seen, has been over the procedures through which learners attain mastery, whether and to what extent they should undertake exercises with a deliberate focus on form, or whether they should pick up the grammar in the process of meaningful interaction. Information about the target language which may be used by teachers and students of the language for learning purposes is presented in pedagogical grammars, and we now examine the concept of pedagogical grammars, as well as a number of recently published books on teaching grammar in the communicative age.

Pedagogical grammars are intended to provide those involved in language teaching (including learners) with information on the grammar of the language for the purposes of teaching and learning, syllabus construction, materials development and so on. While they may reflect current theories of grammatical description and analysis, pedagogical grammars do not necessarily follow a particular grammatical theory or school of thought.

Pit Corder (1988) makes the point that any grammatical presentation will be shaped by the beliefs of the authors on the nature of language, the intended audience, and the purpose for which the grammar was written in the first place. A linguist writing for other linguists in order to present a new grammatical theory will produce a very different work from an applied linguist writing for a foreign language teacher in order to provide material which can be used in the classroom. He exemplifies this point as follows:

| Author | Reader | Object of 'grammar' |
|---|---|---|
| Linguist | Linguist | To illustrate and validate a particular linguistic theory |
| Linguist | Student of linguistics | To teach syntactic theory inductively through its application to a particular language |
| Applied linguist | Educated native speaker | To systematize in linguistic terms the implicit knowledge of the reader |
| Applied linguist | Teacher of the mother tongue | To systematize the implicit or explicit knowledge of the reader in a form which is pedagogically appropriate for his (native speaker) pupils |
| Applied linguist | Teacher of a foreign language | To systematize the implicit or explicit knowledge of the reader in a form which is pedagogically appropriate for his (non-native speaker) pupils |

(Pit Corder 1988: 128)

Rutherford (1980) suggests that the development of some pedagogical grammars involves the principled selection of items which reflect pedagogical experience as well as linguistic theory. He points out that since the development of communicative approaches to language teaching, the selection of structural elements is often constrained by the prior selection of semantic and functional elements. Several books have been published in the wake of the debate on the place of grammar in the curriculum which are aimed at providing teachers with ways of teaching grammar within a communicative context, and it is to three of these that we now turn.

In her book on teaching grammar, McKay (1987) suggests that there are three different views on what it means to 'teach' grammar. The first view is that teaching grammar entails the formal explanation of grammar rules. While learners who receive a great deal of grammatical explanation will end up knowing quite a lot about the language, they will not necessarily be able to put the language to communicative effect. The second view is that teaching grammar is basically a matter of providing learners with practice in mastering common grammatical patterns through a process of analogy rather than explanation. The learners may become fluent in the structures they have been taught, but may not be able to use them appropriately in genuine communication outside the classroom. The third view is that teaching grammar is a matter of giving students the opportunity to use English in a variety of realistic situations. The disadvantage of this approach is that learners will not be able to provide explanations of the grammatical rules of the target language. McKay's text is

> based on the belief that the primary purpose of instruction in grammar is to help our students use English correctly and appropriately. While some classroom time will undoubtedly be devoted to teaching grammar rules and to having students practise grammatical patterns, it is important to remember that such instruction is only the means toward helping out students gain competence and confidence in the language. (McKay 1987: xi–xii)

In other words, explicit treatment of grammar should be seen as a means to an end, rather than an end in itself. Teachers should therefore keep this end in view, regardless of the particular pedagogical techniques and classroom activities they employ.

In the introduction to her book, Ur (1988) raises the issue of whether or not grammar should be explicitly taught. She argues in favour of explicit teaching in the belief that mastering the individual elements of a language, be they lexical, phonological or grammatical, is a valuable means toward eventual ability to communicate in the language. She makes a point which was raised earlier in this book, that learning to do something need not necessarily consist of repeated attempts at the target performance. In other words, learning is not necessarily the same as skilled performance, although at some stage in the learning cycle, it will entail an attempted rehearsal of the skilled performance. However, form-focused exercises should progess to meaningful activities which should themselves ultimately give way to tasks where the emphasis is on successful communication. Ur advocates a fairly traditional four-stage approach to the teaching of grammar items:

1. **Presentation.** Making the structure salient through an input text in which the item appears.
2. **Isolation and explanation.** Ensuring that students understand the various aspects of the structure under investigation.
3. **Practice.** Getting students to absorb and master the language.
4. **Test.** Getting learners to demonstrate mastery.

Frank and Rinvolucri (1987) attempt to provide a range of classroom exercises and activities which, while providing learners with intensive practice in a number of basic morphosyntactic items, do so within a context which stresses 'communicative' rather than 'linguistic' competence, language in action rather than languages as sets of symbols to be manipulated, and ability rather than knowledge. They describe their approach in terms of 'awareness', suggesting that an awareness activity provides control over the students' response to the extent that it is not possible to do the task without having understood the structure being practised, but not the content, which is left up to the learners. In other words, the learners control what is said, while the teacher provides direction on how it is said. 'This adds up to total involvement of the learner's whole person, with total responsibility for what he or she produces in a rather loose framework of predetermined cues' (Frank and Rinvolucri 1987: 7).

In the next section, we look at how these authors have attempted to put these principles into operation.

## 8.6 Pedagogical materials and techniques for teaching grammar

Most contemporary coursebooks and materials for teaching grammar attempt to establish game-like situations in which the repetitive practice of the structure occurs through a task which has a meaningful dimension. In other words, the learner is not simply performing drills. Illustration 8, from Ur, is a good one.

---

ILLUSTRATION 8

### 11.3  Detectives

Affirmative, interrogative and negative of *have*; simple oral repetition.

*Procedure:*   An object to be 'stolen' is decided on – say a coin, or a ring.
One student (the 'detective') is sent out of the room. One of the
remaining students is given the object: he or she is the 'thief'. The
detective returns and tries to find out who is the thief by asking each
participant:
> Do you have it / the ring?

Each participant – including the actual thief – denies guilt, and accuses
someone else:
> No, I don't have it, A has it!

Whereupon the detective turns to A with the same question – and so
on, until everyone has been asked and has denied responsibility. The
detective then has to decide in three guesses who is lying – who 'looks
guilty'. The process is then repeated with another detective and another
thief.

*Variations:*   The activity may be made more lively by encouraging
students to act innocence or indignation as convincingly as they can:
they may change the emphasis or intonation of the set sentences as they
wish, add gesture and so on. Another technique, which abandons
verisimilitude but helps fluency, is to get the class to complete the
round of 'interrogation' as quickly as possible: ('Let's see if we can get
round the whole class in two minutes' ... 'Let's see if we can do it again
in even less time').

Source: P. Ur, *Grammar Practice Activities* (Cambridge University Press,
1988), pp. 123–4. Reproduced by permission.

---

A basic distinction in learning theory is between deductive and inductive learning.
Deductive learning is

> an approach to language teaching in which learners are taught rules and given specific
> information about a language. They then apply these rules when they use the language.
> Language teaching methods which emphasise the study of the grammatical rules of a
> language (for example, the GRAMMAR-TRANSLATION METHOD) make use of the principles of
> deductive learning.
>
> This may be contrasted with inductive learning or learning by induction in which learners
> are not taught grammatical or other types of rules directly but are left to discover or induce
> rules from their experience of using the language. (Richards *et al.* 1985: 73)

Illustrations 9–11 are from the introduction to grammar practice books published
since the beginning of the debate on the place of grammar within the communicative
curriculum. All are aimed at teaching the simple past. From the extracts, it can be
seen that there is considerable divergence in the approaches taken by the authors,
some favouring an inductive approach, while others favour a more deductive
approach.

## ILLUSTRATION 9

### In class

1 Ask the students to write down the 'opposites' of these words:
   good      typing      real      angry      Monday

2 Ask the students to suggest the 'opposites' they have come up with. Jot down the various acceptable 'opposites' on the board.
   *Good* has produced: *naughty, evil, bad, nasty.*

   *Typing* has produced: *hand-writing, reading, walking* (in that typing is a kind of walking with the fingers), *silent writing* etc.

   Get students to explain why they propose a given word as the opposite of one on the list.

3 Write the following scene up on the board and ask the students to write its *opposite* or *reversal*. Don't give examples of how to do this as, if you do, this will reduce the diversity of the students' reactions to the task.

   The waitress came up to Table No. 3 and offered the tall man the menu. He chose and ordered. She went back to the kitchen to get what he wanted.

   Confronted with this task, some students simply put all the sentences into the negative. Others try to find 'opposites' and write:

   'A waiter went down to chair letter C and took away the bill from the short woman.'

4 Group the students in fours to read their 'reversals' to one another.

5 Now tell the students that your are going to tell them the reversal of a bad experience from your own life. We once told this story in class:

   'I went to work as an au pair in France. It was a marvellous family with very few children. My hostess was very kind and understanding. I had almost no work to do and oceans of free time. I had been going to stay for 2 weeks, but in the end I stayed for 6 months.'

6 Ask the students to shut their eyes and think of some bad experience they have had. Also ask them to prepare to tell the experience to someone else, but reversed.

7 Find out how many people have brought back bad experiences to mind, group them with people who haven't and ask them to tell their reversed stories.

8 Ask the listeners to now tell the stories they have heard to others in the group, and so on.

### Rationale

At first sight, the exercise above may seem a little strange, but it provokes very strong listening comprehension, as the listener is doing a double decoding: i) s/he is making sense of the sounds and words of the L2; and ii) s/he is trying to 'reverse' the scene being listened to, to find the real meaning.

### Variation

Instead of bringing sad situations to mind and telling them happily, you could ask the students to bring back happy situations and tell them sadly.

All sorts of opposites can be played, e.g. with: trivial/important
                                        recent/far back in time
                                        selfless/boasting.

Source: C. Frank and M. Rinvolucri, *Grammar in Action* (Hemel Hempstead: Prentice Hall, 1987), pp. 46–7.

## ILLUSTRATION 10

*the Present Progressive and Past Tense*

A grid can also be used to contrast particular verb tenses. For example, in order to contrast the present progressive and past tense, you might begin by giving a command to one of the students such as "Open the window." As the student is opening the window, say "Luvan is opening the window." Then tell the same student to close the window. After he has done this, say, "Luvan closed the window." Then put the following grid on the board.

| PRESENT | PAST |
|---|---|
| 1. Luvan is opening the window. | 2. Luvan closed the window. |

In dealing with any grammatical point in English, two basic approaches are possible. One is an inductive approach in which you strive to help students form generalizations themselves by providing many examples of a particular grammar point. In this case, for example, you would hope that by using many sentences which indicate what class members are doing or have done, students would see how the present progressive and past tense are formed in English.

A second alternative is a deductive approach in which you give explicit attention to the differences in form. In this case, you might ask several short questions such as the following, and then summarize the students' responses.

1. What are the two verbs in sentence 1? (is opening) What has been added to the main verb? (ing)
2. What has been added to the main verb in sentence 2? (d)
3. Which sentence describes something that is going on at the present moment?

Or, rather than using questions, you could, as shown below, underline the distinction in the model and provide a brief explanation of the differences between the two tenses.

| PRESENT | PAST |
|---|---|
| 1. Luvan *is* open*ing* the window. | 2. Luvan clos<u>ed</u> the window. |

Which approach you use will depend on such things as the age of your students and the complexity of the grammar point. With children, an inductive approach will often be the most productive. However, with adults, particularly academically oriented adults, the students may expect and appreciate an explanation of the grammatical rule.

One way to provide further practice in contrasting the present progressive and past tense for reporting actions would be to describe a simple process such as scrambling an egg. First, go through the process and demonstrate each step. Use simple commands such as the following.

1. Crack the egg.
2. Stir the egg.
3. Pour the egg in the pan.
4. Cook the egg.
5. Sit down.
6. Enjoy the egg.

After you go through the process one time, repeat the process, but this time stop as you do each step and ask the students what you are doing. They can then respond with such things as "You are cracking the egg." After you complete each step, you might ask the students, "What did I just do?" They can then answer with such things as "You cracked the egg." Next, have each student describe a simple process for the class and use these demonstrations to further practice the present progressive and past tense for reporting actions.

Source:  S. McKay, *Teaching Grammar: Form, Function and Technique* (Hemel Hempstead: Prentice Hall, 1987), pp. 5–7.

---

ILLUSTRATION 11

### 23.1  Listening to stories

Use of past for narrative; listening comprehension and slot-filling; oral.

*Procedure:*  Tell the students a story – improvising from skeleton notes, or reading out from a text (see BIBLIOGRAPHY for recommended sources). The story should have plenty of action, and be easily comprehensible to the students. Get them to focus on past forms by asking occasionally for a translation of an irregular form, or by stopping and getting them to supply the verb – but not so often as to interfere with overall 'pace' or comprehensibility. After you have finished, ask them to recall some of the sentences in the past that were mentioned in the story – using one-word 'cues' to jog their memories.

*Comment:*  You do not have to finish a single story in one session; use longer stories, or complete books, and read them in serial form, a few minutes each lesson.

### 23.2  Piling up events

Use of past for narrative; repetition and construction of simple sentences based on given past forms; oral, with optional written follow-up.

*Procedure:*  Give each student a verb in the past tense ('sat' or 'stood' or 'gave'). Then start a simple chain of events with the sentence:
> Yesterday I went to town and I bought a loaf of bread...

The first student continues, repeating your sentence but adding a further clause including his or her verb:
> Yesterday I went to town, I bought a loaf of bread and I *sat* on a park bench...

The second continues likewise:
> Yesterday, I went to town, I bought a loaf of bread, I sat on a park bench, and I *stood* at the bus stop...

And so on, until all the students have contributed, or until the chain becomes impossible to remember.

Source: P. Ur, *Grammar Practice Activities* (Cambridge University Press, 1988), p. 213. Reproduced by permission.

---

Illustration 12 is from a self-study book for second and foreign learners of English. You might like to make a note of the similarities and differences between this way of introducing the simple past and the teacher-directed suggestions above.

---

ILLUSTRATION 12

**a)** Study this example:

> Tom: Look! It's raining again.
> Ann:  Oh no, not again. It **rained** all day yesterday too.
>
> **Rained** is the *past simple* tense. We use the past simple to talk about actions or situations in the past.

- I very much **enjoyed** the party.
- Mr Edwards **died** ten years ago.
- When I **lived** in Manchester, I **worked** in a bank.

**b)** Very often the past simple ends in **-ed**:

- We **invited** them to our party but they **decided** not to come.
- The police **stopped** me on my way home last night.
- She **passed** her examination because she **studied** very hard.

For spelling rules see Appendix 3.

But many important verbs are *irregular*. This means that the past simple does *not* end in **-ed**. For example:

leave → **left**   We all **left** the party at 11 o'clock.
go   → **went**   Yesterday I **went** to London to see a friend of mine.
cost → **cost**   This house **cost** £35,000 in 1980.

The past of the verb **be** (**am/is/are**) is **was/were**:

> I/he/she/it **was**        we/you/they **were**
>
> I **was** angry because Tom and Ann **were** late.

For a list of irregular verbs see Appendix 2.

**c)** In past simple questions and negatives we use **did/didn't** + the infinitive (**do/open/rain** etc.):

> it **rained**     **did** it **rain**?     it **didn't** rain

- Ann:  **Did** you **go** out last night, Tom?
  Tom: Yes, I **went** to the cinema. But I **didn't enjoy** the film.
- When **did** Mr Edwards **die**?
- What **did** you **do** at the week-end?
- We **didn't invite** her to the party, so she **didn't come**.
- Why **didn't** you **phone** me on Tuesday?

Note that we normally use **did/didn't** with **have**:

- **Did** you **have** time to write the letter?
- I **didn't have** enough money to buy anything to eat.

But we do *not* use did with the verb be (**was/were**):

- Why **were** you so angry?
- They **weren't** able to come because they **were** very busy.
- **Was** Tom at work yesterday?

For the past simple see also Units 12, 20, 21.

Source: R. Murphy, *English Grammar in Use* (Cambridge University Press, 1985), p. 22. Reproduced by permission.

We now turn to the classroom itself, to see how these various ideas are realised in practice (for further examples from a range of foreign language classrooms, see Peck 1989) . In the two classroom extracts which follow, the two teachers are both trying to teach wh- questions to relatively low-level learners. However, both have very different ways of realising their pedagogical intentions. The first teacher adopts an inductive approach, while the second uses deduction as a teaching strategy.

### *Pre-reading task*

1. What strategies would you expect to see employed in an inductive teaching lesson? What strategies would you expect to see in a deductive lesson?
2. As you read the extract, decide on the teacher's objectives.

### *Classroom extract 8.1: Grammar lesson*

The teacher circulates around the room, asking questions about train travel. The students all have copies of a train timetable.

T: Now . . . back to the timetable. Where do you
catch the train? Where do you catch the train?
[She points to a student in the front row.]

S: Keswick

T: Yeah.
[She turns and writes on the whiteboard '*Where do you catch the train?*'.]

T: Do you know where Keswick is? . . . Okay,
where do you catch the train? At Keswick.
Keswick is near the city – but not the big
railway station. It is about, oh, one kilometre –
two kilometres from the city, and – the big
trains go from Keswick. If you want to catch
the train to Melbourne, or to Sydney, or to
Alice Springs, you go to Keswick. It's the new
railway station. All right. So, where do you
catch the train? At Keswick. Now – what time
. . . what time does the train leave?

Ss: Nine. Nine o'clock. Nine pm. Nine pm.<br>Nine am.

T: [Leans over a student and checks the
timetable] Okay. Depart nine am. So . . . [She
returns to the board.] . . . what can I write
here? What time . . . [She writes '*What time*'
on the board] What comes next, what time
. . . ? Does . . . does . . . [She writes '*does the
train*'.] . . . does the train . . . yes?

S: [inaudible comment]

T: No, what time does the train . . . ? What's
another word for 'depart'? – Leave. What time
does the train . . . leave? [She writes '*leave*' on

the board] Okay, you, you tell me. . . . It leaves
at nine am. Okay, what time does it arrive?

S:  Er, eleven fifty-eight am.

T:  [Leans over his shoulder and checks his
timetable] Okay. Now – where does it arrive at
eleven fifty-eight? At Victor Harbour?

Ss:  No. Goolwa.

T:  No.

Ss:  Goolwa. Goolwa.

T:  Goolwa. Have a look at your map and see if
you can find Goolwa. See if you can find
Goolwa on this map.

S:  Near, er, near the Victor Harbour.

T:  Near Victor Harbour, yeah. [She writes '*What
time*'.] Okay, what comes next? . . . What
time . . . ? What's the question/What time
. . . ? . . . does [does]?

S:  . . . the train arrive . . .

T:  Arrive. [She writes '*does the train arrive at
Goolwa?*'.] All right, so what time does the
train arrive at Goolwa? Okay. What time?

S:  Eleven. Eleven. Eleven fifty.

T:  Eleven fifty . . . eight. What's another way of
saying eleven fifty-eight? Two minutes to . . .
twelve. Yeah, two minutes to twelve. Okay.

[She continues in this fashion, attempting to elicit questions and answers from the students,
and building up the question paradigm on the board until the following pattern is displayed.]

*Where do you catch the train?*
*What time does the train leave?*
*What time does the train arrive at Goolwa?*
*How long does it take to go to Victor Harbour?*
*How long does it take to come back?*
*How long do you spend in Victor Harbour?*
*How much does it cost?*

Without drawing the attention of the students to the board, the teacher gives them
another brochure and timetable, and asks them to find similar information to that
which they have found in relation to the excursion to Victor Harbour.

### Post-reading task

1. In this extract, the teacher is conducting a teacher-fronted question and answer
   session. She is attempting to introduce students to wh- questions with 'do'
   insertion through an inductive approach. Review the extract. Is there any
   evidence that this objective is too difficult for the learners?
2. What modifications would you make to this lesson?

From the difficulties the students are having in generating the required structure, it seems that wh- questions with 'do' are beyond the processing capacity of the students The teacher's attempts at eliciting the question form from the students is not particularly successful, even after several examples are on the board, and she ends up supplying the forms herself. On the other hand, when focusing on the semantic content required by the questions, the students are quite successful.

It would appear that major problem here is that there is a twin focus: on the one hand on the formation of wh- questions with do insertion, and on the other hand, on extracting key information from written brochures. While the task succeeds in its second objective, it fails in the first. In addition, the students do not know what it is that the teacher is trying to do in this part of the lesson, nor whether they should be focusing on meaning or form (or both). I believe that the interaction would have been more successful if the teacher had restricted her focus to a single objective, and if that objective had been spelled out.

The following extract is taken from a class which is very similar to that in extract 8.1 (both consist of low proficiency learners). The grammatical focus of the session (teaching wh- questions) is also similar. However, the teacher is quite different, as is her teaching approach.

### Pre-reading task

As you read this second extract, make a note of the differences between this teacher's approach to the teaching of grammar, and the teacher in the preceding extract.

### Extract 8.2: Teaching grammar through drill and practice

The teacher and students are sitting in a large circle. The teacher has some cards in her hand. She looks at a question.

T: Let's have the question . . . 'live' [She gestures
   with her hand.]
                              S: What do live.
T: No, not 'what', what's the question?
                              S: Where.
T: Where! Good. Where . . . [She leans forward
   and gestures with her hands.]
                              S: Where . . . you . . . live.
T: [Gestures encouragingly] He's nearly there.
   Can you help him?
                              S: Where . . .
[The teacher begins counting the words off on her fingers and repeats each word as the student says them.]
                              S: Where [where] . . . do [do] . . . you [you] . . .
                                 live [live].
T: Okay. Listen [The teacher speaks rapidly and
   makes sweeping gestures with her hands to
   indicate the intonation contour.] Where d'you
   live? Where d'you live? Where d'you live?

Where do you live? Everyone. [She sweeps
her hand around the group.]

S: Where do you live?

T: Okay. Victor, please ask Roberto.

S: Where do you live?

T: Where do you live?

S: I live . . . in Smithfield.

T: Okay, fine. What was number five – the
question – 'languages'?

Ss: What, er , what . . . what . . . what . . .
languages . . .

T: What languages . . .

S: What . . . languages . . . do . . .

T: Do

S: . . . you . . . speak.

T: Yes. What languages do you speak? What
languages do you speak? Remember? What
languages do you speak? Okay, Daniel, ask
Pia.

S: What languages do you speak?

S: I speak English.

T: Uh huh, All right. And in your country . . . I
speak Viet . . .

S: I speak Vietnamese.

T: Good, I speak Vietnamese. And . . .

S: And . . . And a little . . .

T: And a little English. And a little English. And
a little English. And . . . a little [The teacher
pauses, gestures and smiles encouragingly at
one of the male students.]

S: English.

T: Okay. I know you don't like saying you speak
a little English. [laughter] What's the next
one? [She consults her cards.] Question.
Married . . . What was the question?

S: Are. . .

S: Are you married?

T: Uh, huh, are . . . Ask Rosa please.

S: Are you married?

S: Yes, I am.

T: Yes I am. This is my . . . ? [The teacher points
to one of the male students.]

S: This is my wife.

T: Wife? [laughter]

S: Ah, husband.

T: This is my husband. Okay. Have you got.
Have you got any children? Have you got a
pen? Have you got . . . a book? Have you got?

any brothers or sisters? Remember yesterday?
Okay. Helena, could you ask Victor the
question, please?

> S: Have you got any brothers, er, sisters?
> S: Yes. I've got er two brothers, two sisters.

### Post-reading task

1. Which lesson do you think is more successful? Why?
2. What would you have done differently in this lesson?

In contrast with the teacher in extract 8.1, this teacher persists with her probes and, if one student fails to respond appropriately, she asks another rather than supplying the students with the required response herself. Whether the students are able to make the structure part of their productive repertoire is highly doubtful (according to the research of Pienemann and Johnston 1987, the structure is beyond the processing capacity of learners at this level of proficiency). Despite this, in the highly structured, drill-like exercise presented in the transcript, most learners are able to come up with the required structure.

## 8.7 Investigating the teaching and learning of grammar

**Task 8.1**
Record a lesson or lesson segment in which the focus is on teaching an item or aspect of grammar. Analyse the segment. What beliefs emerge about the nature of grammar and learning?

**Task 8.2**
Analyse several coursebooks, looking in particular at the introduction to the teacher's edition. What does the analysis and the exercise and activity types reveal about the author's beliefs about the nature of grammar and learning?

**Task 8.3**
Develop a communicative task (e.g. role play, discussion, problem). Decide what items of grammar learners will need in order to carry out the task successfully. Teach the task to two parallel groups or classes, providing explicit grammar instruction to one group before completing the task but not to the other. Record and analyse the tasks. Were the students who received the explicit instruction better equipped to carry out the task or not? Why or why not?

**Task 8.4**
Develop a communicative task (e.g. role play, discussion, problem) similar to that used in task 8.3. Record some native speakers carrying out the task. Transcribe the

interaction. Teach the task to two parallel groups or classes, allowing one group to study the way a group of native speakers handled the task before completing the task themselves. Record and analyse the tasks. Were the students who received the native speaker model better equipped to carry out the task or not? Why or why not?

**Task 8.5**
Select a grammar point and develop a lesson to teach it inductively and deductively. Teach the lesson to two parallel classes. Record and analyse the lessons. Which seemed the more successful? Why?

## 8.8 Conclusion

In this chapter I have looked at the current status of grammar in the language classroom. I took as my point of departure claims made some years ago that the teaching of grammar was of marginal utility. Since then, a more balanced view has emerged from the literature, a view in which grammar has been reinstated (assuming that, in reality, it had ever been deposed). However, the new approaches, informed by recent advances in linguistic theory and psycholinguistic research, are quite different from approaches which characterised the teaching of grammar in the 1950s and 1960s. In particular, systemic–functional linguistics has provided a principled way of linking context and text, function and form. Advances in linguistic theory have also found their way into pedagogy via the notion of grammatical consciousness-raising. Despite their diversity, the newer approaches have some common features. They bring a much more sophisticated conception of language and learning to pedagogy, and occur within the context of communicative language teaching. The notion that the learning of grammar is a linear, step-by-step process has largely been replaced by an organic, even metamorphical, view in which the development of grammatical competence is seen in terms of process as well as product.

# Chapter Nine

# *Focus on the Learner: Learning Styles and Strategies*

## 9.1 Introduction

In language teaching, research into learning strategies and cognitive styles has been a notable area of growth in recent years (see, for example, Pearson 1988; Reiss 1985; Rubin 1975; Rubin and Thompson 1983; Wenden 1986, 1991). In this chapter, I review this research and consider its implications for language teaching. The implications for methodology in particular are considerable, given evidence which suggests that accommodating learning style and strategy preferences in the classroom 'can result in improved learner satisfaction and attainment' (Willing 1988: 1). This chapter answers the following questions:

1. What are learning styles and strategies?
2. What are the findings from recent theory and research into learning style and strategy preferences by second language learners?
3. Why should we incorporate strategy training into our teaching?
4. What are some techniques for teaching learning strategies and developing skills in learning how to learn?
5. How can learners be encouraged to activate their language outside the classroom?
6. Is there such a thing as the 'good' language learner?

## 9.2 Research into learning styles and strategies

There is a large body of literature on the issues of cognitive style, learning style and learning strategy, and some of this work is being embraced by second and foreign language researchers. While there is obvious overlap between second language acquisition research and learning strategies, research which seeks to link both strands of research is lacking. (A notable exception is work by Rod Ellis – see, for example, Ellis 1987.) As an example of the overlap between these two areas, consider the claim made by Krashen (1981, 1982), referred to in the preceding chapter, that acquisition is a subconscious process, and that grammatical instruction is unimportant for this acquisition to occur. Debate about whether learning/acquisition occurs consciously or subconsciously impinges directly onto learning strategy research, the critical question being: are there certain learners, who, by virtue of their expressed strategy preferences, are better able to benefit from direct grammatical instruction than others?

'Learning style' refers to any individual's preferred ways of going about learning. It is generally considered that one's learning style will result from personality variables, including psychological and cognitive make-up, socio-cultural background, and educational experience. For Willing (1988), an individual's perceptions of his/her own strengths and weaknesses will also have an effect. He also suggests that some aspects of an individual's learning style may be alterable while others may not.

Learning strategies, which we are primarily concerned with in this chapter, are the mental processes which learners employ to learn and use the target language. Faerch and Kasper (1983 and cited in Ellis 1985) refer to these processes as procedural knowledge. Ellis provides the typology of procedural knowledge shown in Figure 9.1.

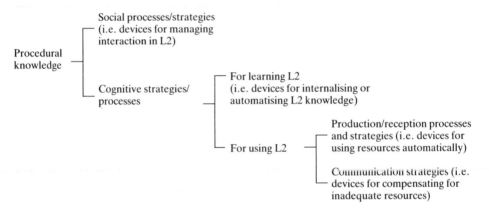

FIGURE 9.1 *Typology of procedural knowledge* (after Ellis 1985: 165).

In this chapter, we are concerned mainly with those cognitive strategies and processes for internalising and automatising L2 knowledge. However, I have included the Ellis typology to show how learning strategies relate to communication and production/reception strategies.

A major problem for learning strategy theorists has been the development of a coherent taxonomy of learning strategy types. Most researchers have developed their own lists, and there is now a plethora of these in the literature, which makes it difficult to compare research findings and suggestions for pedagogy. Ellis (1985) suggests that strategies can be categorised under three broad process types: hypothesis formation, hypothesis testing, and automatisation. Hypothesis formation includes such strategies as simplification and inferencing, and refers to strategies whereby learners come to conclusions about the structure of the target language based on samples of the language, or by transferring from knowledge of one's first language. Hypothesis testing refers to strategies such as trying out rules when communicating with a native speaker and monitoring the speaker's reaction to evaluate whether or not the rule seems to work. Automatisation includes strategies for practising the language. G. Ellis and Sinclair (1989) group strategies according to their macroskill focus (that is, whether they focus on listening, speaking, reading or writing). They provide comprehensive suggestions for listening, speaking, reading and writing as well as for vocabulary and grammar.

Willing (1989) draws a primary distinction between strategies for managing the learning process and strategies for managing information. Managing the learning process involves such things as developing an understanding of one's own language learning preferences, managing communicative situations for learning purposes, practising, monitoring and evaluating. Managing information includes strategies such as attending selectively, associating, categorising, pattern learning and inferencing.

There have been several recent investigations of the learning style and strategy preferences of second and foreign language learners. In a major study of learning styles among adult learners of English as a second language, Willing (1988) obtained data on the learning preferences of 517 learners. Willing was looking for possible correlations between learning preferences and biographical variables. The principal means of data collection was a questionnaire which learners completed in the course of an interview. Low proficiency learners were interviewed in their first language. One of the major aims of the investigation was to explore possible learning style differences attributable to different learner biographical variables. It is widely accepted by teachers that such things as ethnicity, age, etc. will have an effect on preferred ways of learning. The variables investigated by Willing were:

1. Ethnic group
2. Age group
3. Level of previous education
4. Length of residence in Australia
5. Speaking proficiency level
6. Type of learning programme (e.g. whether in full-time or part-time courses)

The study came up with several surprising findings. In the first place, there were certain learning activities which were almost universally popular. In several instances, these were activities which did not enjoy similar popularity amongst teachers as was shown in a follow-up investigation of teachers' preferences by Nunan (1988b). For example, error correction by the teacher was highly valued by almost all learners, while student self-discovery of error was given a low rating. For teachers, the reverse was true.

Perhaps the most surprising finding was that none of the biographical variables correlated significantly with any of the learning preferences.

None of the learning differences as related to personal variables were of a magnitude to permit a blanket generalization about the learning preference of a particular biographical sub-group. Thus, any statement to the effect that 'Chinese are X' or 'South Americans prefer Y', or 'Younger learners like Z' or 'High-school graduates prefer Q', is certain to be inaccurate. The most important single finding of the study was that for any given learning issue, the typical spectrum of opinions on that issue were represented, in virtually the same ratios, within any biographical sub-group. (Willing 1988: 150–1)

This finding, which runs counter to the folk wisdom of the classroom and staff-room, suggests that personality factors are more significant than socio-cultural variables and educational background for learning strategy preferences. Of course, the fact that the study was conducted in a second rather than foreign language environment may have had a significant effect on the outcomes, and it would be useful to replicate the study in foreign language contexts.

One final finding of note was that learners could be categorised by type according to the pattern of their responses on the questionnaire. Learner 'types' and their preferences are set out below.

**Type 1: 'concrete' learners.** These learners tend to like games, pictures, films, video, using cassettes, talking in pairs and practising English outside class.

**Type 2: 'analytical' learners.** These learners liked studying grammar, studying English books and reading newspapers, studying alone, finding their own mistakes and working on problems set by the teacher.

**Type 3: 'communicative' learners.** These students like to learn by watching, listening to native speakers, talking to friends in English and watching television in English, using English out of class in shops, trains, etc., learning new words by hearing them, and learning by conversations.

**Type 4: 'authority-oriented' learners.** These learners preferred the teacher to explain everything, liked to have their own textbook, to write everything in a notebook, to study grammar, learn by reading, and learn new words by seeing them.

The methodological implications of this research are not particularly easy to evaluate. Willing believes that language classes should be constituted on the basis of learner 'types'. In many school contexts, however, this is simply not possible. If such groupings are not possible, due to administrative and resource constraints, it is still desirable to identify the strategy preferences of one's learners by administering a survey/questionnaire similar to the one used by Willing. (This can be found in either Willing 1988 or Nunan 1989b. Ellis and Sinclair 1989 is also an excellent source of questionnaires.)

If your class consists of learners with a range of strategy preferences, then you will need to provide a range of learning options and activities in class. This should be accompanied by opportunities for learners to reflect on and evaluate the activities (ways of doing this are presented later in the chapter.)

The key question is whether there is such a thing as a 'good' learner who can be defined in terms of learning strategies: in other words, do those learners who progress more efficiently and effectively than the average share certain strategy preferences? We look at what the available research has to say on this in the next section.

## 9.3 The 'good' language learner

Much of the research into learning strategy preferences has been concerned with identifying learning strategy preferences with a view to isolating those characteristics of the 'good' language learner. Rubin and Thompson (1983) suggest that 'good' or efficient learners tend to exhibit the following characteristics as they go about learning a second language.

1. Good learners find their own way.
2. Good learners organise information about language.
3. Good learners are creative and experiment with language.
4. Good learners make their own opportunities, and find strategies for getting practice in using the language inside and outside the classroom.
5. Good learners learn to live with uncertainty and develop strategies for making sense of the target language without wanting to understand every word.
6. Good learners use mnemonics (rhymes, word associations, etc. to recall what has been learned).
7. Good learners make errors work.
8. Good learners use linguistic knowledge, including knowledge of their first language in mastering a second language.
9. Good learners let the context (extra-linguistic knowledge and knowledge of the world) help them in comprehension.
10. Good learners learn to make intelligent guesses.
11. Good learners learn chunks of language as wholes and formalised routines to help them perform 'beyond their competence'.
12. Good learners learn production techniques (e.g. techniques for keeping a conversation going).
13. Good learners learn different styles of speech and writing and learn to vary their language according to the formality of the situation.

Recently, I investigated forty-four 'good' language learners in order to find out whether there were any common patterns in their experiences. The learners had all learned English as a foreign language in a variety of Southeast Asian countries including Hong Kong, Thailand, Indonesia, the Philippines, Malaysia and Singapore. They were all 'good' learners in that they had all attained bilingual competence in the language, and all were teachers of English as a foreign language. There were two strands to this research, one which looked at the 'good' language learner, and the other which explored the effect of teachers' learning strategy preferences on their own teaching style. I shall not be concerned with this second strand here.

There were two reasons for selecting language teachers as research subjects. In the first place, by selecting English language teachers it was easier to locate subjects with high levels of proficiency. Secondly, it was felt that because teachers would have the metacognitive and metalinguistic language to conceptualise their experiences, they would be better able to reflect on and articulate their foreign language learning experiences.

Data for the study were provided by a questionnaire and a follow-up interview. The questionnaire was an adaptation of the one used by Willing, and asked subjects to rate thirty statements about learning preferences such as, 'In English classes, I like to learn by reading', 'I like the teacher to explain everything to us', 'I like the teacher to let me find my mistakes', 'I like to study grammar'. Subjects were required to complete the questionnaire on four separate occasions. On each occasion they were required to respond to the questionnaire from four different perspectives:

A  When you learned English, which of the following ways of learning did you like?
B  When you learned English, which of the following ways of learning did you find most helpful?
C  If you were going to learn another language, which of the following ways of learning would you use?
D  Think of the learners you are currently teaching: how do you think they would respond to the questionnaire?

The top ten preferences for each of the categories of response are set out in the following table.

TABLE 9.1  *Top 10 learning strategy preferences of 44 'good' learners of English as a foreign language*

|  | A | B | C | D |
|---|---|---|---|---|
| 1 | Learning by games | Reading newspapers | Talking to L1 speakers | Learning by games |
| 2 | Learning by doing | Watching television | Pictures, films, video | Pictures, films, video |
| 3 | Watching television | Learning by doing | Learning by doing | Learning by doing |
| 4 | Going on excursions | Talking to friends | Talking to friends | Having a coursebook |
| 5 | Pictures, films, video | Practising out of class | Practising out of class | Small group work |
| 6 | Reading newspapers | Talking to L1 speakers | Watching television | Using cassettes |
| 7 | Small group work | Going on excursions | Small group work | Going on excursions |
| 8 | In class conversation | Small group work | In class conversation | Learning by hearing |
| 9 | Talking about interests | In class conversation | Having a coursebook | In class conversation |
| 10 | Talking to friends | Pictures, films, video | Learning by hearing | Talking about interests |

Spearman correlations were calculated for the four variables. The highest correlation was between variables B and C (found most useful/would use next time). The lowest correlation was between variables B and D (found most useful/my students would like).

During the investigation, subjects were asked to record what they found most helpful, and what they found least helpful in learning English as a foreign language. Here are some of their responses. While these were provided as free-form responses, I have classified them under several headings. Despite the different contexts and environments in which the learners learned, the responses are surprisingly homogeneous.

*What did you find most helpful in learning another language?*

1. *Form-focused activities*
   - Constant drilling.
   - When the teacher talked to the class clearly with correct pronunciation.
   - When I had my own textbook and made notes from teacher explanations.

2. *Applying skills to communicative language use outside class*
   - Contact with native speakers.
   - The following helped me most: reading all kinds of printed materials; listening to native speakers through media – radio, television, cinema; writing; studying grammar books; receiving instruction from my mother who was head of the English department in a public school.
   - In general: reading newspapers, magazines and books in English. Also, listening to the radio and television.
   - When I had someone to practise with outside the classroom, at home to foreigners (native speakers).
   - I listened to songs and sang songs myself and watched television, videos and movies; I read interesting novels, and read other media such as newspapers, magazines, advertisements, booklets, all for pleasure; visiting English-speaking countries where I could communicate with native speakers.
   - Practising through conversations and using the media, especially television with subtitles and newspapers. You must have someone who is proficient in the language to speak with in order to learn the language sufficiently well.
   - Social interactions (exposure and practice in the use of the language) at home and with friends.
   - Language taught inside the classroom is not sufficient to make a person a competent speaker in the real world. Children still make mistakes as they follow the structure of their language or make inferences from known languages. In some cases, students are good at talking or story-telling but not good at written language work. I wonder whether the topics for conversations they make could be starting points for syllabus development and the development of other language skills.
   - The language environment, the fact that my family knew and used English, and the radio and television programmes in English all helped.
   - The most useful things I found were practice with other students and exposure to the community using the language (i.e. the target community).

3. *Communicative language use in school*
   - There was a rule in our high school that the only language to be used was English.
   - Everyone spoke English during class and during outdoor activities (e.g. PE, gardening). I also read a lot of books from the library.
   - Reading and proper modelling helped me much in learning another language. Furthermore, whenever rules were given, these were followed by illustrations and realia. To top it all, the exposure to media – both printed and visual, contributed a lot to my learning of the second language.
   - Guidance from the teacher and interactional practice with other students.
   - In general, these helped most: literature (storybooks/story-telling sessions at an early age and self-access reading later on); when it is used as the medium of instruction in all subjects (unconscious [sic] learning); media.

4. *Affective factors*
   - Motivation. I find that motivation is vital to the success of learning a foreign language. I learned Japanese in the university because I had a very close friend who was a Japanese. I was also fascinated with the Japanese culture and people in general. So I found it such a thrill to learn the language and to be able to communicate with my Japanese friend in his own tongue. Although most of our conversations were in English, those times when we spoke in Japanese were helpful. Motivation and the opportunity to use the language are the two most helpful elements in my learning experience.
   - In general, liking the language was most helpful.
   - Strong interest, sheer determination and motivation to learn a second language.
   - I think it is necessary to integrate all four skills in teaching a language. Our basic senses – sight, smell, sound, touch and taste – should be stimulated too when we learn a language. This will make the learning experience a very personal one and we will not feel somewhat detached from the language. Most of the time it is reading ink marks from the book or worksheet – it is too 'cognitive'. I feel it's more exciting to touch something or taste something or see something besides ink marks and learn the language simultaneously. In that way, we can relate to the language in a more natural and ultimate way and we might remember new words/expressions better.

5. *Factors relating to the teacher/teaching*
   - Resourceful teachers who provide interesting ideas and useful background and explanations to, for example, a literature text.

*What did you find least helpful in learning another language?*

1. *Form-focused activities*
   - Reading from textbooks.
   - Grammar lessons during class.

- Enumerating rules of the language and memorising such rules did not help – it only resulted in parroting.
- Language notes from the teacher about grammar, lists of words, reading aloud, one by one around the class.
- Memorising verb patterns, words and conversations.
- Doing grammar exercises; boring and monotonous classwork/activities.

2. *Learning mode*
   - Learning by myself.

3. *Factors relating to the teacher/teaching*
   - I would say 'teacher's talk'. Looking back, I wish he had given me more opportunities to use the language in class, especially speaking it in and outside the classroom. It did help to have him explain everything to us, but it would have been more fun and meaningful had we been given the chance to use the language in more creative ways. Come to think of it, it would have been more fun and challenging if I was thrown into the deep end!
   - Negative criticism (oral) and punishment for wrong answers; dull teachers who do not encourage creativity or who are inactive/cannot be heard clearly.

The most striking thing about this study was the fact that, despite the diverse contexts and environments in which the subjects learned English, practically all agreed that formal classroom instruction was insufficient. Motivation, a preparedness to take risks, and the determination to apply their developing language skills outside the classroom characterised most of the responses from these 'good' language learners (see Beebe 1983 for an interesting study on risk-taking). The free-form responses reinforced the general pattern of responses provided by the questionnaire. Given these responses, I believe that it is premature to reject the notion that there is no correlation between certain learning strategy preferences and the 'good' language learner.

In a follow-up study, a group of advanced second language learners were asked to nominate the things which helped them most and least in learning English. Similar results to those from the foreign language subject were obtained. These are set out below, the items being rank ordered from most to least frequently nominated.

*Things that helped most*
1. Conversation with English speakers /in groups
2. Finding opportunities to practise outside class
3. Accessing media – radio, television, newspapers
4. Formal classes/learning with a teacher
5. Motivation
6. Reading
7. Grammar rules/drills
8. Listening
9. Pronunciation
10. Vocabulary

*Things that helped least*
1. Learning grammar/drills
2. Lack of opportunity to use English outside class
3. Poor teaching
4. Being criticised/punished
5. Practising with L2 speakers/poor L1 speakers
6. Classes too big/too many levels
7. Use L1 too much
8. Accessing media
9. Fear of making mistakes
10. Lack of motivation
11. Childish materials, e.g. picture books
12. Lack of audio-visual facilities
13. Rigid timetables and programmes
14. Reading aloud in classroom
15. Memorising
16. No time to study
17. Writing

Despite the range of responses, there was a large measure of agreement about what helped/did not help these subjects to master a second language. Conversation practice inside and outside the classroom, and opportunities for activating English outside class were by far the most frequently nominated things which facilitated development. Least helpful were grammar drills, these being nominated over twice as often as the next item, lack of opportunity to activate language use outside class.

Data such as these need to be interpreted carefully. For example, they do not mean that we should abandon the teaching of grammar. However, we may need to think again about how we go about teaching it: we need to be more explicit in showing learners how grammar instruction relates to the achievement of communicative objectives, and we need to incorporate into our teaching some of the strategies and techniques discussed in Chapter 8. Findings relating to the limitations of classroom work are more compelling. The data reinforce the desirability of encouraging learners to activate their L2 outside the classroom, and there are numerous ways that this can be achieved, from setting homework to encouraging learners to keep diaries and journals. The foreign language subjects who took part in the study I have just described had many different practical suggestions for practising outside the classroom, and nominated a wide range of activities including the following:

1. Buy a copy of an English language newspaper. Locate the classified advertisements. Find a car/bike/television/washing machine, etc. which would be suitable for you. Say why it is suitable.
2. Listen to an English language news and weather broadcast on the radio. Find out how many separate items there are. What is the forecast maximum temperature for tomorrow?

3. Go into a hotel where English is spoken. Find out the cost of rooms and the availability of facilities.
4. Go into an international airline office. Enquire about the economy/business/first class fares to various places.
5. Go to a bank and fill out an application for a credit card.
6. Visit foreign embassies and make enquiries from the educational, trade and cultural representatives.
7. Go to an American Express office and fill out an application for a card.
8. Look in the telephone book and find the name, address and telephone number of an English language school, the British Council, etc. Call and enquire about English classes.
9. Buy a newspaper and find the employment section. Find all the jobs you would like. How much do they pay? Are they full-time or part-time, permanent or casual?

Here are some additional suggestions from a second language context.

1. Look in your local paper for the restaurant guide. On Saturday evening you want to go with a friend to a restaurant. Your friend likes *seafood*. You want a restaurant with a *view*. It should not be too *expensive*. You want to pay with a credit card.

   Look in the Yellow Pages. Find two seafood restaurants, two licensed restaurants and two restaurants which are are open seven days a week.

2. (a) Get a map of the city from the tourist bureau. Find where you live. Find where you learn English. Trace the route from your home to school.
   (b) Look in a street directory. Use the index to find the page where you live. Now find the spot on the page where you live.
   (c) Write an invitation to a party at your place. Describe how to get there from the city centre.

3. Think about a place you would like to rent. *What suburb is it in? How many bedrooms has it got? Is it a house, or a semi or a unit or a townhouse? How much per week is it?* Buy a newspaper. Find in the 'Rent' section the classified advertisements. Find a place you would like to rent.

   Look in the Yellow Pages. Find some real estate agents. Call two or three agents. Ask: *'Have you got a house/townhouse/flat/semi in* [suburb] *to rent?'*

   If the answer is *'no'* → say *'thank you.'* Hang up.
   If the answer is *'yes'* → ask *'How many bedrooms?'*
                                   *'How much is the rent?'*
                                   *'Thank you.'*
                                   Hang up.
   Imagine you have $1,000,000 to spend. What house would you buy? Look in the newspaper and put a circle around the places you would like to see. Bring the newspaper to school and discuss it with the teacher and the other students.

4. Buy a television programme or find a programme in the newspaper. Put a circle around all the programmes you like.

   Watch tonight's television news or listen to the radio. How many news items were there? What were they about? (Tick the columns.)

| politics | people | sport | money | |
|----------|--------|-------|-------|---|
|          |        |       |       |   |

Give details of one of the news items.

5. Organise a class party. Make a list of all the things you need to buy. Write invitations to a friend, or some friends (e.g. someone in another class) to the party. Don't forget to include the following information:
   • the address
   • the date
   • the time of the party
   • the reason for the party

6. Look in the telephone book. Find the address and telephone number of a Medicare office near where you live. Find the name and telephone number of two private health insurance funds. Ring Medicare and the health insurance funds and ask:
   • What hours are you open on weekdays?
   • Are you open on Saturday?
   • Who is your local doctor?
   • What are the clinic's hours? (When is it open?)
   • What is the 'phone number of the surgery?
   • Who is your local dentist?
   • What are the surgery hours?
   Collect some empty medicine bottles and containers. Bring them along to class to discuss with your teacher.

7. Find the entertainment section of the newspaper. Find three things you would like to do and write them down. Tell a friend about these things.
      Look in the telephone book. Find the page which says: 'Dial it Services'. Find the number for 'What's on in Sydney [or your city]'. Dial the number. What's on? How many different items did you hear? Write down one thing you hear.

## 9.4  A learner-centred approach to language teaching

Work on learning strategies is part of a more general movement within educational theory and practice which takes a learner-centred view of pedagogy. A learner-centred approach is based on a belief that learners will bring to the learning situation different beliefs and attitudes about the nature of language and language learning and that these beliefs and attitudes need to be taken into consideration in the selection of content and learning experiences. (For a detailed analysis of the principles of a learner-centred approach to language teaching, see Nunan 1988b). The approach contrasts with the 'doctor-knows-best' approach which, while it might acknowledge that learners have different preferences and beliefs, discounts these on the grounds that the teacher is the expert and that the learners' views are irrelevant. However, if learners are to be in a position to make informed choices, they need to learn how to make such choices. Informed choice presupposes knowledge, and knowledge presupposes instruction.

Learners, particularly those at more advanced proficiency levels, can be encouraged to reflect on their attitudes, beliefs and preferences by completing attitude surveys and inventories such as the following. The results of such surveys can be used as the basis for subsequent classroom discussions.

Indicate your attitude to the following statements by rating them from 1 (totally disagree) to 5 (totally agree).

Disagree    Agree

*General*

1. Learner behaviour is not fixed, but changes in response to both internal and external pressures. People can and do learn throughout their entire lifetime.  1 2 3 4 5
2. Learners enter learning activities with an organised set of descriptions and feelings about themselves which influence their learning processes.  1 2 3 4 5
3. The past experience a learner brings to any learning activity is both a helpful resource for further learning and an unavoidable potential hinderance.  1 2 3 4 5
4. Part of the learner's past experience is organised and integrated into his self-concept and self-esteem.  1 2 3 4 5
5. When past experience can be applied directly to current experience, learning is facilitated.  1 2 3 4 5
6. Past experience becomes increasingly important as a person grows older  1 2 3 4 5
7. Leaners with a positive self-concept and high self-esteem are more responsive to learning and less threatened by learning environments and the process of change.  1 2 3 4 5
8. Adult learning tends to focus on the problems, concerns, tasks, and needs of the individual's current life situation.  1 2 3 4 5
9. Any group of learners will be heterogeneous in terms of learning and cognitive styles.  1 2 3 4 5

(Extracted from Brundage and MacKeracher 1980: 97–116)

*Language learning*

1. Adults have a right to be involved in curriculum decision making, e.g. selecting content, selecting learning activities and tasks.  1 2 3 4 5
2. Adults learn best if the content relates to their own experience and knowledge.  1 2 3 4 5
3. Adults have fixed ideas about language learning which need to be taken into account in developing language programs.  1 2 3 4 5
4. Adults who have developed skills in learning-how-to-learn are the most effective students.  1 2 3 4 5
5. Adults are less interested in learning for learning's sake than in learning in order to achieve immediate or not too far distant life goals.  1 2 3 4 5

6. Adults have different learning styles and strategies which need to be
   taken into consideration in developing learning programmes.          1 2 3 4 5
7. Adults who have developed skills in self-assessment and self-evaluation
   are the most effective learners.                                      1 2 3 4 5

In addition, all language classes, irrespective of their goals and the types of learner they are catering for, can incorporate elements of learner training. Some of the strategies and skills which can be encouraged are set out in the following list.

| | |
|---|---|
| Monitoring performance | Making errors work |
| Evaluating communication skills | Using formalised routines |
| Evaluating progress | Using linguistic knowledge |
| Evaluating learning tasks | Keeping an interaction going |
| Evaluating content | Developing conversational techniques |
| Evaluating learner groupings | Finding one's own best ways |
| Keeping the conversation going | Following instructions |
| Techniques for memorising | Using an index |
| Identifying patterns in language | Using a learner's dictionary |
| Applying skills in the real world | |

The following sample exercises from Nunan and Lockwood (1989) illustrate some of the tasks and exercises which can be given to learners to develop the sorts of learning skills indicated in the above list. They have been designed for post-beginner learners, and show that learner training need not (and indeed should not) be restricted to advanced learners.

1. How and where do you like learning? Number the following from 1 (best) to 7 (least).
   Learning at home by yourself.          _____
   Learning at home with a friend.        _____
   In class, listening to the teacher.    _____
   In class, working in pairs             _____
   In class, working in groups.           _____
   In class, working alone.               _____
   Working in the self-access centre.     _____
   Talk about you choices with your teacher and the other students.

2. What do you like/don't you like? Tick the box.

| Activity | Like | Don't like | Comments |
|---|---|---|---|
| Learning new words | | | |
| Learning grammar | | | |
| Listening to cassettes | | | |
| Speaking to other students | | | |
| Reading | | | |
| Writing | | | |

Compare your answers with a friend. Talk about them with the teacher.

3. Work in small groups and make a list of all the ways we can use television and radio to help us learn. Compare your list with another group. Talk about your ideas with the teacher.

4. Which activities were easy, and which were hard? Which would you like more/less of? Complete the grid by placing a tick in the relevant column.

| Activity | Easy | Hard | More | Less |
|---|---|---|---|---|
| 1. Tune in | | | | |
| 2. Listen | | | | |
| 3. Read, discuss and write | | | | |
| 4. Read and practise | | | | |
| 5. Language focus | | | | |
| 6. Pronunciation | | | | |
| 7. Role play | | | | |
| 8. Read, compare and write | | | | |
| 9. Out-of-class task | | | | |

Discuss your responses with the teacher and the other students.

5. Do these statements describe the way you learn? Circle the appropriate response.

| | | | |
|---|---|---|---|
| 1. It doesn't matter if I don't understand every word. | | yes | no |
| 2. I try and use new words as soon as I have learnt them. | | yes | no |
| 3. I plan what I am going to say before I speak. | | yes | no |
| 4. If someone doesn't understand me, I try and say it another way. | | yes | no |
| 5. I try to find out my own problems in learning English. | | yes | no |
| 6. My way of learning is different from the rest of the class. | | yes | no |
| 7. I always ask people to explain things I don't understand. | | yes | no |
| 8. Out of class I always try and practise my English. | | yes | no |
| 9. I try not to use my own language out of class. | | yes | no |
| 10. It doesn't bother me if I make mistakes. | | yes | no |

One of the advantages of systematically incorporating into one's teaching these learning-how-to-learn tasks is that learners become aware not only of their own preferred ways of learning, but also of the fact that there are choices, not only in what to learn but also in how to learn. They should encourage learners both to be more flexible in their approaches to learning, and to experiment with a range of learning experiences. I have found learners who are initially antipathetic to group work and other interactive tasks becoming both committed to, and enthusiastic about, such tasks as a result of experimentation and reflection.

## 9.5 Learning strategies in the classroom

In this section, I have included classroom extracts from two different lessons with a teacher who feels that developing skills in learning how to learn, and encouraging learners to activate their language outside the classroom are particularly important.

### Pre-reading task

1. Make a list of the ways in which you might encourage learners to activate their language outside the classroom.
2. As you read the extract, note the ways in which the teacher's beliefs are given practical expression at the level of classroom action.

### Extract 9.1: Developing independent learning skills

The students are sitting in small groups of two to four as the teacher addresses them.

T: Well, students, as you know, this morning
we're going to be looking at ways that we can
help learners improve their English – without a
teacher, without, um, a class to come to.
What've we got all around us that can help us?
Well, the first thing that we're going to be
looking at are these things. [She bends down
and picks up a plastic shopping bag.] Now in
the bag – I've got a bag full of mystery objects
in here – different things, but they all have one
thing in common. We can use them to help
improve our language. Now this is going to be
lucky dip type activity. Have you ever done a
lucky dip?

                               Ss: Yes, yes.

T: Yes. Where you put your hand in and you take
one thing out. I'll do it the first time. Put my
hand in and I'll just bring . . ... something out.
[She pulls out a mirror.] Oh, a mirror. Now
how can this help us improve our language –
you got any ideas? Irene?'

                        S: We can help, er, our voc . . . vocabulary.

T: Vocabulary's one thing, yes. How?

                        S: We can look, er, how we pronounce the words
                        [Mmm] We can look in the mirror and see how
                        our mouth moves.

T: Good. Yes, we can see how our mouth moves
– by looking at our reflection in the mirror. For
example, the sound 'th'. Can you all say 'th'?'

                        Ss: No.

[Laughter]

[The teacher distributes the rest of the objects in the bag and the students, working in groups, spend ten minutes discussing the ways in which the different objects they have chosen can be used for practising English outside the class. The teacher then calls the activity to a halt.]

T: Well, obviously lots of ideas've come out of
that. What I'd like to do is – let's just
summarise the sort of things you've been

·talking about by going round the groups. To
save time, we could just give two or three
strategies that you think somebody could use this
for. And think about not only the language they
can learn, but think *how* they can use them –
right? Well, shall we begin over here at Ziggy and
Maria and Kim's table? Kim, would you like to
begin? How can those help you?

>S: [Holds up the headphones.] This can help me
>to listen the tape and then we can . . . I can
>correct the . . . the pronunciation what I
>speak. And I can learn how to writing . . . and
>dictation from tape.

T: Right, the first point – the listening . . . say
. . . to . . . a, the pre-recorded cassette and
then you speaking and seeing – and then
replaying and matching. It's often good if you
can record your own voice too. . . . Teresa
and Boris? You had the bottle of champagne.

>S: Yes, we had champagne. And I think
>champagne can make, er, a little bit relax [yes]
>when I speak – so it will be good idea to drink a
>little bit champagne . . . [The rest of the class
>laughs.] . . . with some friends, or to invite
>some Australian people and to talk with them
>and drink champagne.

### Extract 9.2: *Learning outside the classroom*

The teacher has spent some time in a teacher-fronted discussion with the class, talking about a
friend of hers who is trying to learn English out of class. She has elicited suggestions from the
students about some of the ways her friend might learn. This provides a context for the next
stage of the lesson, in which students, working in small groups, will read short profiles of other
second language learners, and come up with advice on ways they might go about learning out
of class.

T: [Holding up several sheets of paper] Well, I've
written a few er profiles about other learners I
know. For example, there's Phung, here, who
has a television, but she really doesn't know
how to use that for helping her, right?
Underneath there Demetrios who travels one
hour each day to get to work, and he wants to
know how he can make use of that time.
Right? So, I've written down a little bit of
information about these people. I'm just going
to give you two different people, er, per table.
Read them as a group, and then I'd like you to

discuss and come up with a few other ways and
pieces of advice that would give to help
improve their English.

[The students are given two profiles each, and begin reading and discussing them in small groups. The teacher responds to a query from one of the students]

>S: I watch a film, and I listening to film, how can I do, when I . . . to learn more (more words) words from watching TV?

T: If you hear a new word, don't worry about the
spelling. Just write it down phonetically.

>S: Five new words?

T: Yes, it could be five . . .

>S: For one film?

T: We . . . it depends, er, what level you are. Um,
you could do more – I'm sure you're keen enough
to do more. . . . Well, say ten new words, ten
phrases. [The teacher returns to the front of the
classroom] Okay. Now, what did table one come
up with? How can you help Phung? What advice
would you give her? Maria?

Maria's group has been working with the following worksheet:

---

The following language learners need advice. Can you help them?

Phung has a television but she almost never watches it. Her friends tell her it can help to make her English better, but she does not know how to use it to learn. Should she just watch television? What kinds of programmes should she choose? What can she do while she is watching?

---

>S: We have a story about Ph. . . Phung. She has a television, but she never watch it and I think she's a wrong . . . because her friends tell her television can help her improve her English.

T: What programmes would you recommend?

>S: I think that if she doesn't understand, because it's possible she doesn't understand everything, she can find, have a choice, and she can find any programmes – maybe he has to start with easier programmes for children – cartoons or, doesn't matter what kind of programmes. And I think very useful is Channel SBS [the ethnic television channel] because we can read subtitle . . . and if we don't understand some words we can write and after we can check in dictionary [yes, good]. I think, watch television . . . it's very good and useful for our . . . improving.

T: Right and use a . . . have a piece of paper – jot
down words – don't worry about the spelling.
You can check that later. Good, yes. The
second table. Boris, would you . . . what
advice . . .

## *Post-reading task*

1. Which of these tasks is the more successful? Why?
2. The following quotation is taken from an interview with the teacher concerned. In
   what ways are her beliefs reflected in her teaching?

> As a teacher I see my role as being twofold. One is, yes, I am teaching the language, but
> I feel my other very important role is to assist the learners to take a growing
> responsibility for the management of their own learning. Within our programme,
> learners are with us for only a relatively – a short time, and we have to prepare them so
> that their learning can continue outside, erm, the length of their course. . . . This
> activity came about as a result of a group discussion we had, and in fact we completed a
> survey which showed that their time in the classroom counted for 25 per cent of the time
> they actually spent within an English speaking environment – and by that I mean
> whether they we going shopping or going to the market or picking up children from
> school – watching television. And so I think that really does show that a vast amount of
> their day is – has to be spent with them actively continuing their learning – um, separate
> from with a teacher and with the group. This activity is just a warm-up exercise into it –
> just so that they will promote discussion, and for me to see just where are they at, what
> are their sort of priorities, and how they learn. It's a group activity where they're
> looking at everyday objects that could be used as a stimulus for, um, language learning.'

This classroom extract, and the teacher's comment, illustrate one way in which a
lesson can embody a twin focus on both language and learning by using learning
strategies as the point of focus for the lesson. By setting up an task in which the
learners are required to give advice and opinons, the teacher also achieves her
linguistic aims.

## 9.6 Investigating learning strategy preferences

### Task 9.1
Willing (1989) suggests that all classroom tasks and activities will contain some
implied learning strategy. He provides the following examples:

| **Classroom activity** | **Learning strategy which is implied** |
| --- | --- |
| Read story: learners pay attention to and list names of main characters | Selective focusing of attention |
| Do a role play on a visit to the doctor | Practising in a meaningful context |

| Learners make a list of interactions they have been involved in (in English) over the past week. | Consciously monitoring own use of English |
| Learners do a cloze test | Using contextual clues to 'guess' meaning |

Make a list of five or six of your favourite classroom activities. Analyse these and write down the learning strategy which is implied by each. In other words, what mental steps do you see taking place as a result of the activity. What does this reveal about your beliefs on the nature of language learning? How might you get learners to be aware of the strategies underlying the activities they engage in?

## Task 9.2
Administer the following survey to a group of students.

1. Do you agree or disagree with the learning experiences of these students?

*Student A*
What helped me most to learn English? Let's see – reading all sorts of printed material, listening to native speakers on the radio, television and films, finding opportunities to use
English out of class.

strongly agree/agree/neutral/disagree/strongly disagree

*Student B*
The things that helped me least – well, I would say memorising grammar rules, reading aloud one by one around the class, doing boring grammar exercises.

strongly agree/agree/neutral/disagree/strongly disagree

*Student C*
Language taught inside the classroom is not sufficient to make a person a competent speaker in the real world. Children still make mistakes as they follow the structure of their language or make inferences from known language. In some cases students are good at talking or story telling, but not good at written work. I wonder whether the topics for conversations they make could be the starting points for syllabus development and the development of other language skills.

strongly agree/agree/neutral/disagree/strongly disagree

*Student D*
Practising through conversations and using the media, especially television with subtitles and newspapers. You must have someone who is proficient in the language to speak with in order to learn the language sufficiently well.

strongly agree/agree/neutral/disagree/strongly disagree

*Student E*
I find that motivation is vital in the success of learning a foreign language. Strong interest, sheer determination and motivation to learn a second language were the most important things for me.

strongly agree/agree/neutral/disagree/strongly disagree

*Student F*
I would say 'teacher talk' helped me least. Looking back, I wish he had given me more opportunities to use the language in class, especially speaking it inside and outside the classroom. It would have been more fun and challenging if I was thrown into the deep end!

strongly agree/agree/neutral/disagree/strongly disagree

*Student G*
The thing I liked least was negative oral criticism and punishment for wrong answers. Dull teachers who do not encourage creativity or who are inactive/cannot be heard clearly.

strongly agree/agree/neutral/disagree/strongly disagree

*Student H*
What helped me most was constant drilling, and when I had my own textbook and made notes from teacher explanations.

strongly agree/agree/neutral/disagree/strongly disagree

2. Write down three things that help you most and three things that help you least in learning English.

3. What do you think of yourself as a language learner?

4. *Problem.* I have a group of students who need to improve their conversation skills. I know from my work as a teacher and from the research I have done that the best way for them to improve is to take part in small group discussions, carrying out problem-solving tasks and so on. My problem is that the students do not like talking to each other in groups – they only want to work with me. What should I do?

Discuss the results of the questionnaire with the students. What do they reveal about their learning strategy preferences? What implications do they have for teaching these students?

**Task 9.3**
Develop a list of strategies which students can use to practise their English out of class. Get them to use the strategies over a number of weeks. Ask them to keep a diary of their language learning experiences. At the end of the period of time, review the diaries as a class exercise. To what extent did conscious attention to the activation of language use outside class help improve language skills or alter student attitudes?

**Task 9.4**
Review your programme/coursebook(s) and devise a series of exercises similar to the ones included in the preceding section for developing learning skills. Incorporate these into your teaching. To what extent do they enhance learners perception of their own learning preferences? Do they appear to make your students better learners?

## 9.7 Conclusion

Those involved in learner-centred curriculum development, and learner strategy research and teaching suggest that language programs should have twin goals, one set relating to the development of language skills and the other set relating to the development of learning skills and skills in learning how to learn. In this chapter we have looked at some recent learning strategy research and also at the effect that these suggestions have had on classroom practice.

Data are presented from recent investigations which show that in terms of specific learning strategies and techniques, no one set of strategies or techniques correlates with biographical variables such as ethnicity, education, or type of learning experience. At a more general level, however, there is evidence of agreement among 'good' language learners on what facilitates and impedes successful language development. In particular, developing skills in learning how to learn, and activating one's knowledge outside the classroom seem to be particularly important. I have illustrated and discussed practical ways of achieving these goals.

Like other aspects of methodology such as the teaching of grammar, or teaching the skills of listening, speaking, reading and writing, I have treated learning strategies separately for pedagogical convenience. However, when developing programmes, lessons and units of work, it is important that all of these elements be integrated and sequenced. There are many different ways of achieving this, several of which are described and exemplified in Nunan 1989a. Chapter 11 of this book also provides a detailed example of how various elements can be integrated into a single, coherent unit of work.

# Chapter Ten

## *Focus on the Teacher: Classroom Management and Teacher–Student Interaction*

### 10.1 Introduction

Classroom management and teacher–student interaction are integral to sound methodological practice, as we see in this chapter. In particular, I focus on the language which teachers use. Teacher talk is of crucial importance, not only for the organisation of the classroom but also for the processes of acquisition. It is important for the organisation and management of the classroom because it is through language that teachers either succeed or fail to implement their teaching plans. In terms of acquisition, teacher talk is important because it is probably the major source of comprehensible target language input the learner is likely to receive.

In the first part of the chapter, we look at theory and research into the amount and type of teacher talk, speech modification and its effect on comprehension, teacher questions, explanations and error correction. In succeeding sections, we see how this theory and research can inform and guide our understanding of classroom practices. Key questions addressed in the chapter include:

1. What does classroom research say about the amount and type of teacher talk?
2. Do some types of teacher speech modifications facilitate comprehension more than others?
3. How can teachers improve the effectiveness of their questioning techniques?
4. What types of question stimulate students to maximise their output?
5. How can teachers provide effective feedback to students on their behaviour and language?
6. What is the effect of digressions and extemporisations?

### 10.2 Amount and type of teacher talk

It is not surprising that in all sorts of classrooms, not only those devoted to the teaching and learning of languages, it is the teacher who does by far the most talking. However, teachers who obtain an objective record of their teaching by recording and reviewing their lessons are generally surprised by just how much talking they do. In an in-service programme in which teachers were asked to record and analyse one of their lessons, one of the most frequent comments made by teachers asked what surprised them most, was the amount of talking they did. (For an account of this programme, see Nunan 1990.) Of course, whether or not it is considered a good thing for teachers to spend 70 or 80 per cent of class time talking will depend on the objectives of a lesson and where it fits into the overall scheme of the course or programme. Normative statements sometimes appear that teacher talk is 'bad', and while it can be argued that excessive teacher talk is to be avoided, determining what is or is not 'excessive' will always be a matter of judgement. It can also be argued that in many foreign language classrooms, teacher talk is important in providing learners with the only substantial live target language input they are likely to receive.

When determining the appropriateness or otherwise of the quantity of teacher talk, then, we need to take into account a variety of factors including:

1. The point in the lesson in which the talking occurs.
2. What prompts the teacher talk: whether it is planned or spontaneous, and, if spontaneous, whether the ensuing digression is helpful or not.
3. The value of the talk as potentially useful input for acquisition.

Another issue of concern is code switching between the first and target language by the teacher and the effect of this on pupil talk. In many foreign language classrooms, it has been found that teachers and learners make far greater use of their mother tongue than they do of the target language. Zilm (1989), in an investigation of target language use in her German classes, discovered code-switching was affected by the following factors:

1. The nature of the activity.
2. The teacher's perceptions of how the students learn.
3. Teacher perceptions of the role and functions of the native and target language (for example, English was used exclusively for disciplining student).
4. Student perceptions of the role of the target and native language (students regarded German as the 'end' rather than the means to learning, and tended only to value its use in controlled situations such as set tasks and manipulative drills).
5. The use of English by the teacher.

The relationship between the teacher's use of the first or target language, and the pupils' use of the first or target language was an interesting finding. In a follow-up action research project, Zilm discovered that when she increased her use of German in class, her students' use of German, the target language, rose proportionally. (See also Strong's (1986) research on teachers' target language use in bilingual and submersion classes.)

In the literature, there are literally dozens of investigations of the speech modifications made by teachers. This research follows on from that which has investigated the speech modifications made by primary caregivers to children and by native speakers to non-native speakers (so called motherese and foreigner talk). Investigators have studied a wide range of speech phenomena, including modifications to phonology, lexis, syntax and discourse. In language classrooms, interest in the speech modifications made by teachers is motivated by the hypothesis that these modifications make language more comprehensible, and therefore, potentially more valuable for acquisition. In his extensive review of the literature, Chaudron summarises the research on teacher speech in language classrooms which shows that the following modifications occur:

1. Rates of speech appear to be slower.
2. Pauses, which may be evidence of the speaker planning more, are possibly more frequent and longer.
3. Pronunciation tends to be exaggerated and simplified.
4. Vocabulary use is more basic.
5. Degree of subordination is lower.
6. More declaratives and statements are used than questions.
7. Teachers may self-repeat more frequently.

(Chaudron 1988: 85)

While most studies of teacher speech modifications have taken place in classrooms where the modifications have not been deliberately made, nor manipulated experimentally, there are a number of experimental investigations into the effect of speech modifications on comprehension (and therefore, it is presumed, on acquisition). Some studies have looked at the effect of simplified input, in which the cognitive and linguistic load on the learner is reduced. Others have looked at the effect of elaboration. Elaborated input contains redundant information, the redundancy being achieved through repetition, paraphrase, slower speech and so on. These studies typically present one group of learners with an unmodified listening text and another group with a text which, although containing the same information, is modified in ways hypothesised to enhance comprehension. In their literature review, Parker and Chaudron (1987) conclude that the studies seem to indicate that, 'linguistic simplifications such as simpler syntax and simpler vocabulary do not have as significant an effect on L2 comprehension as elaborative modifications' (p. 6). However, as they point out, the studies tend to confound the different modificational categories. The fact that the criterion measure of comprehension is typically a cloze, multiple choice or true/false test also raises questions about the results of the studies. (In effect, the researchers are implicitly 'defining' comprehension as the ability to complete cloze, multiple choice and true/false questions.)

If future research confirms the value of elaboration over modification, it will strengthen the view that when talking to second language learners, teachers should try to use elaborated rather than simplified language. In other words, they should try to build in redundancy through the use of repetition, paraphrase and rhetorical markers rather than simplifying their grammar and vocabulary.

## 10.3 Teacher questions

Teacher questions have been the focus of research attention in both content classrooms (that is, classrooms devoted to teaching science, mathematics, geography, etc.) and language classrooms for many years (Gerot 1989). This is hardly surprising, given the importance of questions to pedagogy. (Questions are also relatively easy to observe, document and analyse which might also explain their attraction for some researchers.) Despite their importance, Good and Brophy, in commenting on the use of questions in content classrooms, conclude that:

> Unfortunately, in too many classrooms, discussions are parrot-like sessions, with teachers asking a question, receiving a student response, asking a question of a new student and so forth. Such 'discussions' typically are boring and accomplish little other than the assessment of students' factual knowledge. Such assessment is important, but if that is all that is done in discussion, students may come to perceive that the teacher is interested only in finding out who knows the answers. When this occurs, discussion becomes a fragmented ritual rather than a meaningful, enjoyable process. Furthermore, students often do not perceive a clear logical sequence to factual questions. Such questions seem more like an oral test than a lesson intended to teach content or to engage students in a meaningful discussion. (Good and Brophy 1987: 11)

Classroom research has also shown that certain types of questioning behaviour have persisted over many years. Borg *et al.* (1970) point out that factual questions to determine whether or not students know basic information are far more frequent than higher-order questions which encourage students to reflect on their knowledge, attitudes and beliefs, or which require them to follow through and justify a particular line of reasoning.

The following running sequence of teacher questions is extracted from a teacher–student exchange in which the teacher is trying to get the students to talk about an excursion they went on the previous week. It is worth noting that virtually all of the questions are 'closed' requiring little more than yes/no or single-word responses from the students.

Hello, Monica how are you?
Last Wednesday, you went to [name deleted], didn't you?
What did you do on Wednesday?
It was nice, was it?
Did you look at the animals?
What else?
Zdravko, did you go?
What animals did you see?
Was it good?
Can you draw it?
Is it small or big?
What did you do?

[I am grateful to Jill Burton who provided the transcript from which these questions were taken.]

In content classrooms, there has been considerable research on the length of time teachers wait after asking a question. This 'wait time' research is predicated on the belief that it is important for students to have sufficient time to think about questions after they have been asked before attempting to answer them. Rowe (1974, 1986) found that, on average, teachers waited less than a second before calling on a student to respond, and that only a further second was then allowed for the student to answer before the teachers intervened, either supplying the required response themselves, rephrasing the question, or calling on some other student to respond.

Even when given specific training, some teachers never managed to extend their wait time beyond one or two seconds. In those classrooms where teachers did manage to extend their wait time from three to five seconds after asking a question, there was more participation by more students. In particular, the following effects were observed:

1. There was an increase in the average length of student responses.
2. Unsolicited, but appropriate, student responses increased.
3. Failures to respond decreased.
4. There was an increase in speculative responses.
5. There was an increase in student-to-student comparisons of data.
6. Inferential statements increased.
7. Student-initiated questions increased.
8. Students generally made a greater variety of verbal contributions to the lesson.

The issue of wait time is obviously important in language classrooms, not only because of the greater processing time required to comprehend and interpret questions in a second or foreign language but also because of the findings by Rowe. If we believe that acquisition will be maximally facilitated when learners are pushed to the limits of their competence, then, on the evidence of Rowe, wait time should be increased.

The limited amount of research on wait time in language classrooms has yielded mixed results. Shrum and Tech (1985) investigated French and German high school classes and came to similar conclusions as Rowe, finding that wait time following questions was less than two seconds. Long and Crookes (1986) report a similar finding in an investigation of ESL teachers in Hawaii. Holley and King (1971) found that when teachers of German were trained to increase their wait time, the length and complexity of student responses increased.

The study by Long and Crookes found that increased wait time did not lead to greater mastery of content by ESL pupils, although this may have been due to the time scale of the study. If it had been conducted over a longer period of time, the researcher may have obtained a significant result. Unfortunately, Long and Crookes do not report whether increased wait time led to more participation or more complex language by students.

Another issue relevant to the management of learning concerns the distribution of questions. It is generally considered desirable to distribute questions among all students rather than restricting them to a select few. While some students who do not actively participate in lessons do well, the overwhelming evidence presented in this book is that, all other things being equal, students will improve more rapidly if they are actively engaged in interaction than if they are passive. In teacher-fronted interactions, by distributing response opportunities widely, all learners are kept alert and given an opportunity to respond (Good and Brophy 1987: 495). (There are, of course, some students, who might appear to be passive in that they are not responding overtly, but who are, in fact, mentally engaged in their lessons – Bailey, personal communication.)

While most teachers probably imagine that they are even-handed in their treatment of students, they might find, if they obtain an objective record of their teaching, that they favour certain students over others with our questions. Research shows that there is a great deal of variation in the chances afforded to different pupils to speak in class. Jackson and Lahaderne (1967), for example, found that some students were up to twenty-five times more likely to be called upon to speak than others. Furthermore, it is generally the more able students who get called upon. If we accept that one learns to speak by speaking, this means that those most in need of the opportunity to speak are probably given the least amount of classroom talking time.

One way of monitoring this aspect of our teaching is to audiotape or videotape our teaching over several lessons, or get a friend or colleague to observe us, and note down the number of questions we direct to each student. (Techniques for doing this, through the use of seating chart observation records, are set out in Nunan 1989b.) Researchers have also found that there is a tendency for teachers to restrict their questions to certain 'action zones' in the classroom (these are usually towards the front).

One final aspect of questioning behaviour worth looking at is the use of display and referential questions. Display questions are those to which we know the answer (for example, when we hold up a book and ask, 'Is this a book?') Referential questions, on the other hand, are those to which the asker does not know the answer. In classrooms of all kinds, display questions are far more common than referential questions. Outside the classroom, however, they are virtually never used – to begin asking display questions in social situations outside the classroom could lead to highly undesirable consequences.

Several investigations have been carried out into the use of display and referential questions in language classrooms. Long and Sato (1983) looked at forms and functions of teachers' questions. They found significant differences between the types of question that learners encountered in class and out of class: for example, teachers asked more display questions and fewer referential questions. Brock (1986) discovered that teachers could be trained to increase the number of referential questions they ask, and that this prompted students to provide significantly longer and syntactically more complex responses. Nunan (1987a) also found that the use of referential questions by the teacher resulted in more complex language by students. Student interaction was also more like natural discourse (that is, the discourse typical of out-of-class encounters).

The following features, which are characteristic of genuine communication, appear in the data: content-based topic nominations by learners; student–student interactions; an increase in the length and complexity of student turns; the negotiation of meaning by students and teacher, with a concomitant increase in the number of clarification requests and comprehension checks. There is even an instance of a student disagreeing with the teacher. (Nunan 1987a: 143)

Not all researchers agree that the distinction between display and referential questions is a useful one. Van Lier (1988), for example, argues that the distinction is irrelevant, as the function of teacher questions is to elicit learner language, and from this perspective whether or not teachers already know the answer to the question is unimportant.

Elicitation is another common feature of classroom teacher questions. Elicitation methods are designed to extract from students information which might otherwise have been provided by the teacher, and there were many examples in the database for this book of teachers extracting (sometimes painfully) information from students which could have been provided by the teacher in a few seconds.

## 10.4 Feedback on learner performance

Instructing students and providing feedback on performance are probably the two most commonly conceived classroom functions of teachers. In this section we look at some of the managerial and pedagogical aspects of feedback to learners.

Of the various ways in which feedback can be classified, one of the most frequent and simplest distinctions is between positive and negative feedback. For many years, behaviourist-inspired research has found that positive feedback is much more effective than negative feedback in changing pupil behaviour. Positive feedback has two principal functions: to let students know that they have performed correctly, and to increase motivation through praise. In his functional analysis of feedback, Brophy (1981) provides guidelines for effective praise (see Illustration 13).

ILLUSTRATION 13

## GUIDELINES FOR EFFECTIVE PRAISE

| Effective praise | Ineffective praise |
|---|---|
| 1. Is delivered contingently | 1. Is delivered randomly or unsystematically |
| 2. Specifies the particulars of the accomplishment | 2. Is restricted to global positive reactions |
| 3. Shows spontaneity, variety, and other signs of credibility; suggests clear attention to the student's accomplishment | 3. Shows a bland uniformity that suggests a conditioned response made with minimal attention |
| 4. Rewards attainment of specified performance criteria (which can include effort criteria, however) | 4. Rewards mere participation, without consideration of performance processes or outcomes |
| 5. Provides information to students about their competence or the value of their accomplishments | 5. Provides no information at all or gives students information about their status |
| 6. Orients students toward better appreciation of their own task-related behavior and thinking about problem solving | 6. Orients students toward comparing themselves with others and thinking about competing |
| 7. Uses student's own prior accomplishments as the context for describing present accomplishments | 7. Uses the accomplishments of peers as the context for describing student's present accomplishments |
| 8. Is given in recognition of noteworthy effort or success at difficult (for this student) tasks | 8. Is given without regard to the effort expended or the meaning of the accomplishment |
| 9. Attributes success to effort and ability, implying that similar success can be expected in the future. | 9. Attributes success to ability alone or to external factors such as luck or (easy) task difficulty |
| 10. Fosters endogenous attributions (students believe that they expend effort on the task because they enjoy the task and/or want to develop task-relevant skills) | 10. Fosters exogenous attributions (students believe that they expend effort on the task for external reasons—to please the teacher, win a competition or reward, etc.) |
| 11. Focuses students' attention on their own task-relevant behavior | 11. Focuses students' attention on the teacher as an external authority figure who is manipulating them |
| 12. Fosters appreciation of, and desirable attributions about, task-relevant behavior after the process is completed | 12. Intrudes into the ongoing process, distracting attention from task-relevant behavior |

Source: J. Brophy, 'Teacher praise: a functional analysis', *Review of Educational Research*, 51: 5–32 (1981). Reproduced by permission.

Much of the feedback provided by teachers often seems to be rather automatic, and its ultimate effect on the learners is doubtful. Consider the following feedback sequence taken from portion of a lesson.

| Good | All right | Okay | Clock? | Good | Good | Right | Okay | What? |
| Right | Very good | Very good | All right | The . . . ? | | Okay | Right | |

In the lesson from which this sequence was taken, the positive feedback consists of short interjections of 'good' 'okay' and 'all right'. Negative feedback consists exclusively of the teacher repeating the student's response with a rising intonation. All students, even low proficiency students such as the ones taking part in this lesson have no trouble recognising this as a phonologically marked cue indicating that an incorrect response has been given.

In the section on questions, I referred to research which indicated that more able students were much more likely to be given the opportunity to speak than less able students. The research on who gets positive and negative feedback is just as telling:

> When high-achieving students gave a right answer, they were praised 12 percent of the time. Low-achieving students were praised only 6 percent of the time following a right answer. Even though they gave fewer correct answers, low-achieving students received proportionately less praise. Similarly, low achievers were more likely to be criticized for wrong answers. They were criticized 18 percent of the time, and high achievers were criticised 6 percent of the time. Furthermore, teachers were twice as likely to stay with high-achieving students (repeat the question, provide a clue, ask a new question) when they made no response, said 'I don't know,' or answered incorrectly. (Good and Brophy 1987: 32)

It is important that we develop an awareness, not only of the ways in which we provide feedback to learners, but also that we monitor who gets the feedback. It is clear from research that teachers, in general, are not aware of the signals they transmit to individual students. This is particularly important in content classrooms containing both first and second language speakers. Investigations carried out in mixed classrooms indicate that teachers address the non-native speakers much less frequently, that interactions tend to be managerial rather than instructional, and that such learners receive more negative feedback than the native speakers. (For examples of this research, see Laosa 1979, cited in Chaudron 1988, and Schinke-Llano 1983.)

A rather idiosyncratic view of the role of feedback in foreign language teaching is taken by Gattegno who argues that praise and criticism as conventionally delivered breeds a dependency relationship between teacher and learners. In Gattegno's view, learners strive to provide appropriate responses to earn the approval of the teacher, and that this inhibits the development of their own internal criteria for judging the correctness or otherwise of their attempts at using the target language.

> In my approach, I do not correct learners; I only throw them back onto themselves to elaborate further their criteria and to use them more completely. Against a common teachers' demand for immediate correctness through so-called imitation, I take upon

myself the burden of controlling myself so as not to interfere. By doing so I give time to a student to make sense of 'mistakes' (which are precious indicators of the discrepancy between what is and what should be) and to develop exercises that foster progress. (Gattegno 1972: 31)

Whatever the merits or otherwise of this approach (and we look at Gattegno's Silent Way in greater detail in Chapter 12) it is extremely difficult *not* to provide corrective feedback in the classroom. In addition, there is compelling evidence that learners expect feedback. In a major investigation of the learning preferences of adult ESL learners, error correction by the teacher was one of the most highly valued and desired classroom activities (Willing 1988).

## 10.5   Classroom management in action

In the preceding sections we have looked at the role of teacher talk and teacher–student interaction in the management of learning. Research in this area shows that teachers need to pay attention to the amount and type of talking they do, and to evaluate its effectiveness in the light of their pedagogical objectives. Questions are also extremely important, and here we need to monitor the types of question we ask, particularly in terms of their potential to stimulate extended student responses. Another important consideration is wait time, that is, the thinking space we give to students between asking a question and demanding a response. Feedback and error correction are other important aspects of teacher talk, and here we need to monitor, not only how and when such feedback is provided, but also whether the feedback is positive or negative, and who receives the feedback. In the next section we see aspects of teacher talk in action. In this section we see how the ideas and insights set out in the preceding section have been realised at the level of classroom action.

### Pre-reading task

The first classroom extract has been presented in two sequences. While both sequences involve the same teacher, students and materials, the interactions which emerge are very different. As you read these accounts, consider what the differences are between the two interactional sequences focusing in particular on the teacher questions.

### Classroom extract 10.1: Teacher questions

**Sequence 1**
The teacher is working with a small group of students. She stands at the front of the classroom, while the students sit at desks. Most of the students are middle-aged and are from Southeast Asia. They are working with six pictures which show the following road accident. A milk van, swerving to avoid a dog which has run across the road, knocks a boy off his bicycle. A passer-by runs to a public telephone and calls an ambulance. Each student has a set of pictures which has been shuffled up so they are out of sequence.

T:  Can you put the pictures . . . number one,
    number two . . . ?
    [She demonstrates that she wants the students to put the pictures in the sequence in which
    they think the incidents occur. The students do this quickly.]
T:  Finished? Good, good, that was quick. Let me
    have a look.
    [One student looks at the sequence which has been arranged by the person on his left.]
                                    S:  No, this one, you know, hospital, this one first,
                                        telephone, hospital, car.
T:  This the same, same this? [sic] Look at picture
    number one.
                                    S:  Number one.
T:  Yes, can you see, Hing? Where are they?
    Where is this?
                                    Ss: Where are, where are, um, bicycle, bicycle.
T:  The man's on a bicycle, mmm.
                                    S:  And a man behind, behind a car. Bicycle
                                        behind a car. Behind a car.
T:  What's the name of this? What's the name?
    Not in Chinese.
                                    Ss: Van. Van.
T:  Van. What's in the back of the van?
                                    Ss: Milk, milk.
T:  Milk.
                                    Ss: Milk. Milk.
T:  A milk van.
                                    S:  Milk van.
T:  What's this man? . . . Driver.
                                    S:  Driver.
T:  The driver.
                                    S:  The driver.
T:  The milkman.
                                    S:  Millman.
T:  Milkman.
                                    Ss: Milkman.

## Sequence 2

The students and teacher are sitting in a circle. Having completed the activity, the teacher
turns to the students sitting next to her.

T:  Da Sheng, have you been in an accident?
                                    S:  [Pauses] No.
T:  No? Good! Lucky.
                                    S:  Lucky.
[The other students laugh. Several other students are questioned and then a middle-aged
Chinese woman speaks.]
                                    S:  My mother is by bicycle . . . By bicycle, yes,
                                        many, many water.

T:  She had an accident?

S:  In China, my mother is a teacher, my father is a teacher. Oh, she go finish by bicycle, er, go to . . .

S:  House?

S:  No house, go to . . . [pauses]

S:  School?

S:  No school. My mother . . .

T:  Mmm.

S:  Go to her mother.

T:  Oh, your grandmother.

S:  Grandmother. . . . On, yes, by bicycle. By bicycle, oh, is um, accident. [She gestures with her hand.]

T:  In water?

S:  In water, yeah.

T:  In a river?

S:  River, heah, river. . . . Oh, yes, um dead.

Ss:  Dead! Dear! Oh!

T:  Dead? Your mother?

[There is general consternation as the students repeat the story to each other.]

The basic difference between the two sequences is that the first is driven by a sequence of display questions whereas the second is initiated by questions from the teacher to which she does not know the answer. This, as can be seen, has a marked effect on the language produced by the students. In general, the length and complexity of the responses increases. In interactional and discourse terms there are also notable differences: students initiate interactions, nominate topics, disagee with the teacher, and generally use a greater range of language functions. Although such interactions driven by referential questions are extremely rare in the data, when they do occur, they generally stimulate much richer learner language.

The next extract is taken from a class of low proficiency students, many of whom are from Asian first language backgrounds. It illustrates what happens when the teacher digresses in the course of his lesson. Such extemporisations are quite common in the data, although their general utility is questionable.

### Pre-reading task

As you read the extract, think about what causes the teacher to digress. Consider also the net effect of the digression.

### Classroom extract 10.2: Extemporisation

The students, all Asian, and all low proficiency, are sitting in groups on the floor. Each has a set of pictures showing a man getting out of bed, having a shave, having breakfast, and performing a number of other tasks which typically occur between getting up in the morning and going to work. The teacher is describing each action in turn and the students have to find the picture associated with that particular action.

T:  Find the picture of Fred getting out of bed.

[The students rummage through their pictures. Several, who have obviously not understood what the teacher has said, wait until the better students have found the correct picture and then follow suit.]

T:  Put the picture down on your right.

Ss:  Light. Light.

[The teacher calls a halt to the activity. He claps his hands and stands on one leg, pointing down to it.]

T:  What's that? Left or right?

Ss:  Left, left.

T:  What's that?

Ss:  Right.

Ss:  Light.

T:  Not light, right.

Ss:  Right, right

T:  What's that?

Ss:  Left.

T:  What's that?

Ss:  Right.

T:  [Pointing to the light just above his head.]
What's that?

Ss:  Light.

T:  What's that?

Ss:  Light.

T:  All right, that's light. [He points to his right hand.] What's that?

Ss:  Left, left, right.

S:  Less.

T:  Right, right. [He points above his head.]
That's light.

Ss:  Light.

T:  That's right.

Ss:  Right.

T:  [Shakes his left hand.] That?

Ss:  Left.

T:  [Hops on his right leg.] That?

Ss:  Right.

T:  Okay. [The teacher sits on the floor next to the students.] So when I say to put it on the left, you . . .

Ss:  Left.

T:  . . . you [He picks up a card and demonstrates.] . . . put it down there. And on the right – put it down there.

### Post-reading task

What advice would you give this teacher about what to do when an error occurs in the course of a lesson?

One of the problems of error correction is that it generally happens spontaneously. In this extract, we see the teacher having to make an on-line decision about whether or not to correct the pronunciation error. As a participant observer in this lesson, it seemed doubtful to me whether such a digression was of much use to the students, several of whom were clearly mystified by the break in the routine of the lesson. It is also worth noting that the teacher chose not to further digress by correcting the student who mispronounced 'left' as 'less'.

It is something of a truism to say that classrooms are busy, complex places, and it is therefore not surprising that extemporised grammatical explanations and error corrections are not always as clear, consistent or appropriate as we would like them to be. These problem points in teaching can be reduced, if not minimised, by thinking through and deciding in advance which errors you intend to correct, when you intend to correct them (you may, for example, decide not to correct grammatical errors during communicative, meaning-focused tasks), and how you will correct them.

In analysing the lesson transcripts which formed the database for this book, I found that digressions in the form of anecdotes by the teacher were also quite common. In the following teacher-fronted exchange, the teacher digresses to tell an anecdote about something that happened at home. The point and purpose of the anecdote are not entirely clear to the students within the overall structure of the lesson, even though they most commonly occur during the opening phase of a lesson, or during a changeover point from one activity to another.

### Classroom extract 10.3: Digressions

The teacher has spent several minutes at the beginning of the lesson talking about what the students have done over the weekend. She then asks them about their trip to an animal and conservation reserve during the preceding week where they saw native Australian animals.

T: We have a possum at home . . .

　　　　　　　　　　　　S: Emu.

T: . . . at our house . . . roof, it goes in the roof.

　　　　　　　　　　　　S: Smells.

T: Yes, it smells. It makes a lot of noise. My husband got a trap – you know a trap? You want to catch . . . [She demonstrates the process of catching an animal with a trap.]

　　　　　　　　　　　　Ss: Ah! Yes, yes, yes. Oh!

T: He got a trap and he caught the possum . . . [She demonstrates again.] . . . in the trap and it was at night time – eleven o'clock at night

and he was very worried. Oh, poor possum,
poor possum, possum will be . . . Oh, oh, oh, I
must go now up to the hills. Let it free. So he
gets dressed to go up to the hills and pulls on
his boots and his gloves because the possum
may bite. He goes to the cage to pick it up. The
door is open . . . and the possum goes away.

S: Yes.

T: So, that was the possum. Ok, erm, so last
Wednesday, you went to [name deleted] to the
park and saw a lot of animals. What did you do
with [teacher's name deleted] on Thursday
and Friday?

### Post-reading task

What is the net effect of this digression? Do you think that digressions such as this
fulfil a useful function? If so, what?

Another feature of the data were the speech modifications made by teachers. These
are exemplified in extract 10.4 where the teacher modifies her speech, presumably to
facilitate comprehension. As with other features of their language, the teachers were
unaware of these modifications, and were greatly surprised when presented with the
transcripts.

### Pre-reading task

Make a note of the speech modifications as you encounter them. (Note, in particular,
the ungrammatical utterances.)

### Classroom extract 10.4: Teacher speech modifications

The teacher is talking to her students about road accidents and safety.

T: In Australia, er, bicycle, er, we wear a helmet.

S: Helmet.
Ss: Yes, yes.

T: Special helmet. [She gestures to show them
what she means.]

Ss: Ohh.
S: Malaysia, same, same.

T: Same in Malaysia?

Ss: Yes, yes.
S: Moto, moto.

T: In China, a little or a lot?

S: Motor. Some motor bicycle.

T: Motor bike.

S:  Yes, yes. Bicycle, no. China, bicycle no. Motor, yes.

T:  Ah huh!

S:  Cap, cap.

S:  Cap.

S:  Hat on, hat, hat.

T:  Hat. [It is not clear here whether she is confirming the utterance of the preceding speaker or correcting the student who said 'cap'.]

Ss:  Hat. Hat.

T:  Ah, in Australia, motor bike, yes. Yes, yes, yes. Bicycle, yes, good. [Oh!] Children, special helmet [Helmet], Helmet, mmm. Special helmet.

### Post-reading task

1.  What is the overall effect of the speech modifications?
2.  What advice would you give to this teacher about her teacher talk?

The final extract illustrates another commonly employed technique: the use of elicitation as a device for extracting information from the students which might otherwise have been provided by the teacher. While this can be an effective device for eliciting learner contributions, and getting students involved, it can be overdone.

### Classroom extract 10.5 Elicitation

The teacher and students are discussing a forthcoming classroom test, about which the students are seeking some additional clarification.

T:  The questions will be on different subjects, so, er, well, one will be about, er, well, some of the questions will be about politics and some of them will be about, er . . . what?

S:  History.

T:  History. Yes, politics and history and, um, and . . . ?

S:  Grammar.

T:  Grammar's good, yes . . . but the grammar questions were too easy.

Ss:  No. Yes, ha, like before. You can use . . . [Inaudible]

T:  Why? . . . The hardest grammar question I could think up – the hardest one, I wasn't even sure about the answer, and you got it.

S:  Yes.

T: Really! I'm going to have to go to a professor
   and ask him to make questions for this class.
   Grammar questions that Azzam can't answer.
   [The students all laugh at this.]

T: Anyway, that's, um, Thursday . . . yeah,
   Thursday. Ah, but today, er, we're going to do
   something different . . .

                                      S: . . . yes . . .

T: . . . today, er, we're going to do something
   where we, er, listen to a conversation – er, in
   fact, we're not going to listen to one
   conversation. How many conversations're we
   going to listen to?

                                      S: Three?

T: How do you know?

                                      S: Because, er, you will need, er, three tapes and
   three points.

T: Three?

                                      S: Points.

T: What?

                                      S: Power points. [power points = electrical
   sockets]

T: Power points. If I need three power points and
   three tape recorders, you correctly assume
   that I'm going to give you three conversations,
   and that's true. And all the conversations will
   be different, but they will all be on the
   same . . . ?

                                    Ss: Subject. Subject.

T: The same?

                                    Ss: Subject. Subject.

T: Right, they'll all be on the same subject.
   Different conversations, but the same subject.
   And so, I'm going to later in the lesson divide
   the class into three . . . ?

                                    S: Groups.

T: Right! And each group, each group . . . ?

                                    S: Listens.

T: Ah huh!

### Post-reading task

Do you feel the elicitation is overdone or not?

The extracts presented in this section illustrate some of the issues and outcomes revealed by research into teacher–learner interaction in both content classrooms and language classrooms. Many of the outcomes of content classroom research, such as findings on wait time, have particular pertinence for language classrooms, where language is both message and medium. These and other extracts presented in the book underline the importance of teachers being aware of the research, and of contesting the outcomes of such research in their own classrooms.

## 10.6 Investigating teacher talk

**Task 10.1**
Record your teaching over several lessons. (Alternatively, if you are not teaching, and cannot get access to a class, see whether you can obtain a recorded sample from someone else's classroom.) Select one lesson for analysis, and, if it is your own classroom, estimate the amount of time you talked as a percentage of the lesson as a whole. If you are analysing someone else's lesson, ask them to estimate how much of the lesson was spent in teacher talk. Now measure the amount of teacher talk there is and express this as a percentage of the total lesson.

How accurate was your (or your colleague's) estimate? Were you surprised by the amount of teacher talk?

**Task 10.2**
1. Using the recorded lesson from task 10.1, analyse the teacher talk.
2. At what stage in the lesson does the talk occur?
3. What prompts the teacher talk?
4. Is it planned, or spontaneous? (If spontaneous, is the digression helpful or not in terms of the lesson as a whole?)
5. Does the talk seem to be comprehensible to the students?

**Task 10.3**
1. Using the recorded lesson from task 10.1, or another lesson, investigate the issue of wait time. How long does the teacher wait after asking questions?
2. What percentage of questions does the teacher answer her/himself?
3. Make a list of the strategies adopted by the teacher when students fail to respond, or fail to provide the required response.

**Task 10.4**
1. Audiotape or videotape a lesson (alternatively, get a friend or colleague to sit in on a lesson and make a record of the distribution of questions in the lesson).
2. Does the record show that you favour certain students over others?
3. Are these the better students?
4. Do you favour male students over female students or vice versa?
5. Do you tend to direct your questions to one part of the room rather than another?
6. Do you think you should modify your practice as a result of your investigation?

**Task 10.5**

1. Record a lesson in which you provide no negative or positive feedback to the learners. What is the reaction of the learners?
2. Review the audio- or videotaped lesson. Did you, in fact, inadvertently provide feedback?
3. How difficult was it not to provide feedback?
4. Survey a group of learners and find out what they think about the issue of teacher feedback.

## 10.7 Conclusion

Teacher action and teacher–learner interaction are important aspects of classroom life, and there are many facets to structuring and managing learning. In this chapter I have focused in particular on teacher language, suggesting that this is central to effective classroom management and organisation. In the body of the chapter, we surveyed relevant research into the amount and type of teacher talk, teacher questions, feedback, instructions and explanations. I also presented a number of classroom interactions which serve to contextualise and exemplify research outcomes. As with other aspects of teaching, it is extremely valuable for us as teachers to monitor and experiment with different aspects of classroom management, and this can be achieved through small-scale research projects of the type set out in the final section of the chapter.

# Chapter Eleven

# *Materials Development*

## 11.1 Introduction

In this chapter we take up some of the issues surrounding the selection, adaptation and creation of teaching materials. While the focus of attention will be principally on the evaluation, adaptation and use of commercially produced materials, we shall also look at teacher-developed materials. As we shall see, materials, whether commercially developed or teacher-produced, are an important element within the curriculum, and are often the most tangible and visible aspect of it. While the syllabus defines the goals and objectives, the linguistic and experiential content, instructional materials can put flesh on the bones of these specifications. Richards and Rodgers (1986) suggest that instructional materials can provide detailed specifications of content, even in the absence of a syllabus. They give guidance to teachers on both the intensity of coverage and the amount of attention demanded by particular content or pedagogical tasks. They can help define the goals of the syllabus, and the roles of teachers and learners within the instructional process (Wright 1987). Some are designed to be used by inexperienced or poorly trained teachers, while others are intended to replace the teacher completely. In fact, the best materials, if used in the ways intended by their author, can be a useful professional development tool.

The chapter answers the following questions:

1. What are the criteria by which materials can be evaluated?
2. In what ways can one research materials in use?
3. What is the relationship between materials and methods?
4. What are some key principles for materials design?
5. How can different task and activity types be integrated into units of work?

## 11.2 Commercial materials

There is a certain amount of controversy associated with the use of commercial materials, particularly coursebooks. Swales (1980), for example, refers to the textbook 'problem' in *English for Specific Purposes*. One of the major concerns is that any given coursebook will be incapable of catering for the diversity of needs which exists in most language classrooms. The adoption of a particular coursebook or textbook series by a government ministry or educational authority is often fraught with controversy, and commercial publishers expend a great deal of time, effort and money in promoting and securing contracts for their materials. On the positive side, the best commercial materials fulfil an important teacher education function, and remove much of the burden and time involved in creating materials from scratch. The creation of materials can be particularly burdensome in foreign (as opposed to second) language contexts, where authentic source and stimulus material may not be readily available.

When selecting commercial materials it is important to match the materials with the goals and objectives of the programme, and to ensure that they are consistent with one's beliefs about the nature of language and learning, as well as with one's learners' attitudes, beliefs and preferences. Evaluating and selecting commercial materials is not an easy task. As Low (1989) points out, rather like the evaluation of hi-fi equipment, it remains something of a 'black art', even when supported by empirical investigations (see below). 'Designing appropriate materials is not a science; it is a strange mixture of imagination, insight and analytical reasoning, and this fact must be recognised when the materials are assessed' (Low 1989: 153). Nevertheless, the selection processes can be greatly facilitated by the use of systematic materials evaluation procedures which help ensure that materials are consistent with the needs and interests of the learners they are intended to serve, as well as being in harmony with institutional ideologies on the nature of language and learning.

Sheldon (1988) provides an extensive checklist of questions which can aid in the selection of commerical materials. He proposes that materials should be evaluated according to criteria such as their rationale, accessibility, layout and ease of use. A somewhat more accessible list of evaluative questions is provided by Breen and Candlin (1987). Their checklist invites the teacher to adopt a critical stance toward the materials' aims, appropriateness and utility. (These questions are reproduced in task 11.1 at the end of this chapter.)

Littlejohn and Windeatt (1989) propose a more modest scheme for assessing commercial materials. They suggest that materials can be evaluated from six different perspectives:

1. The general or subject knowledge contained in the materials.
2. Views on the nature and acquisition of knowledge.
3. Views on the nature of language learning.
4. Role relations implicit in materials.
5. Opportunities for the development of cognitive abilities.
6. The values and attitudes inherent in the materials.

Content areas covered in materials include the use of fictionalised characters and events, general interest (which often reflects the materials writer's guess about what might interest learners), academic subject matter, a focus on language itself, and literature. Littlejohn and Windeatt also add learning how to learn (see Chapter 9) and specific purpose content to the list.

In considering the views on the nature and acquisition of knowledge inherent in materials, Littlejohn and Windeatt make reference to work in general education by sociologists of knowledge such as Young (1971), who have pointed out that what gets included in materials largely defines what may count as 'legitimate' knowledge. The way materials are organised and presented, as well as the types of content and activities, will help to shape the learner's view of language. They provide examples of grammatical explanations which convey the simplistic and sometimes erroneous notion that the grammatical system consists of objective watertight rules, and that gaining 'knowledge' in language learning is basically a matter of accumulating objective facts. (Rutherford, 1987, provides an incisive critique of this 'accumulated entities' view of language learning.) Beliefs on the nature of learning can also be inferred from an examination of teaching materials. These will often relate to psychological and/or psycholinguistic theories of language learning or acquisition and may be explicitly spelled out in the introduction to the materials. (Some of the more prominent psychological models which have informed the development of approaches and methods in language teaching are discussed in the next chapter.) The importance of role relationships in the classroom is being increasingly recognised within the profession. A key variable here is the amount of initiative and control which learners are allowed to exercise and the extent to which they are active participants in the learning process. Wright (1987) provides the most comprehensive treatment available on roles of teachers, learners and materials in language class-rooms. (See also the discussion later in this chapter.)

In discussing the opportunities provided by materials for cognitive development, Littlejohn and Windeatt contrast the 'empty bucket' view of learning with its emphasis on the accumulation of linguistic knowledge with a more active approach in which learners are encouraged to negotiate and interpret meaning and engage in problem-solving activities which challenge them cognitively as well as linguistically. They suggest that if this latter view becomes more widely accepted, we shall see a re-orientation away from 'language learning as reproduction' to 'language learning as problem solving'. Beyond problem-solving, we have problem 'posing'. This more critical perspective is presented in Candlin (1984) and developed in Candlin (forth-coming).

The final area in which materials can be critiqued relates to the values and attitude which are inherent in them: it is possible to evaluate materials for their sexism, racism and so on. Littlejohn and Windeatt provide examples of textbooks which are biased in numerous subtle and not so subtle ways. For example, one book showed only two black people, one of whom was a muscular athlete, the other a manual worker. Another contained over thirty references to smoking and drinking in the first twenty-five pages, perhaps thereby 'legitimising and sanctioning such behaviour'.

Littlejohn and Windeatt conclude their survey of perspectives on materials design by posing the following evaluative questions:

1.  Do the materials extend the learner's 'general' or 'specialist' knowledge?
2.  What view of knowledge do the materials present? What implications might this have for how learners attempt to learn?
3.  Do the materials develop the learner's understanding of what is involved in language learning and how they may help themselves?
4.  How do the materials structure the teacher–learner relationship? What 'frame' if any is placed on classroom interaction?
5.  Do the materials develop the learners' general cognitive abilities? Is language learning presented as reproduction or as problem solving?
6.  What social attitudes do the materials present?

(Littlejohn and Windeatt 1989: 174)

The discussion in this section underlines the deeply ideological nature of language learning and teaching as reflected in the materials which provide the springboard for pedagogical action. Materials only take on value in context, and the social and cultural context in which they will be used must underpin their evaluation and selection. It could be claimed that the values implicit in the assertions made in this section reflect western, and even Anglo-Saxon views of language and learning which may not be appropriate in other contexts. This is something which only those with detailed knowledge of particular contexts can answer. However, there needs to be some caution in rushing to judgement on new ways of learning. Learners have an infinite capacity to surprise, and there is a danger that the claim of cultural in-appropriacy may be used as an excuse for refraining from action. It may also block classroom initiatives which the learners themselves might welcome. In the final analysis, we can only judge the efficacy of materials by evaluating them in contexts of use, and it is to this particular issue that we now turn.

## 11.3 Research on materials in use

A major theme of this book is the need to relate theory, research and methods to classroom action. This is also important in the case of materials. While the checklists provided by Sheldon, Littlejohn and Windeatt are extremely valuable, they only enable us to evaluate materials in a preliminary way. Most of the questions on such things as rationale, availability, layout and appropriacy relate to issues which are external to the classroom. Any comprehensive evaluation also needs to collect data on the actual use of materials in the classroom, and while we can exercise profes-sional judgement in answering questions such as, 'does the introduction, practice, and recycling of new linguistic items seem to be shallow/steep enough for your students?', ultimately, such questions can only be settled with reference to their actual use.

There are, in fact, comparatively few empirical investigations of materials develop-ment and use in the classroom. One study, reported in Nunan (1988b), investigated the possible differences between inexperienced and experienced teachers in realising teaching resources in the classroom. Twenty-six teachers, who were differentiated according to their years of experience, were given an authentic listening text and an accompanying set of worksheets, and asked to prepare and teach a unit of work based on the materials. They were asked to provide detailed information on the following:

1.  The aims of the unit.
2.  The length of time it took to teach the unit (including the time allocated to different learner configurations: teacher-fronted, small groups, pair and in-dividualised work).
3.  An indication of how the unit was introduced.
4.  A description of the steps in the lesson.
5.  A description of any changes that were made to the unit.
6.  An evaluation of student reaction to the material.
7.  An indication of intention to use similar materials in future.
8.  An indication of the best liked feature of the material.
9.  An indication of the least liked features.
10. An estimation of the suitability of the materials for the designated learner group.

A great deal of data were generated by the study, and it is beyond the scope of this chapter to report on all of these. Some of the major outcomes are worth noting, however. Eleven different aims were nominated by the teachers, as follows:

1.  Listening for gist.
2.  Vocabulary development.
3.  Identifying key words.
4.  Listening for specific information.
5.  Revision of previous language points.
6.  Developing fluency.
7.  Encouraging prediction.
8.  Promoting discussion.
9.  Developing functional skills.
10. Introducing theme 'shopping'.
11. Developing listening skills.

Despite some minor variations, there was nothing in the data to suggest that the more experienced teachers selected aims that were qualitatively different from those selected by the less experienced teachers. The major difference between the experienced and inexperienced teachers was in the amount of time taken to teach the materials, the number of steps in the unit of work, and the learner configurations. Average unit length of the most experienced group of teachers (more than eight years' experience) was 164 minutes, compared with 98 minutes for the least experienced group (less than four years' experience). However, in terms of learner configuration, the less experienced teachers had a more equitable balance between teacher-fronted, small group, pair-work and individual work. The two most experienced groups of teachers spent 64 and 70 per cent of their time on teacher-fronted activities, while the less experienced groups spent 41.2 and 42.7 per cent of their time on such activities. My original interpretation of these data was that the more experienced teachers felt that the materials, given their innovative nature, 'needed more teacher mediation, explanation and support'. Crawford (1989), however, suggests that the data could equally well indicate a more balanced treatment by less experienced teachers reflecting their more recent teacher education experiences which might, for example, have sensitised them to the importance of group and pair-work. In overall terms, however, it seemed that no significant differences between the more and less experienced teachers emerged. In the study, it was concluded that in terms of materials development and exploitation, experience needs to be coupled with other aspects of professional development: '"Classroom experience is more than duration (endurance!); it is variety and intensity. Professional development programmes are about structuring and evaluating that experience" (Burton, personal communication). In addition to experience, teachers need the time, opportunity and support to reflect on that experience through a variety of professional development activities which should include professional development programmes, collegiate consultations and action research projects' (Nunan 1988b: 115).

## 11.4  Materials and methods

In Chapter 12 we look in detail at some of the more prominent methods which have made their appearance over the past forty years or so. Without wishing to pre-empt the issues covered there, it is worth considering the important role that materials have played in different language teaching methods. In their book on different approaches and methods in language teaching, Richards and Rodgers (1986) have pointed out that different methods imply very different roles for, and role relationships between teacher and learners. The same also holds for materials. For example:

> The role of instructional materials within a functional/communicative methodology might be specified in the following terms:
> 1. Materials will focus on the communicative abilities of interpretation, expression, and negotiation.
> 2. Materials will focus on understandable, relevant, and interesting exchanges of information, rather than on the presentation of grammatical form.
> 3. Materials will involve different kinds of texts and different kinds of media, which the learners can use to develop their competence through a variety of different activities and tasks.
> (Richards and Rodgers 1986: 25)

In his article on materials, Rossner (1988) focuses in particular on the role of materials in communicative language teaching. He argues that while classroom practice has continued its 'circumspect and patchy evolution', there has been a significant change in materials, particularly in the range of materials available and in the attitude of materials writers to issues of selection and grading. In Rossner's view, teachers look to materials to provide new information on how language works at a formal level, to provide focused practice in manipulating language forms and in practising sub-skills, to provide 'comprehensible input' (we look in some detail at the nature and function of 'comprehensible input' in Chapter 12), grammatical and communicative 'consciousness-raising' on the part of learners, to provide opportunities for simulating and rehearsing communicative situations to be encountered outside the language classroom, for testing and self-assessment, and for increasing motivation and interest in learning. Of these, Rossner considers the provision of comprehensible input, consciousness-raising and rehearsal the roles which have been particularly enhanced by communicative language teaching.

The work of writers such as Richards and Rodgers (1986) and Rossner (1988) (who are authors of major coursebook series) illustrates the theory-laden nature of all aspects of language teaching, even the so-called practical business of writing materials. Despite the need for pragmatism, the decisions made by coursebook writers are inevitably influenced by theoretical statements and research outcomes in applied linguistics. They will also be influenced by other factors, not the least of which is the rather conservative outlook and unwillingness of commercial publishers to take risks, a conservatism which reflects the dangers and expense associated with producing commercial materials.

Despite the dramatic improvements in foreign language materials with the advent of communicative language teaching, Rossner (1988) articulates a number of worries. In the first place, current materials tend to overburden the user with an embarrassment of riches. (Breen and Candlin, 1987, have also pointed to the abundance of data at the expense of process in commercial materials.) This creates more work for the teacher, who is forced to spend more time coming to grips with the materials, and creates the possibility that language lessons may become a fragmented 'cabaret' of unintegrated activities. Secondly, few materials provide opportunities for genuine communication with a 'real' purpose. (Given the fact that these are related to learners' needs, Rossner asks whether published materials can ever provide such activities.) Thirdly, in Rossner's view, British and American publishers have too much power, and project cultural attitudes which are inappropriate to the needs of the vast majority of learners of English as a foreign language.

## 11.5 Materials design

In the preceding section, one of the problems raised by Rossner relates to the potential for fragmentation of materials developed since the advent of communicative language teaching. The problems of grading, sequencing and integration, so crucial to the development of coherent language programs, are the constant pre-occupation of syllabus designers and materials developers. Materials design exists at the interface of syllabus design and methodology, and issues associated with sequencing illustrate the difficulty of separating syllabus design from methodology.

(Nunan 1988a). Fragmentation is evident in many recently published coursebooks, particularly those aimed at low proficiency learners. Consider, for example, the following sequence of activities:

Read a short passage and dialogue based on the passage.

Answer comprehension questions about the passage.

Repeat the dialogue based on the passage.

Work with a partner. Ask questions about the passage and complete a form based on the content of the passage.

Study a diagram related to the passage and describe it.

Look at a map related to the passage and answer a series of comprehension questions.

Unless the lesson based on such a sequence of activities is carefully structured and sequenced, the learners are likely to perceive the lesson as confusing, unprincipled and piecemeal; although, of course, this very much depends on the skill of the teacher in linking together the various activities in the lesson.

Several solutions have been sought to problems of integration, among them, the topic solution, the text solution and the storyline solution. The topic solution is probably the most common. Units of work are organised around topics which provide internal coherence to the units of work (although the problem of the external coherence between units remains). Topics can reflect the needs of the learners, general interest, other content areas such as science, geography, etc. Having selected a topic, the materials writer collects or creates texts and tasks around the topic. (Legutke and Thomas, 1991, address this and other issues in their book on process and experience in language learning.) The following list of topics are taken from a coursebook for newly arrived immigrants and short-term visitors, and the perceived needs of the learners are reflected in the topics

| Unit 1 | First contact | Unit 9 | Sightseeing |
|--------|---------------|--------|-------------|
| Unit 2 | Getting about | Unit 10 | News and weather |
| Unit 3 | Entertainment | Unit 11 | Jobs |
| Unit 4 | Meeting people | Unit 12 | Communications |
| Unit 5 | Money | Unit 13 | Eating out |
| Unit 6 | Housing | Unit 14 | Education |
| Unit 7 | Health | Unit 15 | Holidays |
| Unit 8 | Transport | | |

These contrast with the topics in a foreign language course such as that by Swan and Walter (1985) which includes the natural world, wildlife, advertising, crime and prisons, travel and exploration, music, love and marriage, national culture.

An alternative, although related approach is to begin, not with a topic, but a type of text. This is an approach advocated by proponents of genre-based teaching. Units of work are organised around 'narratives', 'descriptions', 'expositions', etc., and learners are taught the generic structure of these text types, as well as the way the texts are realised linguistically. One of the great advantages of beginning with authentic written or spoken texts is that classroom work is referenced against the type of language which learners will encounter outside the classroom. Cathcart (1989) argues that classroom language models must be based on authentic native speaker/native speaker discourse. She provides empirical evidence to show that 'simulated excerpts may serve to mislead students about the nature of everyday inter-actions' (Cathcart 1989: 105) (For an extended discussion on the use of authentic data in communicative language teaching, see Nunan 1989a.)

In reality, the teacher and textbook writer will probably juggle topic, text and task elements in creating materials, beginning, perhaps with a topic such as 'finding accommodation', collecting aural and written texts relating to the topic, and then creating activities which reflect the communicative needs of the learners in relation to the topic. This procedure is one which can be readily adopted/adapted by teachers with access to authentic sources of data. As an example of the procedure, consider the development of the following unit of work from a set of draft materials based on topic, text and task.

**Step 1:** Select topic – Finding accommodation

**Step 2:** Collect data
Recorded conversation between estate agent and client
Newspaper advertisements
Pictures/illustrations of different types of housing
Reading passage from real estate institute brochure

**Step 3:** Determine what learners will need to do in relation to the texts
For example:
Read newspaper 'To Let' advertisements
Make enquiries about homes to let
Talk about housing and furniture
Get basic information from newspaper articles

**Step 4:** Create pedagogical activities/procedures
For example:
Listening for gist
Role play
Information gap

**Step 5:** Analyse texts and activities to determine the language elements
For example:
Cohesion: I'm ringing about a semi. Is it still available?
Adjectives: big, close, cheap, small, new, expensive
Present continuous: I'm looking for a flat
Wh- questions: who, what, where, how much/many
Existential 'there': There is/are

**Step 6:** Create activities focusing on language elements
For example:
Cloze passage
Sentence sequencing exercise
Match question and answer exercise

**Step 7:**  Create activities focusing on learning skills/strategies
For example:
> Think about the tasks in this unit and in small groups decide which were useful/not useful.
> Discuss your answers with the rest of the class.

**Step 8:**  Create application tasks
For example:
> Think about a place you would like to rent.
> What area is it in? How many bedrooms has it got? Is it a house, or flat, or a condominium? How much per week is it?
> Buy a newspaper. Find the classified advertisements.
> Find the 'To Let' section. Find a place you would like to rent.

(Adapted from Nunan and Lockwood 1989)

Low (1989) outlines a number of procedures for developing units of work. He suggests that the tradtional four-phase unit structure, which was reflected in materials design, is as follows:

1.  Presentation: (a) of language to be learned.
                   (b) of language description.
2.  Controlled exploitation.
3.  Free exploitation (generalising to areas other than those in the presentation).
4.  Synthesis (pulling disparate strands together and sometimes creating an 'end-product').

Materials incorporating this four-stage procedure typically took a reading or listening text as their point of departure. Initial exploitation exercises included comprehension questions, repetition and grammatical drills. The rigidity inherent in this approach, along with shortcomings in the psychological model on which it was based (see the discussion on behaviourism in the next chapter) led to a search for alternatives. Among the options discussed by Low are 'feeding and bleeding solutions', 'the writing last solution' and the 'storyline solution'.

Feeding and bleeding solutions focus on the relationship between presentation materials, or input texts, and the exercises which accompany them. A 'feeding' relationship exists when succeeding tasks can only be completed if those which precede it have been successfully carried out. Bleeding relationships occur when the initial task takes away from the value of the second, for example, when the solution to a problem is provided before the problem itself. An example of the feeding solution is given in Illustration 14.

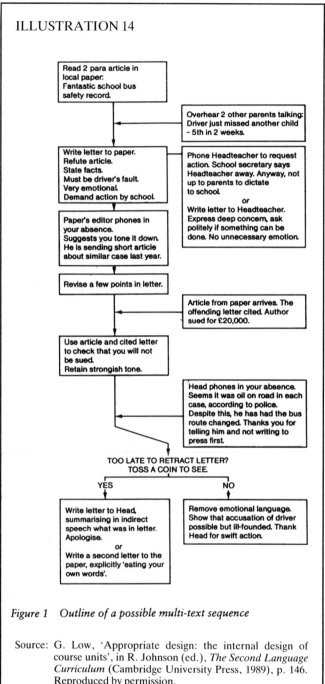

*Figure 1    Outline of a possible multi-text sequence*

Source: G. Low, 'Appropriate design: the internal design of course units', in R. Johnson (ed.), *The Second Language Curriculum* (Cambridge University Press, 1989), p. 146. Reproduced by permission.

The writing last solution, as the name implies, is one in which a writing task occurs at the conclusion of the unit of work and serves to integrate the work that has gone before. Although not devoted exclusively to writing, the application task in the eight-stage procedure from Nunan and Lockwood (1989) discussed above is intended to fulfil this function.

The storyline solution, in which a narrative serial is presented one episode at a time, has been popular in commerical coursebooks over many years. Graves and Rein (1988) present a mystery entitiled 'Moon of India', about a famous necklace which disappears from a New York City museum. Problems confronting authors incorporating stories into their materials include the difficulty of presenting subtle or sophisticated content at low proficiency levels and the frequent negative reaction from adult learners to detective stories. Corbel attempts to overcome these problems with his variation to the storyline solution which he calls the 'action sequence' approach. In this approach, the storyline and attendant exercises make up the whole of the course. Materials are designed through a four-stage procedure:

1. Identify the learners' areas of interest in broad thematic terms.
2. Identify a series of communication situations related to that theme and link them to form an action sequence.
3. Select or devise materials appropriate to the situations in the action sequence.
4. Choose language points to focus on from the materials.

(Corbel 1985: 74)

## 11.6 Materials adaptation

Most commercially produced materials can be adapted to fit a range of needs and goals not originally envisaged by the materials writiers. However, before adapting materials, it should be kept in mind that materials from reputable authors and publishers have been carefully written and extensively trialled, and it is therefore advisable to teach such materials at least once in the ways suggested by the author before experimenting and adapting them.

In this section, I illustrate the way in which a teacher adapted a unit from a set of commerical materials to suit her own purposes. The unit on which the lesson was based contained a tape consisting of two parts. Part A was a description of five people, Keith, Sue, John, Alexandra and Jane. Part B consisted of an authentic interview with each of these people. The students' book contained photographs of each of the five individuals, along with a blank information table.

The original materials required the students to listen to the descriptions and interviews, extract key information about the people and use this information to complete a grid. However, the teacher who used this material wanted to give the lesson an interactive dimension in which the students worked together, negotiating with each other, in order to complete the task.

## *Pre-reading task*

Before reading the extract, consider ways in which you might modify the materials to provide an interactive dimension.

## *Classroom extract 11.1 Using commercial materials in the classroom*

The lesson evolved through five tasks.

**Task 1:  Warmer**
The teacher revises vocabulary, and the questions one asks to extract personal information.

T:  Height – yep. Height. Height. And, weight.
     What about, not so much weight, but . . .
     What do you call this? [Slim] What's the word
     for this, when you describe somebody if
     they're slim or fat or thin? This begins with 'B'
     . . . If they're strong or thin.
                                    S:  Body?
T:  Body? No. [Laughter] Good guess. What
     about build? Build? Build. Somebody's build.
     If you talk about somebody's build. You
     describe if they're slim, or thin or maybe fat or
     maybe strong. Like a building. [Oh] Like a
     building. Build. Like a building. A house
     somebody's built. Anything else? Hair.
     Height. What about this? [Gestures to
     clothing]
                                    S:  Clothes.
T:  Clothes. Clothes. What's the question?
     [inaud.] Not colour. What's the question for
     clothes, you ask – the question – for clothes?
     What . . .. The question. Come on, we did this
     last week. Can you remember? The question?
                           S:  What clothes do you like?
                           S:  What kind of a clothes do you like?
T:  Not like.
                                    S:  Wear.
T:  Wear, yeah. What's the question? Wear.

**Task 2:  Talking about the photographs**
The teacher gets the students to study the photographs and say as much as they can about the people in them.

T:  Okay, just looking at the pictures, just looking
     at the pictures – what can you tell about these
     people? Obviously you don't know their
     name, do you? You don't know their name.

Maybe you can guess . . . how old they are,
guess their age, or their . . . if they're married,
. . . children. Have a think about these
people. In twos – two, two, two two two.
Maybe you can talk together about what you
think about them – what these people're like.
From the photos. Do you think they're
married? How old are they?
[The students talk together and the teacher circulates, asking and responding to questions.]

### Task 3:  Listening for key information
The teacher gives out and explains the following grid.

| Name | Keith | Sue | John | Alexandra | Jane |
|------|-------|-----|------|-----------|------|
| Age | | | | | |
| Married? | | | | | |
| Children? | | | | | |
| Ages? | | | | | |
| Job | | | | | |
| Height | | | | | |
| Hair | | | | | |
| Build | | | | | |
| Clothes | | | | | |
| Hours worked | | | | | |
| Interests | | | | | |
| Books read | | | | | |
| Smokes | | | | | |
| Drinks | | | | | |
| Church | | | | | |

T:  What we're going to do is listen to some
information about these people. And I want
you to decide which photograph matches
which information. Let's have a look at the
side here. Let's see, it says 'age', 'married' it's
a question mark whether we're single, married
or single. Children. Maybe they've got
children, maybe they haven't. Yes or no. Job.
Height. Hair. Build. And clothes. What's the
question again, with clothes.

Ss:  What are . . . What are you wearing?

T:  What're you wearing, what's he wearing or she
wearing?
[The students then listen to descriptions of the people and work in pairs to complete the grid.]

### Task 4:  Sequencing the conversation
The final two tasks in the lesson use the authentic interviews as their input data. Given the
length and difficulty of the language, the teacher decides to provide the learners with a staged

introduction to the tape. She also wants to encourage the learners to co-operate and to interact with each other in the course of completing the listening tasks. She achieves these objectives by letting the students see the first interview. The students are put into groups of three and provided with a photocopy of the tapescript which is cut into chunks. The students are required to sequence the conversation. They are then given the opportunity to listen to the tape and to check that their sequence was correct.

T: I'll give you five minutes to do this, five
   minutes.
[The students work in their groups for several minutes.]
T: Two minutes.
T: Come on, this group's nearly finished. One
   minute. One minute left.
T: Okay, we'll listen to the conversation now.
   Okay, so as you're listening to the
   conversation, can you check your sequence?
[The students listen to the interview and check that their strips of paper are correctly sequenced.]

### Task 5: Split listening
For the final part of the lesson, the class is divided into two groups, and each group is given its own recorder and tape. Group A listens to interviews with Keith and Sue. Group B listens to interviews with John and Jane. The students completed their part of the grid, group B returns, and students from group B form pairs with students from group A.
T: Okay, before we start, I want you to ask the
   proper questions. So please don't just look and
   copy. What you have to do is okay, Keith. First
   question. What's the first question? What . . .
   [hours] hours does he work? Interests. What's
   the question?
                                  S: What are his interests.
T: What . . .
                                  Ss: . . . . are
T: . . . his interests. Again.
                                  Ss: What are his interests?
T: What are his interests. Next question. What's
   the question? What . . . ?
                                  S: What kind of books . . .
T: What kind of books – does he read? – Smokes?
                                  Ss: Do you smoke?
T: Keith. Does he smoke
                                  Ss: Does he smoke?
[The paired students sit back-to-back and ask and answer questions to complete their grids. To complete the lesson, the teacher gets students to match the photos and the names.]

In this extract, we see a teacher modifying a set of commercial materials to suit her pedagogical ends. While she liked the authentic nature of the tape, she wanted her students to be active rather than passive listeners. Therefore, she modified the materials, creating information gaps which required the learners to work collaboratively in order to complete the tasks successfully. Of course, there are many situations and pedagogical contexts in which one would want to use the materials in the ways intended by the authors. However, I have included this classroom extract to illustrate the fact that one need not be tied to the procedures recommended in a teacher's book. Modifications should be made with reference to one's pedagogical goals, and only after one has become thoroughly familiar with the materials themselves.

## 11.7 Investigating materials

**Task 11.1**
Review the following list of evaluative questions from Breen and Candlin (1987) and select those which you feel are most appropriate/pertinent to your own situation. Construct a checklist based on these questions and evaluate the materials you are currently using or are contemplating using. Get one or two colleagues to carry out the same task and compare results. Are there marked divergences of opinion? How do you account for these?

---

PHASE ONE: Initial questions
I *What do the materials aim to do and what do they contain?*
   1. When they finish their course, what should your learners know of and about the target language?
   2. What should they be able to do in and with the language?
   3. What knowledge about language and what guidance for using language appropriately for different purposes in various situations are offered in the materials?
   4. What do the materials offer which your learners will need to know?
   5. What do the materials offer which the learners will need to be able to do?
   6. What is missing from the materials?

II *What do the materials make your learners do while they are learning?*
   7. How do you think you best learn a language? What is most useful for learners to do to help them learn?
   8. What procedure or sequence of work does the learner have to follow in order to be successful at the task?
   9. Which types of task seem to be most conducive to learning?
  10. Which helpful ways of learning seem to be missing from the tasks provided in the materials?

III *How do the materials expect you to teach your learners in the classroom?*
  11. What can I do as a teacher which can best help my learners to learn a new language?
  12. What are you expected to do to help your learners work successfully through the materials?
  13. Do materials give you enough freedom to adopt those roles which for you are most helpful to learners discovering a new language?

14. Are you asked to take on roles you do not regard as appropriate?
15. Do the materials limit what you want to do as a teacher in using them with your learners?

IV *Are materials the only resource in classroom language learning?*
16. What contributions can a classroom and its participants make to learning and teaching languages?
17. Which of your contributions to classroom work are referred to and extended in the materials: your contribution as a teacher; your learners' contributions (as individuals or as a group); or the contributions of other classroom resources?
18. During classroom work, which of those contributions are additional to those referred to and extended in the materials?

PHASE TWO: Your learners and the materials

I *Are the materials appropriate to your learners' needs and interests?*
19. How and to what extent do the materials fit your learners' long-term goals in learning the language and/or following your course?
20. How far do the materials directly call on what your learners already know *of* and *about* the language, and extend what they can already do *with* and *in* the language?
21. How far do the materials meet the immediate language learning needs of your learners as they perceive them?
22. Which subject matter (topics, themes, ideas) in the materials is likely to be interesting and relevant to your learners?
23. In what ways do the materials involve your learners' values, attitudes and feelings?
24. Which skills do the materials highlight and what kinds of opportunities are provided to develop them?
25. How much time and space, proportionately, is devoted to each skill?
26. How is your learner expected to make use of his/her skills?
27. How are the learners required to communicate when working with the materials?
28. How much time and space, proportionately, is devoted to your learners expressing meaning?
30. How and how far can your materials meet the desire of individual learners to focus at certain moments on the development of a particular skill or ability use?

II *Are the materials appropriate to your learners' own approaches to language learning?*
31. On what basis is the content of the material sequenced?
32. On what basis are the different parts of the material divided into 'units' or 'lessons', and into different sub-parts of units/lessons?
33. On what basis do the materials offer continuity? How are relationships made between 'earlier' and 'later' parts?
34. To what extent and in what ways can your learners impose their own sequencing, dividing up and continuity on the materials as they work with them?

III *Are the materials appropriate to the classroom teaching/learning process?*

---

## Task 11.2

1. Evaluate a set of commercial materials against the six areas outlined by Littlejohn and Windeatt in section 11.2.

2. Did the evaluation reveal aspects of the materials which were not immediately apparent from a casual inspection?
3. What were the major weaknesses, and how might these be redressed?

**Task 11.3**
Select a reading or listening text and some attendant activities or worksheets. Get three or four colleagues (more, if possible) to teach the materials and provide you with the following information:

1. The aims of the unit.
2. The length of time it took to teach the unit (including the time allocated to teacher-fronted, small group, pair and individual tasks).
3. How the unit was introduced.
4. The steps in the lesson.
5. Changes that were made to the activities or worksheets.
6. An evaluation of student reaction to the material.
7. An indication of intention to use similar materials in future.
8. An indication of the best liked feature of the material.
9. An indication of the least liked features.
10. An estimation of the suitability of the materials for the designated learner group.

Review the data provided by your colleagues. What similarities and differences are apparent in their treatment of the materials? How would you account for these? Are they related to the teachers' education and experience? To what extent are their theories of language and learning reflected in the choices they made?

**Task 11.4**
Richards and Rodgers (1986) suggest that a particular design for an instructional system will imply a particular set of roles for materials. Examine a set of materials with which you are familiar and analyse them in terms of their role within the instructional system.

**Task 11.5**
1. Develop a unit of work following the eight-step procedure set out in section 11.5. Teach the unit and record the lessons.
2. Review the lessons and evaluate the materials.
3. Did anything unexpected happen?
4. Did the materials take longer to teach than expected?
5. What modifications would you make to the materials?
6. What modifications would you make to the materials development procedure?

**Task 11.6**
1. Develop a unit of work following the 'feeding' procedure developed by Low. Teach the unit and record the lesson or lessons.
2. Review the lessons and evaluate the materials.

3. Did anything unexpected happen?
4. Did the materials take longer to teach than expected?
5. What modifications would you make to the materials?
6. What modifications would you make to the materials development procedure?

**Task 11.7**
In this chapter we looked at some of the philosophical and ideological issues associated with commercial materials. The ideological principles underpinning a textbook, as well as the writer's beliefs about the nature of language and learning, can be inferred from the texts and tasks that make up the materials. They are also usually explicitly referred to in the introduction to the teacher's edition. This is evident in the following extracts. As you read these, consider what the authors' beliefs are, and what types of activities you would be likely to encounter in the books themselves.

**1**
Reading and Listening are developed by using an extensive range of authentic and semi-authentic material, which exposes the learner to varieties of language they are likely to encounter in real life. In particular, the recorded listening material involves a number of different speakers with both native and non-native accents. Speaking and Writing are also carefully developed in a number of communicative activities, such as role plays and problem-solving sessions. (Garton-Sprengler and Greenall 1986: viii)

**2**
Most people seem to learn a language if it is 'tidied up' for them. This helps them to focus on high-priority language and to see the grammatical regularities. However, learners also need to encounter a certain amount of 'untidy' natural language (even if this seems too difficult for them). Without this unstructured input, people's unconscious mechanisms for acquiring languages may not operate effectively. A course should cater for both these ways of approaching a language (sometimes called 'learning' and 'acquisition' respectively). The use of unsimplified authentic materials may require a change in learner expectations: many students and teachers are used only to texts in which every new word and structure has to be explained and learnt. (Swan and Walter 1987: vii)

**3**
With the development of communicative language teaching, the importance of accuracy has sometimes been neglected in favour of encouraging fluency in spoken English. It seems clear that a balanced approach where both fluency and accuracy are developed is essential if students are to do more than simply 'survive' in English-speaking situations. . . . Students cannot suddenly and miraculously achieve accuracy in spoken English. The best they can hope for is a progressive improvement in accuracy. Correction is an essential tool to guide students towards improvement but there is no point in correcting every error that is made. Instead, the teacher should concentrate on correcting relevant errors. . . . Even though most of the activities in this book focus on accuracy, the teacher must be extremely gentle and tactful when correcting errors. Sensitive or diffident students often feel that they are being reprimanded or even mocked if they are told they are 'wrong'. Even well-adjusted average students can be upset by tactless or aggressive correction techniques. (Jones 1985: 5–6)

## 11.8 Conclusion

In this chapter we have looked at some of the issues surrounding the development, evaluation and use of language teaching materials. Materials are an important component within the curriculum, and are often the most tangible and 'visible' component of pedagogy. While the evaluation of materials can be partly carried out outside the classroom (such a task being greatly facilitated by the checklists and evaluative questions presented in the body of this chapter), their real potential – or lack of potential – can only be evaluated in relation to real learners in real classrooms. In keeping with the other chapters of this book, then, I have suggested that the development or evaluation of materials should be largely based on the collection and analysis of classroom data.

In the next chapter we turn to the issue of 'methods'. Some of the themes which appeared in this chapter are developed there, and we look among other things at the different roles that materials play in different teaching methods.

# Chapter Twelve

# Language Teaching Methods: A Critical Analysis

## 12.1 Introduction

For much of its history, language teaching has been obsessed with a search for the 'right' method. It was felt that somewhere or other there was a method which would work for all learners in all contexts, and that once such a method had been found the language teaching 'problem' would be solved once and for all (Richards 1987). More recently, it has been realised that there never was and probably never will be a method for all, and the focus in recent years has been on the development of classroom tasks and activities which are consonant with what we know about processes of second language acquisition, and which are also in keeping with the dynamics of the classroom itself.

Given this shift away from a focus on methods, it might seem odd that a chapter of this book is devoted to the subject. I have provided a description and critique of some of the more prominent methods which have made their appearance in the market place for two reasons. In the first place, it is valuable for teachers to be aware of where we have come from as a profession. It is also interesting to note the ways in which theoretical and ideological beliefs about the nature of language and learning as well as the results of empirical research, have been realised at the level of pedagogical action. Lastly, I should like to give readers themselves the opportunity to evaluate some of the methods which have influenced and which continue to influence classroom practices and teaching materials.

I have chosen to assign methods to three categories: the psychological tradition, the humanistic tradition and the second language acquisition tradition. While any act of categorisation will often mask important differences between category members, I believe that the groupings highlight essential similarities between the different methods in each category.

The chapter answers the following questions:

1. What has been the contribution of disciplines such as linguistics, psychology and sociology to the development of language teaching methods?
2. What are the key characteristics, strengths and weaknesses of the more prominent methods?

3. Why is it dangerous to base second language teaching on insights supposedly derived from research into first language acquisition?

## 12.2 The psychological tradition

The psychological tradition refers to methods which take as their principal point of departure psychological theories of learning which were not, in the first instance, developed specifically to inform language learning and teaching, but which were more general. In this, they contrast with methods developed within the SLA tradition. The methods we shall look at in this section are audio-lingualism and cognitive code learning.

### *Audio-lingualism*

Audio-lingualism has probably had a greater impact on second and foreign language teaching than any other method. Unlike some of the more loosely formulated methods which grew out of humanistic psychology, and which we shall examine in the next section, it consists of a highly coherent and well developed classroom pedagogy, with clear links between theory and practice. It was, in fact, the first approach which could be said to have developed a 'technology' of teaching, developing in the 1940s and 1950s as a reaction against more traditional methods, and purporting to be based on 'scientific' principles. One of the interesting aspects of language teaching methodology over the past thirty years or so has been the relationship between theory and research in disciplines such as linguistics, psychology, sociology and anthropology, and language teaching. In the case of audio-lingualism, a principal rationale was provided by behaviourist psychology and structural linguistics.

The name most consistently associated with behaviourism is B. F. Skinner who developed his model from the early theoretical and empirical work of Pavlov and Watson (see, for example, Skinner 1957). Skinner added a new dimension to this earlier work by applying the Pavlovian principles of animal behaviour to the study of human behaviour. In doing this, he created a new concept called operant conditioning which placed more emphasis on the consequences of a stimulus or stimuli than on the stimuli themselves. Skinner accounted for learning in terms of the reinforcement of these stimulated consequences or responses. In his excellent analysis of principles and practices in language teaching, Brown provides the following account of the way reinforcement was supposed to result in learning:

> According to Skinner, the events or stimuli – the reinforcers – that follow a response and that tend to strengthen behaviour or increase the probability of a recurrence of that response constitute a powerful force in the control of human behaviour. Reinforcers are far stronger aspects for learning than mere association of a prior stimulus with a following response, as in the classical conditioning model. We are governed by the consequences of

our behaviour, and therefore Skinner felt we ought, in studying human behaviour, to study the effect of those consequences. And if we wish to control behaviour, say, to teach somebody something, we ought to attend carefully to reinforcers. (Brown 1987: 63)

Parallel to the development of behaviourism in psychology was the growing influence of structural linguistics. Both fields were mutually supportive. On the behaviourist side Skinner had plenty to say about the way language worked, and on the linguistic side, Leonard Bloomfield (1933), the most noted of the structural linguists, had a great deal to say about the psychological aspects of language learning. Bloomfield and his associates were anthropologists, and developed an interest in linguistics because they wanted to document the languages of the American Indians. They found that the traditional tools of linguistic analysis and description were inadequate for this task, and so they developed tools of their own. In the process, they also created new attitudes towards language and language learning. These articulated extremely well with the ideas emerging from behaviourists. For instance, they noted that while the Indians could use their language they could not describe it. From this, they concluded that the memorising of rules and grammatical paradigms were not very useful for learning second or foreign languages, and that in consequence, teachers ought to teach the language rather than teaching about it.

Rather than using the grammatical categories developed for analysing classical languages, they tried to analyse each new language in its own terms, maintaining that as each language is basically different, each demands its own form of structural analysis. They attempted to isolate significant linguistic structures and patterns which were segmented into smaller and smaller constituents, which were considered to be the basic building blocks of the language under investigation. This technique for linguistic analysis had a pervasive influence on the selection of input for language teaching, and also on the development of classroom activities. The development of patterns and substitution drills represented a marriage of structural linguistic analysis and behaviourist habit formation. In patterns such as:

| The pen | is on | the desk |
|---------|-------|----------|
| book    | under | chair    |
| ruler   | by    | table    |
| pencil  |       |          |

the intention was to inculcate the structure NP + 'be' + preposition + NP through a process of drilling. The rationale for the selection of structures came from structural linguistics, while the rationale for the ways these were exploited in the classroom came from behaviourist psychology.

Having examined the background to audio-lingualism, I should now like to look at the ways in which the method manifested itself in the classroom. Moulton (1963) suggests that behaviourism and structuralism provide us with five key characteristics which need to be taken into consideration in designing language programmes.

1. Language is speech, not writing.
2. A language is a set of habits.

3. Teach the language, not about the language.
4. A language is what native speakers say, not what someone thinks they ought to say.
5. Languages are different.

Perhaps the characteristic which owes most to bahaviourism is the second, relating to learning as habit formation. Bloomfield (1933), while basically a linguist, had a great deal to say about the psychological processes of language learning. He described L1 acquisition as occurring through the following five steps.

1. The baby babbles, eventually gaining the habit of repeating a given mouth movement when it hears its corresponding sound.
2. When someone says 'doll' in the baby's presence, the child hears 'dad' and repeats 'da'. This signals the beginning of imitation.
3. The mother says 'doll' so often that the child forms a new habit. The sight of the doll stimulates the child to say 'da'.
4. The next step is for the child to say 'da' when the doll is not present, and for the mother to interpret this as a request for the doll.
5. The final step is for the child's pronunciation to come into line with that of the parent, i.e. the child's utterance 'da' moves in the direction of 'doll'. Faulty pronunciation will not be rewarded and will, as a consequence, be extinguished.

Those involved in second language pedagogy assumed that these processes also underlie second language learning. Classroom environments were therefore arranged in which there was a maximum amount of repetition on the part of the learners. The teacher was supposed to reward those utterances coming closest to the model provided by the teacher or a tape, and to extinguish those utterances which did not. A typical lesson might look something like the following:

1. Present the new language item to be learned, giving a clear demonstration of its meaning, through non-verbal means.
2. Model the target pattern using a number of examples.
3. The whole class engages in mimicry-memorisation following the teacher's model.
4. Progressive substitution drill with the whole class, followed by the class divided into two, followed by individual responses.
5. Repeat the first four steps using negative versions of the target structure.
6. Repeat the first four steps using interrogative versions of the target structure.
7. Check for transfer using previously unrehearsed cues. Solicit both whole class and individual responses.

The presentation and practice stages are the heart of audio-lingualism. As the presentations were to be done exclusively in the target language, it was vitally important that they be as clear and unambiguous as possible. The demonstration and accompanying language item should leave no doubt in the learner's mind as to what the language meant. At the early stages of learning, structures were exemplified through actions by the teacher, pictures and items of realia which either already existed in the classroom or could be readily brought in. For inexperienced teachers, audio-lingualism provided a clear set of procedures, methods, principles and even 'recipes' to follow. It was also based on theories which were inadequate as explanations of human learning.

Audio-lingualism suffered in the two-pronged attack on behaviourism and structural linguistics. In 1957, Skinner published *Verbal Behaviour*, a comprehensive behaviourist account of language development. Shortly afterwards, Chomsky (1959) published his now famous critique of Skinner's book. This critique was based on Chomsky's own model of linguistics, transformational generative grammar.

The transformationalists demonstrated that there were aspects of the child's emerging linguistic system which could simply not be accounted for in terms of stimulus–response psychology. Some of the forms which children used could not have been attained through imitation because they were simply never used by adults. One well-known example is the use of irregular past tense forms. Children commonly start out using the correct forms, for example, 'went', and 'ran', and then pass through a stage of using the deviant forms 'goed' and 'runned'. Cognitive psychologists and transformational linguists argued that the child has constructed his/her own simplified rule on the operation of the simple past – add 'ed' to the root form of the verb.

It was examples such as this which served to undermine behaviourism as a plausible psychological theory of language development. It also supported the transformational view that language acquisition was basically rule governed. A spate of experiments into child language development showed that children did not follow adult grammatical models, but developed their own internally consistent grammars. Deviations from adult models were not random abberations, but were systematic, and it was concluded that children were devising rules and then testing them out against reality. When they received disconfirming evidence, they modified their rule and moved their language in the direction of the adult model. (It must be added that the persistence of the deviant forms, often for several years, posed a challenge to this hypothesis-formation theory of language acquisition.)

### Cognitive code learning

Transformational grammar and cognitive psychology gave rise to their own method – cognitive code learning, although this never attained the prominence or pervasiveness of audio-lingualism. (For a comparative analysis of audio-lingualism and cognitive code learning, see Diller 1978.) If the high priests of behaviourism and structural linguistics were Skinner and Bloomfield, their transformational and cognitive counterparts were Chomsky and Ausubel. The major departure of cognitive psychology from behaviourism was that cognitivism viewed the learning process as a two-way process between the organism and its environment. The ability of the organism to act on the environment contrasts with the behaviourist view that the organism is basically the passive recipient of outside stimuli. Linguists working within the framework provided by cognitive psychology were able to demonstrate that there were aspects of a child's emerging linguistic system which simply could not be accounted for in terms of the reaction of an organism (the learner) to its environment. Rather, it was believed that language development could be characterised by rule governed creativity. With a finite number of grammatical rules and a limited vocabulary, we can create an infinite number of sentences, many of which may never have been uttered before. This incidentally is another argument against behaviourism – it would take thousands of lifetimes to learn all the sentences of a language through a process of stimulus–response.

Cognitive code learning de-emphasises the role of rote learning, along with the techniques of mimicry and memorisation. Some cognitive courses do have drills, especially substitiution and transformation drills, but these have a different rationale and use from behaviourist drills. Cognitivism also accepts the value of rules – it is felt that a few carefully chosen examples of rules in operation can be an important short-cut to learning. New knowledge, however, should always be linked to prior know-ledge, and at the beginning of a lesson the teacher should try to establish a mental set which encourages learners to invoke their prior knowledge as a preliminary to new learning. Also, rather than preventing learners from consciously thinking and talking about the language, there should be activities in which this is actively en-couraged. The emphasis at all times should be on language learning as an active, intelligent, rule-seeking, problem-solving process in which learners are encouraged to reflect upon and discuss the way the target language operates.

In devising cognitively based lessons, the presentation of target language items can be managed either deductively or inductively. In deductive learning, a situation is created in which the target item is embedded in a meaningful context. Learners are told the rule and then given the opportunity to apply it to several practice items or examples. In inductive learning, the student is given a number of examples and asked to work out the rule through a process of guided discovery. This is different from the inductive techniques used in audio-lingualism, because in the former approach the learner would not be expected to come to a conscious formulation of the rule, nor be able to articulate it.

There are numerous other points of contact between audio-lingualism and cog-nitivism. For example, the cognitivists are much more sanguine about mistakes, rejecting the behaviourist notion that if learners make mistakes they will learn these deviant forms which will have to be 'unlearned' later. Cognitivists believe that making mistakes is an important part of the learning process, that such mistakes provide disconfirming instances which are important in learning a new concept or rule.

Chastain provides the following useful summary of the essential differences be-tween the two psychological theories underlying the methods we have looked at in this section.

> Cognitive interpretations of learning assign a central and dominant role to the processes that are subject to the individual's control. An individual's knowledge does not consist of conditioned behaviour but of assimilated information within her cognitive resources that makes her behaviour possible and controls it. Rote learning and motor learning are considered to be relatively unimportant in the explanation of basic and higher mental

activity. The extrapolation of learning outcomes from animal to human subjects is rejected. The role of the teacher is to recognise the importance of the student's mental assets and mental activity in learning. In the final analysis, learning resides within the learner: the teacher's task is to organise the material being presented in such a manner that what is to be learned will be meaningful to the learner. To do this he is obliged to consider the student's existing cognitive structure. . . . His next obligation is to try to couch the material in such a fashion that the learners can relate the content to their existing fund of knowledge. (Chastain 1976: 144)

## 12.3 The humanistic tradition

In this section, I should like to discuss a number of methods which advocate a diverse range of classroom techniques, but which, nonetheless, share a common point of departure. The thing which sets apart the methods I have chosen to deal with in this section is not sets of linguistic or psychological tenets, but a common belief in the primacy of affective and emotional factors within the learning process. Proponents of these methods believe that if learners can be encouraged to adopt the right attitudes, interests and motivation in the target language and culture, as well as in the learning environment in which they find themselves, then successful learning will occur, and that if these affective factors are not right, then no set of techniques is likely to succeed, regardless of how carefully they have been devised or how solidly based on the latest theory and research. As you read of the classroom techniques proposed by methods derived from humanistic psychology, you might like to note just how inhumane some of these appear to be.

Perhaps the best known proponent of humanism in language learning is Earl Stevick (see, for example, Stevick 1982) who, while he has not developed his own method, has been an enthusiastic champion and interpreter of humanistic methods in language teaching. Others include Curran (1972; 1976), who developed Community Language Learning, Gattegno (1972) who created the Silent Way, and Lozanov who produced the approach known as Suggestopedia. Stevick, who has taken up and extended the work of Curran, Gattegno and Lozanov, became interested in applying principles of humanistic psychology to language learning and teaching after he became dissatisfied with both audio-lingual habit theory and cognitive code learning. Why is it, he asked, that both of these methods were capable of working extremely well (or extremely badly), when both were the logical antithesis of each other and therefore mutually incompatible? He came to the conclusion that success or failure in language teaching depends not so much on whether one adopts inductive or deductive techniques for teaching grammar, nor whether one engages in meaningful practice rather than in pattern drills, but in the extent to which one caters to the learner's affective domain. In other words, the actual classroom techniques, the bases on which we select materials, and the sorts of activities in which we have our learners engage, matter less than certain other basic principles which could be used in audio-lingualism, cognitive code learning, or any other number of approaches.

Perhaps the most important article of faith is that the learner's emotional attitude towards the teacher, towards fellow learners, and towards the target language and culture, is the single most important variable in language learning. It is crucial, not only to take account of this factor, but to give it a central place in the selection of content, materials and learning activities. The other principle shared by these diverse methods is that teaching should be made subservient to learning. In this learner-centred view of language development, the emphasis at all times should be on the learners, not the teacher. In fact, the most extreme proponents of this view argue that it is not really possible to teach anybody anything, except in a superficial sense – all that the teacher can do is to attempt to establish the optimal conditions whereby learning can come about through the learner's own efforts.

This view of learning has obvious implications for teachers, particularly for the ways they define their classroom roles (for an excellent discussion on roles of teachers and learners, see Wright 1987.) Stevick points out that learner-centredness does not imply that teachers should abandon the classroom to the learners, that there are a number of legitimate teacher functions in learner- as well as teacher-centred classrooms. While learners may be able to learn languages independently, given the right conditions and environment, these conditions and environment are extremely rare.

According to Stevick, the five most important functions of the teacher are as follows:

1. The cognitive function. The teacher possesses knowedge desired by the student about the target language and culture. We, the teachers, have this knowledge, which the students expect us to impart to them.
2. The classroom management function. Our students and the society in which we work expect us to take responsibility for how the students' time is used in class. The students rely on our training and experience with materials, schedules and techniques.
3. Practical goals. Here Stevick is referring to the goals which students and society have for language courses. The teacher is expected to take these vaguely thought out or articulated goals and give them practical expression in language teaching syllabuses.
4. The personal or interpersonal function. As teachers with the desired skills, knowledge and expertise, we have a great deal of power in the classroom and it is our responsibility to set the tone or interpersonal classroom climate. The atmosphere we set will determine whether the students' non-linguistic emotional needs are met in the classroom.
5. The final function is closely related to the fourth, but is more subtle. It has to do with the warmth and enthusiasm that the teacher radiates – the 'vibes' that he or she puts out. According to Stevick, this is the most important function of all.

### Community Language Learning

When establishing an effective emotional climate, the first thing that has to be dealt with is the learners' anxiety. In the initial stages, at least, learning another language is probably the most anxiety provoking activity an individual can undertake in the classroom. For learners to be relaxed enough and confident enough to exploit fully the opportunities which present themselves, the teacher has to ensure that there is a large degree of cohesiveness and trust built up among the members of the group. Learners are unlikely to make the necessary commitment in groups in which they have little or no support. The method which focuses most assiduously on building trust is Community Language Learning (CLL), or, as it is sometimes called, Counseling-Learning (the latter title reflects its creator, Curran's, early work as a counsellor.) The primary aim of CLL is to create a genuinely warm and supportive 'community' among the learners and gradually to move them from complete dependence on the teacher to complete autonomy.

The method, which assumes a group of homogeneous first language learners working with a bilingual teacher, works in the following way. The learners are first seated in a closed circle with the teacher on the outside. When learners want to say something, they call the teacher across and whisper whatever it is they want to communicate to the teacher in the L1. The teacher whispers back an L2 translation, and the learner then repeats this to the group. The process continues for some time, the learners' utterances being recorded on tape. At the end of the session, the group generally has a lengthy taped interaction, all in the target language. This is subsequently replayed, analysed and used as the basis of more formal language work.

While the method was initially developed to teach homogeneous classes, it has been modified for use with heterogeneous language groups. With intermediate learners, a problem-solving task can be set and the class can be placed into small groups, each with a cassette recorder, to solve the problem and at the same time record their conversation . The teacher keeps out of the way and allows the learners to complete the task autonomously. At the end of the allotted time, each small group replays its cassette. In a follow-up session, the teacher, having transcribed parts of the small group discussions, distributes these to the class. Students go through the transcriptions and correct the errors; such self-correction sessions supposedly increasing the sense of power which learners have over their own learning. The teacher can also use the transcripts as the basis for a grammar lesson or review.

Community Language Learning has several weaknesses which can trap the unwary or inexperienced teacher. In the first instance, the lesson can take unexpected and even dangerous directions. The method is pitched directly at the emotions and attitudes of the learners, and can release negative as well as positive emotions. The approach may awaken interpersonal hostilities that are difficult to control or channel into more positive directions. These may, in fact, destroy the very cohesion and solidarity which the method is supposed to create. There may also be difficulties in trying to use the approach with learners who, due to their previous learning experiences, may be antagonistic towards the teacher for taking a low classroom profile, and may express the belief that the teacher is not doing his/her job. If this method or any other were to be imposed on a group of unwilling learners, it would be highly unlikely that a positive climate will emerge.

In their critique of the method, Richards and Rodgers summarise a number of other shortcomings in the following way:

> Critics of Community Language Learning question the appropriateness of the counselling metaphor on which it is predicated, asking for evidence that language learning in classrooms indeed parallels the processes that characterize psychological counselling. Questions also arise about whether teachers should attempt counselling without special training. CLL procedures were largely developed and tested with groups of college-age Americans. The problems and successes experienced by one or two different client groups may not necessarily represent language learning universals. Other concerns have been expressed concerning the lack of a syllabus, which makes objective unclear and evaluation difficult to accomplish, and the focus on fluency rather than accuracy, which may lead to inadequate control of the grammatical system of the target language. (Richards and Rodgers 1986: 126)

### The Silent Way

Another prominent humanistic method is the Silent Way, devised by Gattegno (1972). Classroom extract 12.1 has been taken from Gattegno. Unlike the other extracts in this book, it is a fictionalised account rather than a genuine piece of interaction. Nonetheless, it purports to reflect what happens in an initial Silent Way lesson.

### Pre-reading task

1. As you read the extract, think what would be your reaction to an initial lesson such as this.
2. Consider also the ways in which the method contrasts with Community Language Learning.

### Classroom extract 12.1: A Silent Way lesson

> Let us imagine that we are looking at a class of interested students of any age (6 or 11 or 14 or adults), and that the teacher enters the room for the first time. The class knows that it will study a foreign language, and the teacher is determined not to use one single word of the vernacular, which he may know, or which may even be his mother tongue.
>
> The approach is, as I have insisted, most artifical. The box of colored rods that the teacher places on his desk is all he carries. He opens it and draws out of it one rod and shows it to the class while saying in the foreign language the word for rod, with the indefinite article if it exists in that language. He puts it down in silence and picks up another of a different color and says the same (one or two) words again and so on, going through seven or eight rods and never asking for anything. The intrigued students have attentively noted the events and heard some noises which to them will seem the same while their eyes see only

different objects and a repetition of the same action. Without any fuss the teacher then lifts a rod and asks in mime for the sounds he uttered. Bewildered, the class would not respond, in general, but the teacher says 'a rod' and asks again in mime for another effort from the class. Invariably someone guesses (perhaps from the habits ingrained in traditional teaching) that the teacher wants back what he gave. When in his own way the pupil says something approximating what the teacher said, the teacher may smile or nod, showing how content he is at being understood. At the next trial almost the whole class repeats the sounds for a rod (very approximately in most cases). The teacher does not inquire whether some students are thinking of a piece of wood, others of lifting something, or something different. Contact has been established without the vernacular, and that is all that was wanted so far.

The teacher then introduces the names for four or five of the colors, giving the sounds for 'a blue rod,' 'a black rod,' 'a red rod,' 'a yellow rod,' 'a green rod,' or any other combination of the ten colors available. Because the names of the colors are now added the pupils can no longer imagine that different expressions mean the same action and are forced to conclude that the teacher is giving the phrases that summarily describe these objects. The exercise is now shifted to practice in uttering the foreign sounds for the six or seven objects, so that as soon as one rod replaces another, one utterance replaces another, which would be the case in vernacular. (Gattegno 1972: 35–6)

While the Silent Way differs significantly from Community Language Learning, it does share a belief in the importance of the inner state of the learner in the learning process. For Gattegno, the author of the Silent Way, the learning of a first and subsequent languages is a mysterious, even mystical process. Like Curran, he emphasises the need to develop in learners an autonomy from the teacher and the teaching situation. He also claims that the method is learner-centred in that teaching is subordinated to learning. Despite these claims, the method is highly controlled, and extremely manipulative of the students.

The mystical dimension to the method is captured in the following extracts from Gattegno:

From outside, one could say that it is the different structures of languages that cause the insecurity, and that if one knew enough of the foreign grammar, and had a sufficiently wide vocabulary, all would be well. This unfortunately is not the case. Grammar is not of much help, nor even is a rich vocabulary. Only when one is really imbued with the literature or soaked in the environment of the people using the language can one express oneself in speech or writing as a native would. It is the spirit of a language that has to get hold of one's mind and dictate the expressions that sound right and fully convey the meaning to native listeners or readers. . . . We can trace the first elements of the spirit of a language to the unconscious surrender of our sensitivity to what is conveyed by the background of noise in each language. . . . Surrender to the melody of a language, as to music, will bring to our unconscious all of the spirit of a language that has been stored in the melody. It cannot be reached otherwise. (Gattegno 1972: 20–2)

In extract 12.1 we see an attempt to realise some of these principles in action. The learners are placed in a situation in which their attention is closely focused on a limited amount of language – common actions associated with the manipulation of a number of coloured rods. The teacher provides the minimum number of target language models, and the learners, from the very beginning, are required to work things out for themselves. Despite the rather mystical quality of Gattegno's writing, and the highly idiosyncratic nature of the lesson we have just seen, the approach is less radical than might at first appear. As Richards and Rodgers point out, the syllabus is highly conventional, and the classroom techniques themselves are in many ways not so different from audio-lingual techniques, centring on the accurate repetition of the teacher's model sentences. The innovative nature of the method rests in the way in which classroom activities are organised, 'the indirect role the teacher is required to assume in directing and monitoring learner performance, the responsibility placed upon learners to figure out and test their hypotheses about how the language works, and the materials used to elicit and practise language' (Richards and Rodgers 1986: 111).

### Suggestopedia

The final method we shall look at in this section is Suggestopedia. Lozonov, who developed the method, believes that the human mind is capable of prodigious feats of memory if learning takes place under the appropriate conditions. He attempts to realise the hidden potential of the mind by getting students to learn in a state of deep relaxation bordering on hypnosis. This hypnotic state is brought about through yogic techniques of relaxation, rhythmic breathing, and listening to readings by the teacher which are synchronised to music. The use of music is supposed to activate the left hemisphere of the brain, which, in consequence is designed to facilitate 'holistic' learning.

Suggestopedia is one of the few methods whose claims have been put to the empirical test. Wagner and Tilney (1983) set up an experiment to test the claim that, through Suggestopedia, students could learn huge amounts of vocabulary. (It had been claimed that, through Suggestopedia, students could learn between one thousand and three thousand words per day – Ostrander and Schroeder 1981.) In a formal experiment utilising control and experimental groups, Wagner and Tilney set out to teach three hundred German words to native English speakers over a five week period. When the results were analysed, they found that, contrary to the claims of proponents of Suggestopedia, 'those taught by a traditional class-room method learned significantly more vocabulary than those taught by Super-learning techniques . . . Although scrupulous care to preserve "Superlearning" methodology was taken in this investigation, accelerated learning could not be substantiated' (p. 5). In his review of Suggestopedia, Scovel (1979) attacks the method, suggesting that its author attempts to legitimise the method through the use of scholarly citations and terminological jargon (Lozonov's writings are spiked with expressions such as 'suggestive–desuggestive ritual placebo systems'), while in reality, there is nothing particularly scientific about the method. In Scovel's view, the language teaching profession has very little to gain from the 'pseudo-science of suggestology'.

## 12.4 The second language acquisition tradition

The third methodological tradition I have identified encompasses methods which draw directly on research and theory into first and second language acquisition, and attempt to apply this theory and research to the second language classroom. While earlier methods such as audio-lingualism and cognitive code learning also relied heavily on what were seen as the conditions underlying first language development, the more recent methods are different in that they claim to be based on substantial empirical research into language development.

The most persuasive advocate of the acquisitionist tradition is Krashen. His two publications, *Second Language Acquisition and Second Language Learning* and *Principles and Practice of Second Language Acquisition* set out the central principles of the tradition, along with the research which is purported to provide a rationale for the principles. Along with Terrell (Krashen and Terrell 1983) he has developed a method based on these principles called the Natural Approach.

Of the various principles set out by Krashen, the best known and most controversial is the suggestion that there are two distinct mental processes operating in second language development. The first of these is the acquisition process, while the second is the learning process. The acquisition process is very similar, if not identical, to what goes on in first language acquisition, whereas learning is a conscious process, an interim device to help the learner cope with the target language in the short term. For anything more than the most rudimentary facility in the target language, subconscious acquisition rather than conscious learning must occur. When a second language learner is communicating in the language, the consciously learned rules do not help generate utterances but merely help the learner monitor or censor the language. The way these processes are supposed to operate, and the links with first language development are constantly explicated by Krashen:

> Language acquisition is very similar to the process children use in acquiring first and second languages. It requires meaningful interaction in the target language – natural communication – in which speakers are concerned not with the form of the utterances but with the messages they are conveying and understanding. . . . Conscious learning is available to the performer only as a Monitor. In general, utterances are initiated by the acquired system – our fluency in production is based on what we have 'picked up' through active communication. Our 'formal' knowledge of the second language, our conscious learning, may be used to alter the output of the acquired system, sometimes before and sometimes after the utterance is produced. We make these changes to improve accuracy, and the use of the Monitor has this effect. (Krashen 1981: 1)

If second language acquisition operated in exactly the same way as first language acquisition, then all second language learners, given sufficient time, should develop bilingual competence in the language. This, of course, does not occur, and in order to account for this Krashen introduces what he calls an affective 'filter'. If the learner is anxious, has negative feelings towards the target language or learning situation, is under stress, etc. then the input which should feed the acquisition process is blocked. The creation of the affective filter is a nice example of the tinkering to the model in the face of constant criticism, which, in effect, renders the hypothesis unfalsifiable.

According to Krashen, several essential characteristics or conditions exist in first language acquisition. The first of these is the 'here and now' principle which suggests that whenever language is directed to the child it is used to refer to some action, entity or event that is occurring in the immediate environment. The child is enabled to comprehend the language through the non-verbal clues with which the language is associated. Secondly, language directed to young children is simplified, carefully structured and contains many repetitions. The third characteristic is that the focus of the language is firmly on meaning rather than form. The child acquires the forms through subconscious acquisition. In addition, children comprehend new language forms long before they produce them.

## The Natural Approach

The Natural Approach is based on the conditions which Krashen argues underlie all successful language acquisition, whether it be the acquisition of a first or a second language. The following sample activities, taken from Krashen and Terrell's (1983) book on the Natural Approach are all designed to provide comprehensible input, which, according to the authors, is the most important element in language acquisition.

### Affective–humanistic activities

These activities are designed to involve students' feelings, opinions, desires, reactions, ideas and experiences. They include dialogues, interviews, preference ranking, personal charts and tables, revealing information about yourself, activities using the imagination. Although quite varied, all of these activities focus on meaning not form, and attempt to lower the affective filter. 'Personal charts and tables' (Illustration 15) is an example of an affective–humanistic activity.

ILLUSTRATION 15

### Personal Charts and Tables

The use of charts and tables was introduced in Chapter Four as a means of providing comprehensible input while requiring only one-word or short answers. But they can also be used at more advanced levels. Their role in providing input is the same, but the questions in the input can be more open, allowing the students opportunities for more complex responses.

The construction of tables of information about the students in a particular class, for example, can serve as a basis for interesting discussions. In the following example, the instructor has begun to create a chart of the weekly routines of the class members on the chalkboard.

|  | Monday | Wednesday | Saturday |
|---|---|---|---|
| John | works | studies | plays baseball |
| Jim | studies | has baseball practice | works in supermarket |
| Louise | studies | has swim team practice | plays waterpolo |
| Herman | works at record store | lifts weights | visits friends |

After the chart is completed it can serve as a basis for lively questions and discussions which provide the desired comprehensible input. The level of the discussion depends on the level of the class. For students only beginning the "speech emerges" stage, the following questions would be appropriate:

*Who has baseball practice on Wednesdays? What does John do on Saturdays? Does Herman lift weights on Wednesdays?*

As the students' ability to produce increases, so does the difficulty level of the instructor's input.

*Does Jim have baseball practice on Wednesdays? What team is he on? What position does he play? Who plays water polo on Saturdays? Why does she play on Saturdays? Does she ever play during the week? Does she play for fun only or is she on a team? What position does she play? Do girls and women ordinarily play water polo? Why? Why not? Do you suppose Louise knows how to swim? Well? Why?*

Charts may also be created so that the students first fill out the chart with personal information and then this information serves as a basis for the class follow-up discussion. In the following chart for a beginning Spanish course, the students are asked to say whether or not they did certain activities yesterday, and if so at what time of the day. The activities include: Did you wash your car? Did you go to the beach? Did you watch television? Did you clean house? and so forth.

Source:  S. Krashen and T. Terrell, *The Natural Approach* (Oxford: Pergamon, 1983), pp. 103–104. Reproduced by permission.

## Problem-solving activities

In these activities, students are involved in finding a correct answer to a question, problem or situation. Comprehensible input in these activities is supplied by the teacher when providing explanations, and by the students when working together in small groups. One type of problem-solving activity is called 'tasks and series'.

In the tasks model, the instructor or students choose a specific activity. Suppose, for example, the topic is 'washing a car'. There will be three stages in the activity. In the initial stage, the instructor will guide the students in developing the vocabulary necessary to talk about the activity. Then together the class and instructor create utterances to describe the sequence of events to complete the activity. For example, in the above activity the class might say, *First I look for a bucket and a sponge or some rags. Then I park the car in the driveway. I use the hose to wash the car first with water only.* These utterances are developed slowly with interspersed discussion. *Which is better to use, a sponge or a clean rag? Should you use soap or other cleaners (such as detergents) to wash a car?* During the final stage, after the sequence is constructed, the discussion will broaden to include questions and discussion concerning the specific activity in the students' own lives. How often do you wash your car? When? Where? Do you enjoy it? Why? Why not? (Krashen and Terrell 1983: 108–109)

## Games

In the Natural Approach, games are not a 'frill' but an important element in the acquisition process. They qualify as an acquisition activity because of their value in providing comprehensible input.

> It is simple in many games to focus on particular words. One common technique is to make up illogical combinations and ask the students (in teams if desired) to figure out what is wrong with the combination. For example,
> *What is strange about:*
>   *a bird swimming*      *a television laughing*
>   *a table eating*       *a person flying*
>   *a tree crying*
> In such games it is easy to provide comprehensible input in the discussion: *Has anyone ever seen a bird swimming? (I have.) What kinds of birds swim? (penguins). Has everyone seen a penguin? Do you know what a penguin is? (a black and white bird). Where do penguins live? (where it's cold). That's right, they prefer cold climates. Can penguins fly? (no, they walk and swim). Are they good at walking? Can they walk fast? (no). They're clumsy (new word).* Other games focus mainly on discussion. In one such game each student has a word or a description written on a sign taped to their backs which others can see but they cannot. They may ask any question they want of the other students or the other students may try to give them clues to help them figure out what is written on the sign. In this case comprehensible input is student interlanguage. (Krashen and Terrell 1983: 121–2)

## Content activities

These are activities which focus on learning something other than language, such as the academic subject matter of mathematics, science, etc.

> Examples of content activities include slide shows, panels, individual reports and presentations, 'show and tell' activities, music, films, film strips, television reports, news broadcasts, guest lectures, native speaker visitors, readings and discussions about any part of the target language or culture. (Krashen and Terrell 1983: 123–4)

Like most of the other methods discussed in this chapter, the Natural Approach contains activities which, in themselves, are generally unexceptional. It is only when they are elevated to the status of a movement, and when they are fed to learners as an unvarying diet that they pose a problem to pedagogy. My major criticism of these 'acquisitionist' methods is that they oversimplify the nature of first language acquisition, and mislead teachers by suggesting that it is possible to recreate in the classroom the conditions underlying successful first language acquisition. I shall expand on this point after we have looked at the last of our methods.

### The Total Physical Response

Another elaborate methodology erected on principles supposedly derived from insights into first language acquisition parades under the rather lurid title, Total Physical Response. Asher, who developed the method, focuses in particular on two characteristics of first language acquisition. The first of these is that the child gets a vast amount of comprehensible input before beginning to speak. Young children comprehend language which is far in excess of their ability to produce. Secondly, there is a lot of physical manipulation and action language accompanying early input. 'Throw the ball to Daddy', 'Put your arm through here', etc. This action language, encouraging physical manipulation, is couched in the imperative.

Asher derived three key principles from his beliefs about the nature of first language acquisition:

1. We should stress comprehension rather than production at the beginning levels of second language instruction (the first ten to twelve hours should be devoted exclusively to input according to Asher) with no demands on the learners to generate the target structure themselves.
2. We should obey the 'here and now' principle.
3. We should provide input to the learners by getting them to carry out commands. These commands should be couched in the imperative.

### Classroom extract 12.2:  A Total Physical Response lesson

The following detailed lesson outline is taken from Asher (1988) which contains 53 TPR lessons based on a training log kept by an ESL instructor. As you read the extract, you might like to consider the extent to which the interactions really do simulate the environment in which a first language is acquired.

## CLASSROOM EXTRACT 12.2

*Let's begin.* Using hand signals, motion four students to come up to the front of the classroom. Then gesture for two students to sit on either side of you facing the class. Other students in the class are often seated in a semi-circle so that there is a rather large space for the action.

Then say, "Stand up!" and immediately stand up as you motion the students seated on either side of you to stand up. Next say, "Sit down!" and immediately sit down along with the four students. If any student tries to repeat what you have said, signal silence by touching your lips with your index finger. Then say, "Stand up!" and the group, including the instructor, should stand up; and then "Sit down!" and all sit down. Repeat the utterance "Stand up!" and "Sit down!" each followed by the appropriate action until all respond confidently, without hesitation.

Then the command is "Walk!" and all walk forward. The next commands are "Stop!" "Turn!" "Walk!" "Stop!" "Turn!" "Walk!" "Stop!" "Jump!" "Turn!" "Walk!" "Stop!" "Jump!" "Turn!" "Sit down!"

By observing the hesitation or non-hesitation of students, you can make decisions as to how many more times you should model with the students. For cues about student readiness to try it alone, after uttering a command, delay your own response slightly to give the students a chance to show they understand and to decrease their dependency on you.

When you think the students are ready to try it themselves, sit down and utter commands which the students as a group act out. As you progress in a routine, it is important to vary the order of commands so that students do not memorize a fixed sequence.

By observing the group, you can decide when individuals are ready to try it alone. Certain students seem more confident and ready than others, so begin with those people. One by one, use gestures to invite each student to try it alone. Next, invite students from the audience to try. If you can memorize each student's first name in the beginning of the class while you take roll, you can then call out individuals from the audience with, "Juan, stand up!" "Walk!" and so forth.

Of course the concept of a command implies an authoritarian harshness, but this is not what is being advocated. The commands are given firmly but with gentleness and pleasantness. The kindness, compassion, and consideration of the instructor will be signaled in the tone of voice, posture and facial expressions. You are the student's ally and they will sense this in the way you direct their behavior.

Another hint is this: Students will be quite literal in their interpretation of what an utterance means. You must be careful to make "clean" responses that are uncluttered with extraneous movements or gestures. For example, one instructor would say "Turn!" then unconsciously move his head in either direction and then turn. Whenever the students heard "Turn!" they would swivel their heads from side to side and then turn. Remember, the students are watching every move you make and if you add irrelevant cues, they will internalize them as a false part of the meaning.

When the students can individually respond quickly and accurately to "Stand up!" "Sit down!" "Turn around!" "Walk!" "Stop!" and "Jump!" they are ready for an expansion of utterances that will move students to different locations in the room. With a few students, begin the expansion with:

Point to the door. (*You and the students point to the door.*)
Point to the chair. (*You and the students point to the chair.*)
Point to the table. (*You and the students point to the table.*)

After you have uttered the commands and pointed with the students, say:

Point to the door. Walk to the door. (*You and the students point to the door; then you all walk to the door.*)

Touch the door. (*You all touch the door.*)

Now try:

Point to the chair. Walk to the chair. (*You all point to the chair; then walk to the chair.*)

Touch the chair. (*You all touch the chair.*)

Next try:

Point to the table. Walk to the table. (*You all point to the table and then walk to the table.*)

Touch the table. (*You all touch the table.*)

At this point, say:

Point to a chair. (*Each student points to a chair.*)

Walk to a chair. (*The students walk to their chairs.*)

Sit down. (*The students sit down.*)

You sit down also and direct *individual* students with commands as:

Maria, stand up. (*Maria, who is sitting next to you, stands up.*)

Walk to the table. (*Maria walks to the table.*)

Point to the door. (*Maria points to the door.*)

Walk to the door and touch the door. (*Maria walks to the door and touches the door.*)

**Novelty**

Maria, point to a chair. (*Maria points to a chair.*)

Jump to the chair. (*You have now uttered a novel command—one Maria has not heard before.*)

She has heard "Jump" and "Walk to the chair," but *not* "Jump to the chair." Usually, Maria will delight you and the other students by responding correctly. If not, you demonstrate by uttering:

Jump to the table. (*Then you jump to the table.*)

Or perhaps you say,

Juan, stand up. (*Juan stands up.*)

Then you say,

Juan, jump to the door. (*Usually Juan will respond correctly by jumping to the door.*)

Then return to Maria with,

Maria, jump to the chair.

Now try.

Eduardo, stand up. (*Eduardo, who was in the audience, stands up.*)

Eduardo, walk to the table. (*He walks to the table.*)

Now point to the table. (*He points to the table.*)

Now touch the table. (*He touches the table.*)

Next try:

Eduardo, point to a chair. (*He points to a chair.*)

Walk to the chair and sit down. (*He walks to a chair and sits down.*)

Now try a novel command with Eduardo. He has been responding quickly and confidently to utterances he has heard you use to direct other students. Try a recombination of familiar constituents (i.e., a novel command). Try this:

Eduardo, stand up. (*He stands up.*)

Walk to the table. (*He walks to the table.*)

Now sit on the table.

Usually Eduardo will not disappoint you, but if he does not respond, do *not* press him by repeating the novel command. Rather, say:

Walk to the table (*and you walk to the table*).

Sit on the table (*and you sit on the table*).

Or, illustrate with another student by saying:

Maria, sit on the chair. (*Maria sits on the chair.*)

Maria, stand up. (*She stands up.*)

Maria, sit on the chair. (*She sits down on the chair.*)

Maria, stand up and walk to the table. (*She walks to the table.*)

Maria, sit on the table.

With practice you will become extremely skilled at recombining utterances to produce novel commands which students respond to correctly. Novelty is not meant to trick the student. We expect a successful response to each novel utterance. The intent is first to encourage flexibility in understanding the target language in the richness of recombinations. Secondly, novelty is a keen motivator. The surprises will delight both you and the students. And thirdly, student self-confidence is enhanced because they are aware that they instantly understood an unfamiliar utterance—one they had never heard before in training.

Source: J. J. Asher, *Learning Another Language Through Actions: The Complete Teacher's Guidebook*, 3rd edn (Los Gatos, Ca.: Sky Oaks Productions, 1988), pp. 66–9. Reproduced by permission.

An analysis of L1 child–parent interaction shows that that the assumptions made by people such as Krashen, Terrell and Asher about L1 acquisition and its application to second language learning are, in the main, naive, simplistic and, in some cases, simply wrong. A study cited in Nunan (1991) provides only very partial support for the claims of Krashen and Asher. In this study, the primary caregiver makes numerous references to events which are displaced in time and space. In addition, there is plenty of evidence that the child attends consciously to the nature and functions of language. Lastly, the data show that the child is very active in the construction of her new language, and that active production as well as comprehension is an important part of her language development.

Gathercole (1988) also takes issue with some of the assumptions made by second language acquisition researchers about first language acquisition. She reviews what the L1 research has to say about the beliefs that comprehension precedes production, that first language development is systematic and rule-governed, and that the basic stimulus to acquisition is the need to communicate. In relation to priority of comprehension over production, Gathercole cites research which shows that the relationship is not unidirectional, and that there are some structures where correct production precedes comprehension. For example, two-year-old children are able to use wh- words *where* and *what* appropriately, but have great difficulty in comprehending them. The finding that word order rules are rigidly used in production, but not relied on in comprehension also supports the notion that comprehension and production may invoke very different cognitive operations. Gathercole concludes from her review of the relevant L1 literature that extrapolations to second language acquisition tend to be characterised by inaccuracies and half-truths. 'It is not the case that comprehension always precedes production, nor that all learning is systematic and involves rule-governed behaviour, nor that communication is always the primary motivating force behind acquisition. (p. 428).

## 12.5 Investigating methods

**Task 12.1**
Select a grammatical structure and construct a TPR lesson similar to the one outlined in the preceding section. Teach, record and review the lesson. How successful was it? What was the reaction of the students? Were students able to respond appropriately to novel utterances?

**Task 12.2**
Select one or two recently published coursebooks and analyse the tasks and activities they contain. To what extent do the books reflect principles from the different methods we have looked at in this chapter? Is there any evidence of a persistence of audio-lingual techniques? How might you account for this?

**Task 12.3**

If possible, find a teacher who subscribes to one of the methods analysed in this chapter. Record and analyse the teacher's lesson. In what ways does the lesson support or violate the principles underlying the method? What modifications does the teacher make and why?

## 12.6 Conclusion

In his comprehensive review of classroom tasks, Long (1989) vigorously attacks the language teaching profession's preoccupation with methods, claiming that it says nothing about what to teach. In addition, as we have seen in this book, the analysis of classroom transcripts of lessons based on different methods shows that, in general, similarities outweigh differences. In other words, once they reach the classroom, 'methods' generally become subsumed within the larger concerns of classroom management and organisation.

From the perspective of language taken here, the two major shortcomings of the 'methods' approaches to language teaching are, firstly, that they exist as packages of precepts which are imported into the classroom, rather than being derived from a close observation and analysis of what actually goes on in the classroom. Secondly, there is a real danger that they may divorce language from the contexts and purposes for its existence.

This is not to say that individual methods do not have any redeeming features. There are aspects of all methods which might usefully be incorporated into one's classroom practice. However, individual classroom exercises and techniques need to be derived in the first instance from a consideration of the purposes to which the language will potentially be put, and the functions it will fulfil. Lastly, the claims made by champions of one method or another need to be treated with caution – after all, we have yet to devise a method which is capable of teaching anybody anything.

# References

Acton, W. 1984. Changing fossilized pronunciation. *TESOL Quarterly*, 18 (1): 71–85.

Alderson, J. C. and A. H. Urquhart (eds). 1984. *Reading in a Foreign Language*. London: Longman.

Anderson, A. and T. Lynch. 1988. *Listening*. Oxford: Oxford University Press.

Anderson, R. (ed.). 1981. *New Dimensions in Second Language Acquisition Research*. Rowley, Mass.: Newbury House.

Asher, J. 1988. *Learning Another Language Through Actions: The Complete Teacher's Guidebook*, 3rd edn. Los Gatos, Ca.: Sky Oaks Productions.

Aslanian, Y. 1985. Investigating the reading problems of ESL students: An alternative. *ELT Journal*, 39 (1): 20–7.

Bailey, N., C. Madden, and S. Krashen. 1974. Is there a 'natural sequence' in adult second language learning? *Language Learning*, 24: 235–43.

Barnes, D. 1975. *From Communication to Curriculum*. Harmondsworth: Penguin.

Bartlett, F. C. 1932. *Remembering: A Study in Experimental and Social Psychology*. Cambridge: Cambridge University Press.

Beebe, L. 1983. Risk-taking and the language learner. In H. Seliger and M. H. Long (eds), *Classroom Oriented Research in Second Language Acquisition*. Rowley, Mass.: Newbury House.

Bell, J. and B. Burnaby. 1984. *Handbook for ESL Literacy*. Toronto: OISE.

Bialystock, E. 1981. Some evidence for the integrity and interaction of two knowledge sources. In R. Anderson (ed.), *New Dimensions in Second Language Acquisition Research*. Rowley, Mass.: Newbury House.

Bialystock, E. 1982. On the relationship between knowing and using linguistic forms. *Applied Linguistics*, 3 (3): 181–206.

Bloomfield, L. 1933. *Language*. New York: Holt.

Borg, W., M. Kelley, P. Langer and M. Gall. 1970. *The Mini-course: A Micro-teaching Approach to Teacher Education*. Beverley Hills, Ca.: Macmillan Educational Services.

Bransford, J. D. and M. K. Johnson. 1972. Contextual prerequisites for understanding: some investigations of comprehension and recall. *Journal of Verbal Learning and Verbal Behaviour*, 11.

Breen, M. 1984. Processes in syllabus design. In C. Brumfit (ed.), *General English Syllabus Design*. Oxford: Pergamon.

Breen, M. 1985. The social context for language learning – a neglected situation. *Studies in Second Language Acquisition*, 7.

Breen, M. and C. N. Candlin. 1980. The essentials of a communicative curriculum in language teaching. *Applied Linguistics*, 1 (2), 89–112.

Breen, M. and C. N. Candlin. 1987. Which materials? A consumer's and designer's guide. In L. Sheldon (ed.), *ELT Textbooks and Materials: Problems in Evaluation and Development.* ELT Document 126. London: Modern English Publications.

Brinton, D., M. A. Snow and M. B. Wesche. 1989. *Content Based Second Language Instruction.* New York: Newbury House.

Brock, C. 1986. The effects of referential questions on ESL classroom discourse, *TESOL Quarterly*, 20 (1): 47–59.

Brophy, J. 1981. Teacher praise: a functional analysis. *Review of Educational Research*, 51: 5–32.

Brown, D. 1974. Advanced vocabulary teaching: the problem of collocation. *RELC Journal*, 5 (2): 1–11.

Brown, G. 1990. *Listening to Spoken English*, 2nd edn. London: Longman.

Brown, G. and G. Yule. 1983a. *Discourse Analysis*. Cambridge: Cambridge University Press.

Brown, G. and G. Yule. 1983b. *Teaching the Spoken Language*. Cambridge: Cambridge University Press.

Brown, G., A. Anderson, R. Shillcock and G. Yule. 1984. *Teaching Talk: Strategies for Production and Assessment*. Cambridge: Cambridge University Press.

Brown, H. D. 1987. *Principles of Language Learning and Teaching*. Englewood Cliffs: Prentice Hall.

Brown, K. and S. Hood. 1989. *Writing Matters*. Cambridge: Cambridge University Press.

Brown, R. 1973. *A First Language*. London: Allen and Unwin.

Brundage, D. H. and MacKeracher. 1980. *Adult Learning Principles and their Application to Program Planning*. Ontario: Ontario Institute for Studies in Education.

Bruton, G. and V. Samuda. 1980. Learner and teacher roles in the treatment of oral error in group work. *RELC Journal*, 11 (3): 49–63.

Butt, D. 1989. *Living with English*. Sydney: Macquarie University.

Bygate, M. 1987. *Speaking*. Oxford: Oxford University Press.

Bygate, M. 1988. Units of oral expression and language learning in small group interaction. *Applied Linguistics*, 9 (1): 59–82.

Byrne, D. 1973. *Listening Comprehension 1*. London: Longman.

Byrne, D. and G. Walsh. 1973. *Listening Comprehension I Pronunciation Practice Teacher's Book*. London: Longman.

Cambourne, B. 1979. How important is theory to the reading teacher? *Australian Journal of Reading*, 2: 78–90.

Cancino, H., E. Rosansky and J. Schumann. 1978. The acquisition of English negatives and interrogatives by native Spanish speakers. In E. Hatch (ed.), *Second Language Acquisition: A Book of Readings*. Rowley, Mass.: Newbury House.

Candlin, C. N. 1984. Syllabus design as a critical process. In C. Brumfit (ed.), *General English Syllabus Design*. Oxford: Pergamon.

Candlin, C. N. (forthcoming) *Critical Perspectives on Second Language Teaching*. London: Longman.

Candlin, C. N. and M. Hennessy. 1990. The *Macquarie Learner's Dictionary*. Presentation to the Style Council '90 Conference, Macquarie University, July 1990.

Carrell, P., J. Devine and D. Eskey (eds). 1988. *Interactive Approaches to Second Language Reading*. Cambridge: Cambridge University Press.

Carter, R. and M. McCarthy. 1988. *Vocabulary and Language Teaching*. London: Longman.

Cathcart, R. 1989. Authentic discourse and the survival English curriculum. *TESOL Quarterly*, 23 (1): 105–26.

Channell, J. 1988. Psycholinguistic considerations in the study of L2 vocabulary acquisition. In R. Carter and M. McCarthy, *Vocabulary and Language Teaching*. London: Longman.

Chastain, K. 1976. *Developing Second Language Skills*. New York: Rand–McNally.

Chaudron, C. 1988. *Second Language Classrooms: Research on Teaching and Learning*. Cambridge: Cambridge University Press.

Chomsky, N. 1959. A review of B. F. Skinner's Verbal Behaviour. *Language*, 35: 26–58.

Cicourel, A. 1973. *Cognitive Sociology: Language and Meaning in Social Interaction*. Harmondsworth: Penguin.

Corbel, C. 1985. The 'action sequence' approach to course design. *Prospect*, 1 (1).

Corder, S. Pit. 1988. Pedagogic grammars. In W. Rutherford and M. Sharwood-Smith. (eds), *Grammar and Second Language Teaching*. New York: Newbury House.

Craik, F. and R. Lockhart. 1972. Levels of processing: a framework for memory record. *Journal of Verbal Learning and Verbal Behaviour*, 11: 67–84.

Crawford, J. 1989. Curriculum change in ESL. Paper presented at the QATESOL Conference, Brisbane, June 1989.

Curran, C. 1972. *Counseling-Learning: A Whole Person Model for Education*. New York: Grune and Stratton.

Curran, C. 1976. *Counseling-Learning in Second Languages*. Apple River, Ill.: Apple River Press.

Dijk, T. van. 1977. *Text and Context: Explorations in the Semantics and Pragmatics of Discourse*. London: Longman.

Diller, K. 1978. *The Language Teaching Controversy*. Rowley, Mass.: Newbury House.

Doughty, C. and T. Pica. 1986. 'Information gap' tasks: do they facilitate second language acquisition? *TESOL Quarterly*, 20 (2).

Duff, P. 1986. Another look at interlanguage talk: taking task to task. In R. Day (ed.), *Talking to Learn*. Rowley, Mass.: Newbury House.

Dulay, H. and M. Burt. 1973. Should we teach children syntax? *Language Learning*, 23: 235–52.

Dulay, H. and M. Burt. 1974a. Natural sequences in child second language acquisition. *Language Learning*, 24: 37–53.

Dulay, H. and M. Burt. 1974b. A new perspective on the creative construction process in child second language acquisition. *Language Learning*, 24: 253–78.

Dulay, H., M. Burt, and S. Krashen. 1982. *Language Two*. Oxford: Pergamon.

Economou, D. 1985. *Coffee Break: A Course in Understanding Authentic Australian Casual Conversation*. Sydney: Adult Migrant Education Service.

Edmonson, W. 1981. *Spoken Discourse: A Model for Analysis*. London: Longman.

Eisenstein, M., N. Bailey and C. Madden. 1982. It takes two: contrasting tasks and contrasting structures. *TESOL Quarterly*, 16: 381–93.

Ellis, G. and B. Sinclair. 1989. *Learning to Learn English*. Cambridge: Cambridge University Press.

Ellis, R. 1984. *Classroom Second Language Development*. Oxford: Pergamon.

Ellis, R. 1985. *Understanding Second Language Acquisition*. Oxford: Oxford University Press.

Ellis, R. 1987. Learning strategies and second language acquisition. Paper presented at the AILA International Convestion, Sydney University, August 1987.

Faerch, C. and G. Kasper. 1983. Procedural knowledge as a component of foreign language learners' communicative competence. In H. Boete and W. Herrlitz (eds), *Kommunikation im (Sprach-) Unterricht*. Utrecht.

Fox, L. 1979. On acquiring an adequate second language vocabulary. *Journal of Basic Writing*, 2 (3): 68–75.

Frank, C. and M. Rinvolucri. 1987. *Grammar in Action*. Hemel Hempstead: Prentice Hall.

Gairns, R. and S. Redman. 1986. *Working with Words*. Cambridge: Cambridge University Press.

Garton-Sprengler, J. and S. Greenall. 1986. *BBC Beginner's English*. London: BBC.

Gathercole, V. 1988. Some myths you may have heard about first language acquisition. *TESOL Quarterly*, 22 (3): 407-35.

Gattegno, C. 1972. *Teaching Foreign Languages in School the Silent Way*. New York: Educational Solutions.

Gerot, L. 1990. A question of legitimate answers. PhD dissertation. Macquarie University, Sydney.

Good, T. and J. Brophy. 1987. *Looking in Classrooms*. New York: Harper and Row.

Goodman, Y. M. and C. L. Burke. 1972. *Reading Miscue Inventory Manual: Procedure for Diagnosis and Remediation*. New York: Macmillan.

Graves, K. and D. Rein. 1988. *East–West*. Book 1. Oxford: Oxford University Press.

Halliday, M. A. K. 1985a. *An Introduction to Functional Grammar*. London: Arnold.

Halliday, M. A. K. 1985b. *Spoken and Written Language*. Victoria: Deakin University Press.

Halliday, M. A. K. and R. Hasan. 1976. *Cohesion in English*. London: Longman.

Halliday, M. A. K. and R. Hasan. 1985. *Language, Context and Text: Aspects of Language in a Social-Semiotic Perspective*. Victoria: Deakin University Press.

Hatch, E. 1978. Discourse analysis and second language acquisition. In E. Hatch (ed.), *Second Language Acquisition: A Book of Readings*. Rowley, Mass.: Newbury House.

Hammond, J. 1987. Oral and written language in the educational context. Paper presented at the 8th World Congress of Applied Linguistics, Sydney University, August 1987.

Hammond, J. 1989. Grammar and language teaching. In D. Nunan (ed.), *Working Papers in Linguistics*. Vol. 1. School of English and Linguistics, Macquarie University, Sydney.

Hamp-Lyons, L. and B. Heasley. 1987. *Study Writing*. Cambridge: Cambridge University Press.

Hatch, E. (ed.). 1978. *Second Language Acquisition: A Book of Readings*. Rowley, Mass.: Newbury House.

Hockett, C. 1958. *A Course in Linguistics*. New York: Macmillan.

Holley, F. and J. King. 1971. Imitation and correction in foreign language learning. *Modern Language Journal*, 55: 494-8.

Hollon, W. 1968. *The Great American Desert*. New York: Washington Square Press.

Honeyfield, J. 1977. Word frequency and the importance of context in vocabulary learning. *RELC Journal*, 8: 35–42.

Horowitz, D. 1986. Process, not product: less than meets the eye. *TESOL Quarterly*, 20 (1): 141-4.

Howatt, A. 1984. *A History of English Language Teaching*. Oxford: Oxford University Press.

Hyltenstam, K. and M. Pienemann (eds). 1985. *Modelling and Assessing Second Language Acquisition*. Clevedon, Avon: Multilingual Matters.

Jackson, P. and H. Lahaderne. 1967. Inequalities of teacher–pupil contacts. *Psychology in the Schools*, 4: 204–8.

James, C. 1980. *Contrastive Analysis*. London: Longman.

Johnston, M. 1985. *Syntactic and Morphological Progressions in Learner English*. Canberra:

Department of Immigration and Ethnic Affairs.

Jones, L. 1985. *Use of English. Teacher's Book*. Cambridge: Cambridge University Press.

Kelly, L. 1969. *Twenty-five Centuries of Language Teaching*. Rowley, Mass.: Newbury House.

Kemmis, S. and R. McTaggart (eds). 1988. *The Action Research Planner*. Victoria: Deakin University Press.

Kenworthy, J. 1987. *Teaching English Pronunciation*. London: Longman.

Knowles, G. 1987. *Patterns of Spoken English*. London: Longman.

Kolers, P. and M. Katzmann. 1966. Naming sequentially presented letters and words. *Language and Speech*, 9: 54–95.

Krashen, S. 1981. *Second Language Acquisition and Second Language Learning*. Oxford: Pergamon.

Krashen, S. 1982. *Principles and Practice in Second Language Acquisition*. Oxford: Pergamon.

Krashen, S. and T. Terrell. 1983. *The Natural Approach*. Oxford: Pergamon.

Kruse, A. 1979. Vocabulary in context. *ELT Journal*, 33 (3): 207–13.

La Forge, P. 1983. *Counselling and Culture in Second Language Acquisition*. Oxford: Pergamon.

Labov, W. 1972. *Language in the Inner City: Studies in the Black English Vernacular*. Philadelphia: University of Pennsylvania Press.

Lapp, R. 1984 (cited in Richards 1990). The process approach to writing: towards a curriculum for international students. MA dissertation, University of Hawaii.

Larsen-Freeman, D. 1975. The acquisition of grammatical morphemes by adult ESL students. *TESOL Quarterly*, 9: 409–30.

Larsen-Freeman, D. 1976. An explanation for the morpheme acquisition order of second language learners. *Language Learning*, 26 (1): 125–34.

Larsen-Freeman, D. and M. Long. 1991. *An Introduction to Second Language Acquisition Research*. London: Longman.

Laosa, L. 1979. Inequality in the classroom: observational research on teacher–student interaction. *Aztlan*, 8: 409–20.

Legutke, M. and H. Thomas. 1991. *Process and Experience in the Language Classroom*. London: Longman.

Liberman, A., K. Harris, H. Hoffman and B. Griffith. 1957. The discrimination of speech sounds within and across phoneme boundaries. *Journal of Experimental Psychology*, 54: 358–68.

Lier, L. van. 1988. *The Classroom and the Language Learner*. London: Longman.

Littlejohn, A. and S. Windeatt. 1988. Beyond language learning: perspective on materials design. In R. K. Johnson (ed.), *The Second Language Curriculum*. Cambridge: Cambridge University Press.

Long, M. H. 1981. Questions in foreigner talk discourse. *Language Learning*, 31: 1.

Long, M. H. 1983. Does instruction make a difference? *TESOL Quarterly*, 17 (3): 359–82.

Long, M. 1985. Input and second language acquisition theory. In S. Gass and C. Madden (eds), *Input in Second Language Acquisition*. Rowley, Mass.: Newbury House.

Long, M. H. 1989. Task, group, and task-group interaction. Plenary address to the RELC Regional Seminar, Singapore, April 1989.

Long, M., L. Adams, M. McLean and F. Castanos. 1976. Doing things with words: verbal interaction in lockstep and small group classroom situations. In R. Crymes and J. Fanselow (eds), *On TESOL '76*. Washington DC: TESOL.

Long, M. and C. Sato. 1983. Classroom foreigner talk discourse: forms and functions of teachers' questions. In H. Seliger and M. Long (eds). *Classroom Oriented Research in Second Language Acquisition.* Rowley, Mass.: Newbury House.

Long, M. and G. Crookes. 1986. Intervention points in second language classroom processes. In B. B. Das (ed.), *Patterns of Classroom Interaction in Southeast Asia.* Singapore: RELC.

Low, G. 1989. Appropriate design: the internal design of course units. In R. K. Johnson (ed.), *The Second Language Curriculum.* Cambridge: Cambridge University Press.

Lozanov, G. 1979. *Suggestology and Outlines of Suggestopedy.* New York: Gordon and Breach.

McKay, S. 1987. *Teaching Grammar: Form, Function and Technique.* Hemel Hempstead: Prentice Hall.

Martin, J. 1985. *Factual Writing: Exploring and Challenging Social Reality.* Geelong: Deakin University Press.

Maugham, W. S. 1969. *Maugham's Malaysian Stories.* Kuala Lumpur: Heinemann Educational Books.

Mohan, B. 1986. *Language and Content.* Reading, Mass.: Addison-Wesley.

Morgan, J. and M. Sellner. 1980. Discourse and linguistic theory. In R. Spiro, B. Bruce and W. Brewer (eds), *Theoretical Issues in Reading Comprehension.* Hillsdale: Erlbaum.

Moulton, W. 1963. Linguistics and language teaching in the United States 1940–1960. *IRAL*, 1: 21–41.

Murphy, R. 1985. *English Grammar in Use.* Cambridge: Cambridge University Press.

Nattinger, J. 1988. Some current trends in vocabulary teaching. In R. Carter and M. McCarthy, *Vocabulary and Language Teaching.* London: Longman.

Nunan, D. 1985. Content familiarity and the perception of textual relationships in second language reading. *RELC Journal*, 16 (1): 43–51.

Nunan, D. 1987a. Communicative language teaching: making it work. *ELT Journal*, 41 (2).

Nunan, D. 1987b. Methodological issues in research. In D. Nunan (ed.), *Applying Second Language Acquisition Research.* Adelaide: NCRC.

Nunan, D. 1988a. *Syllabus Design.* Oxford: Oxford University Press.

Nunan, D. 1988b. *The Learner-centred Curriculum.* Cambridge: Cambridge University Press.

Nunan, D. 1988c. Learning strategy preferences of students in Southeast Asia. Paper presented at the Annual ILE Conference, Hong Kong, November 1988.

Nunan, D. 1989a. *Designing Tasks for the Communicative Classroom.* Cambridge: Cambridge University Press.

Nunan, D. 1989b. *Understanding Language Classrooms: A Guide for Teacher Initiated Action.* Hemel Hempstead: Prentice Hall.

Nunan, D. (ed.). 1989c. *Beginning Reading and Writing: A Curriculum Framework for Adult Second Language Learners.* Sydney: National Centre for English Language Teaching and Research.

Nunan, D. 1990. Action research in the language classroom. In J. Richards and D. Nunan. (eds), *Second Language Teacher Education.* Cambridge: Cambridge University Press.

Nunan, D. 1991. *Research Methods in Applied Linguistics.* Sydney: NCELTR.

Nunan, D. and J. Lockwood. 1989. *The Australian English Course* (pilot edition). Sydney: Cambridge University Press.

Odlin, T. 1989. *Language Transfer.* Cambridge: Cambridge University Press.

Ogden, C. 1930. *Basic English: A General Introduction.* London: Kegan Paul.

Oller, J. 1979. *Language Tests at School.* London: Longman.

Ostrander, S., and L. Schroeder. 1981. *Superlearning.* London: Sphere Books.

Palmberg, R. 1988. Computer games and foreign-language vocabulary learning. *ELT*

*Journal*, 42 (4): 247–52.

Parker, K. and C. Chaudron. 1987. The effects of linguistic simplification and elaborative modifications on L2 comprehension. Paper presented at the 21st Annual TESOL Convention, Miami Beach, April 1987.

Pearson, E. 1988. Learner strategies and learner interviews. *ELT Journal*, 42 (3).

Pearson, P. D. and D. Johnson. 1978. *Teaching Reading Comprehension*. New York: Holt, Rinehart and Winston.

Peck, T. 1989. *Teachers at Work*. Hemel Hempstead: Prentice Hall.

Pennington, M. and J. Richards. 1986. Pronunciation revisited. *TESOL Quarterly*, 20 (2): 207–25.

Pica, T. 1985. Linguistic simplicity and learnability. In K. Hyltenstam and M. Pienemann (eds), *Modelling and Assessing Second Language Acquisition*. Clevedon, Avon.: Multilingual Matters.

Pica, T. and C. Doughty. 1985. Input and interaction in the communicative language classroom: a comparison of teacher-fronted and group activities. In S. Gass and C. Madden. (eds), *Input in Second Language Acquisition*. Rowley, Mass.: Newbury House.

Pienemann, M. and M. Johnston. 1987. Factors influencing the development of language proficiency. In D. Nunan (ed.), *Applying Second Language Acquisition Research*. Adelaide: NCRC.

Porter, P. 1983. Variations in the conversations of adult learners of English as a function of the proficiency level of the participants. PhD dissertation, Stanford University.

Porter, P. 1986. How learners talk to each other: input and interaction in task-centered discussions. In R. Day (ed.), *Talking to Learn: Conversation in Second Language Acquisition*. Rowley, Mass.: Newbury House.

Reiss, M. A. 1985. The good language learner: another look. *The Canadian Modern Language Review*, 41 (3).

Renouf, A. 1984. Corpus development at Birmingham University. In J. Aarts and W. Meijs (eds), *Corpus Linguistics: Recent Developments in the Use of Computer Corpora in English Language Research*. Amsterdam: Rodopi.

Richards, I. 1943. *Basic English and Its Uses*. London: Kegan Paul.

Richards, J. 1974. Word lists: problems and prospects. *RELC Journal*, 5 (2): 69–84.

Richards, J. 1987. Beyond methods: alternative approaches to instructional design in language teaching. *Prospect*, 3 (1): 11–30.

Richards, J. C. 1989. Profile of an effective L2 reading teacher. *Prospect*, 4 (2), 13–29.

Richards, J. 1990. *The Language Teaching Matrix*. Cambridge: Cambridge University Press.

Richards, J., J. Platt, and H. Weber. 1985. *Longman Dictionary of Applied Linguistics*. London: Longman.

Richards, J. and T. Rodgers. 1986. *Approaches and Methods in Language Teaching*. Cambridge: Cambridge University Press.

Rivers, W. 1983. *Communicating Naturally in a Second Language*. Cambridge: Cambridge University Press.

Rivers, W. and M. Temperley. 1978. *A Practical Guide to the Teaching of English as a Second or Foreign Language*. New York: Oxford University Press.

Rodrigues, R. J. 1985. Moving away from writing-process workshop. *English Journal*, 74: 24–7.

Rossner, R. 1988. Materials for communicative language teaching and learning. *Annual Review of Applied Linguistics*, 8: 140–63.

Rost, M. 1989. *Listening*. London: Longman.

Rost, M. 1991. *Listening In Action*, Hemel Hempstead: Prentice Hall.

Rowe, M. 1974. Wait-time and rewards as instructional variables, their influence on language, logic and fate control: Part I – Wait-time. *Journal of Research on Science Teaching*, 11: 81–94.

Rowe, M. 1986. Wait time: Slowing down may be a way of speeding up. *Journal of Teacher Education*, 37: 43–50.

Rubin, J. 1975. What the 'good language learner' can teach us? *TESOL Quarterly*, 9 (1): 41–51.

Rubin, J. and I. Thompson. 1983. *How to Be a More Successful Language Learner*. New York: Heinle and Heinle.

Rudzka, B., J. Channell, Y. Putseys and P. Ostyn. 1981. *The Words You Need*. London: Macmillan.

Rutherford, W. 1980. Aspects of pedagogical grammar. *Applied Linguistics*, 1 (1): 60–73.

Rutherford, W. 1987. *Second Language Grammar: Learning and Teaching*. London: Longman.

Rutherford, W. and M. Sharwood-Smith (eds). 1988. *Grammar and Second Language Teaching*. New York: Newbury House.

Sato, C. 1985. Task variation in interlanguage phonology. In S. Gass and E. Varonis (eds), *Input in Second Language Acquisition*. Rowley, Mass.: Newbury House.

Schinke-Llano, L. 1983. Foreigner talk in content classrooms. In H. Seliger and M. Long (eds), *Classroom Oriented Research in Second Language Classrooms*. Rowley, Mass.: Newbury House.

Schmidt, R. and S. Frota. 1986. Developing basic conversational ability in a second language: a case study of an adult learner of Portuguese. In R. Day (ed.), *Talking to Learn: Conversation in Second Language Acquisition*. Rowley, Mass.: Newbury House.

Scholes, R. 1968. Phonemic interference as a perceptual phenomenon. *Language and Speech*, 11: 86–103.

Scovel, T. 1979. Review of Suggestology and outlines of Suggestopedy by George Lozanov. *TESOL Quarterly*, 13: 255–66.

Sharwood-Smith, M. 1988. Consciousness raising and the second language learner. In W. Rutherford and M. Sharwood-Smith (eds), *Grammar and Second Language Teaching*. New York: Newbury House.

Sheldon, L. 1988. Evaluating ELT textbooks and materials. *ELT Journal*, 42 (4): 237–46.

Shrum, J. and V. Tech. 1985. Wait-time and the use of target or native languages. *Foreign Language Annals*, 18: 304–13.

Skinner, B. F. 1957. *Verbal Behaviour*. New York: Appleton Crofts.

Sinclair, J. McH. and A. Renouf. 1988. A lexical syllabus for language learning. In R. Carter and M. McCarthy. *Vocabulary and Language Teaching*. London: Longman.

Smith, F. 1978. *Understanding Reading: A Psycholinguistic Analysis of Reading and Learning to Read*. New York: Holt, Rinehart and Winston.

Stanovich, K. 1980. Toward an interactive–compensatory model of individual differences in the development of reading fluency. *Reading Research Quarterly*, 16: 32–71.

Steffensen, M. 1981. Register, Cohesion and Cross-cultural Reading Comprehension. Technical Report No. 220. Centre for the Study of Reading, University of Illinois, Champaign, Illinois.

Stenhouse, L. 1975. An *Introduction to Curriculum Research and Development*. London: Heinemann.

Stern, H. H. 1983. *Fundamental Concepts of Language Teaching*. Oxford: Oxford University Press.

Stevick, E. 1976. *Memory, Meaning and Method*. Rowley, Mass.: Newbury House.

Stevick, E. 1982. *Teaching and Learning Languages*. Cambridge: Cambridge University Press.

Strong, M. 1986. Teacher's language to limited English speakers in bilingual and submersion classrooms. In R. Day (ed.), *Talking to Learn: Conversation in Second Language Acquisition*. Rowley, Mass.: Newbury House.

Summers, D. 1988. The role of dictionaries in language learning. In R. Carter and M. McCarthy, *Vocabulary and Language Teaching*. London: Longman.

Swaffar, J., K. Arens, and M. Morgan. 1982. Teacher classroom practices: redefining method as task hierarchy. *Modern Language Journal*, 66 (1).

Swales, J. 1980. ESP: the textbook problem. *ESP Journal*, 1 (1): 11–23.

Swain, M. 1985. Communicative competence: some roles for comprehensible input and comprehensible output in its development. In S. Gass and C. Madden (eds), *Input in Second Language Acquisition*. Rowley, Mass.: Newbury House.

Swan, M. and B. Smith (eds). 1987. *Learner English: A Teacher's Guide to Interference and Other Problems*. Cambridge: Cambridge University Press.

Swan, M. and C. Walter. 1985. *The Cambridge English Course*. Book 2. Cambridge: Cambridge University Press.

Tarone, E. 1982. Systematicity and attention in interlanguage. *Language Learning*, 32: 69–84.

Tarone, E. 1983. On the variability of interlanguage systems. *Applied Linguistics*, 4: 142–63.

Ur, P. 1988. *Grammar Practice Activities*. Cambridge: Cambridge University Press.

Wagner, M. and G. Tilney. 1983. The effect of 'Superlearning techniques' on the vocabulary acquisition and alpha brainwave production of language learners. *TESOL Quarterly*, 17 (1): 5–17.

Wajnryb, R. 1986. *Grammar Workout: The Dictogloss Approach*. Sydney: Melting Pot Press.

Wajnryb, R. 1988. *Grammar Workout 2: The Dictogloss Approach*. Sydney: Melting Pot Press.

Wallace, C. 1988. *Learning to Read in a Multicultural Society*. London: Prentice Hall.

Walter, C. 1982. *Authentic Reading: A Course in Reading Skills for Upper-Intermediate Students*. Cambridge: Cambridge University Press.

Wenden, A. 1986. Helping language learners think about learning. *ELT Journal*, 40 (1).

Wenden, A. 1991. *Learner Strategies for Learner Autonomy*. Hemel Hempstead: Prentice Hall.

West, M. 1960. *Teaching English in Difficult Circumstances*. London: Longman.

Widdowson, H. G. 1978. *Teaching Language as Communication*. Oxford: Oxford University Press.

Widdowson, H. G. 1979. *Explorations in Applied Linguistics*. Oxford: Oxford University Press.

Widdowson, H. G. 1983. *Learning Purpose and Language Use*. Oxford: Oxford University Press.

Widdowson, H. G. 1990. *Aspects of Language Teaching*. Oxford: Oxford University Press.

Wilkins, D. 1976. *Notional Syllabuses*. Oxford: Oxford University Press.

Willing, K. 1988. *Learning Strategies in Adult Migrant Education*. Adelaide: NCRC.

Willing, K. 1989. *Teaching How to Learn: Learning Strategies in ESL*. Sydney: National Centre for English Language Teaching and Research.

Willis, D. 1990. *The Lexical Syllabus*. London: Collins.

Wolfson, N. and E. Judd (eds). 1983. *Sociolinguistics and Language Acquisition*. Rowley, Mass.: Newbury House.

Wright, T. 1987. *Roles of Teachers and Learners*. Oxford: Oxford University Press.

Yorkey, R. 1970. *Study Skills for Students of English as a Second Language*. New York: McGraw-Hill.

Young, M. (ed.). 1971. *Knowledge and Control*. London: Collier–Macmillan.

Zamel, V. 1982. Writing: the process of discovering meaning. *TESOL Quarterly*, 16 (2): 195–209.

Zamel, V. 1987. Recent research on writing pedagogy. *TESOL Quarterly*, 21 (4): 697–715.

Zilm, M. 1989. *Investigating the Role of Code Switching in Oral Language in the Classroom*. Adelaide: Languages and Multicultural Centre.

# Author Index

# Subject Index